Leadership
and Early Years Professionalism

Jennie Lindon
Lance Lindon

HODDER
EDUCATION

Dedication

To Julian Toland

Orders: please contact Bookpoint Ltd, 130 Milton Park, Abingdon, Oxon OX14 4SB. Telephone: (44) 01235 827720. Fax: (44) 01235 400454. Lines are open from 9.00–5.00, Monday to Saturday, with a 24-hour message answering service. You can also order through our website **www.hoddereducation.co.uk**

British Library Cataloguing in Publication Data
A catalogue record for this title is available from the British Library

ISBN: 978 1 4441 4424 6

This Edition Published 2012
Impression number   10 9 8 7 6 5 4 3 2
Year   2014, 2013, 2012

Hachette UK's policy is to use papers that are natural, renewable and recyclable products and made from wood grown in sustainable forests. The logging and manufacturing processes are expected to conform to the environmental regulations of the country of origin.

Cover photo © Ingram Publishing Ltd.

Typeset by DC Graphic Design Limited, Swanley Village, Kent.
Printed in Great Britain for Hodder Education, An Hachette UK Company, 338 Euston Road, London NW1 3BH by CPI Group (UK) Ltd, Croydon, CR0 4YY.

Contents

Acknowledgements

We appreciate what we have learned over the years from listening to many experienced practitioners, team leaders, advisors and consultants. Special thanks for recent conversations with Anna Batty (Head, Millom Children's Centre, Cumbria); Julian Grenier (Early Years Advisor, Tower Hamlets and previously head of Kate Greenaway Children's Centre, London); Sharon Hogan (Head of Centre, Early Excellence and previously Head of Canterbury Nursery School and Centre for Children and Families, Bradford); Laura Henry (Childcare Consultancy Ltd); and Maureen Lee (Director, Best Practice Network).

Our thanks also go to the heads and teams of Buckingham's Nursery School (Leek), Grove House Children's Centre (Southall), Little Learners Nursery School (Skegness), Kennet Day Nursery (Reading), Pound Park Children's Centre (Charlton, London), Randolph Beresford Children's Centre (White City, London), Red Hen Day Nursery (Legbourne) and Southlands Kindergarten and Crèche (Newcastle-under-Lyme). Many thanks also to the large number of early years professionals who have been happy to talk within conferences, in particular the networks of Bournemouth, Poole & Dorset; Hampshire, Southampton & the Isle of Wight; and Devon.

Our examples in the book use fictional settings and these names – so far as we can establish – are not used by any existing provision. We have woven in our experience with people and places. However, none of these imagined early years people or places represents any of the individuals or teams whom we have just thanked.

SDI®, Strength Deployment Inventory®, and Relationship Awareness®, are registered trademarks of Personal Strengths Publishing, Inc. Carlsbad, CA, USA.

Leadership for early years provision

Over the first decade of the 21st century, the nature of leadership and leaders in early years provision has become a much discussed professional issue. Programmes and courses about leadership have multiplied for early years practitioners. Leadership now features as a module, or part of one, in many of the Foundation and Early Childhood Studies degrees. Different types of leadership are promoted as appropriate for the sector, and in particular for the growing number of practitioners with Early Years Professional (EYP) status.

This book will explore different approaches to understanding leadership and the implications for practice in any organisation, but especially for early years provision. The aim of this first chapter is to explore key basic issues of leadership and management, and to discuss the ways in which leadership has largely been discussed within the literature on early childhood studies.

The main sections in this chapter are:
- why leadership rather than management
- leadership as a key issue for early years
- a very female workforce.

Why leadership rather than management

The title of this book includes the word 'leadership' and not 'management' – that was a deliberate choice. It is valuable professionally to understand the difference between being a leader and being a manager. The skills of management are important for the smooth running of any organisation – and early years provision is no exception. The skills of leadership differ from those typically associated with management and are needed most when existing patterns of working are called into question. If the future were as well known as the past, the secure skills of management would work perfectly well and the need for leadership would be much less than it is today.

Work and organisations

Leadership is all around us and happens all the time in social and family life. To a greater or lesser extent, most people are leaders at some point. When friendship groups try to decide what to do, it is unlikely that the same person will lead every time. Some people will take a clear lead over where to eat or what to do at the weekend. One friend may definitely be the person to lead the group across an unfamiliar part of town or city. The choice of leader tends to be based on knowledge or experience, or at least your belief that the leader has it. In some instances you will lead in organising activities; at other times you will be a follower. You may be a contented follower because the leader helps you access new experiences that you enjoy.

In one's personal life the whole process of leadership is rarely formal; discussion and decision making are informal. Similarly, at home, family members or adult partners usually divide up domestic responsibilities and lead different areas of domestic life. At home or with friends, people usually work out leadership issues with each other. We often do not think of leadership in a personal and social context. However, when the term 'leadership' is brought into the formal organisational context, many people feel confused or uneasy about it. Can I do this? Do I have any experience? Does it mean being bossy?

Take another **perspective**

Think about your life with family, friends and acquaintances.

- Can you see patterns of leadership in the different parts of your non-work life?
- Are you sometimes the leader?
- What determines who leads at different times in your social group of friends, or in your family life?

Structure and systems

Any work organisation aims to operate in a rational and coordinated way to reach defined goals, although daily working life is often rather more messy. The primary way that organisations seek to achieve this rational coordination is through defining the tasks that need to be done and the best way to get these done, and putting in place the people and resources necessary to deliver the results. In practice this means that organisations, unlike social groups, have both structure and systems. This description is as true of early years provision as it is of the commercial world.

Structure is the way that the working of any organisation is subdivided into different areas that make sense in terms of what it needs to do. In the commercial world there may be departments such as sales or operations. In early years provision a smaller nursery may have age-based rooms. A large centre may be divided into day care, a nursery school section and parent support services. A second part of structure is provided by the hierarchy of levels of seniority and the definition of individual roles and responsibilities. In early years provision there will be someone who heads up the whole setting, one or more deputies and maybe room leaders.

Systems are all the different processes designed to provide what this organisation needs in terms of information, tools and controls to deliver the outcomes required. Like any organisation, early years provision has a range of procedures that need to be followed, for instance over recruitment of staff or offering places to families. Settings need efficient systems to track attendance and payment of fees, and sometimes these work methods will include use of computer software.

What does it mean?

Structure: the way that any organisation is subdivided into different areas of the work and also into different individual roles and levels of seniority.

Systems: the processes designed to provide the necessary information, tools and controls for the organisation to meet its aims.

Leader or manager?

A focus on the structural element helps to make progress in identifying the distinction between leader and manager. At one level this is very simple. If you are appointed to the position by a superior or committee with the authority to appoint and have people directly reporting to you, you are a manager. Even with the tight budgets of much early years provision, you are probably also paid at a higher rate for the manager's position. This working definition aligns well with some of the meanings you will find in a dictionary definition for 'manage' or 'manager', which tend to include the concepts of controlling, administering and taking charge.

Typically, the manager is responsible for organising the work of their staff and the many details that affect operations day to day. In the business world, managers have long been responsible for giving some sort of formal performance appraisal, a development which has reached parts of early years provision. Within a hierarchy, some staff members will operate like junior managers, with responsibility for organising and supervising some aspects of work.

Only people in a superior position can appoint managers. In some cases, such as the community nursery model, the management committee may have considerable influence over the appointment. There will be a choice over title and some settings prefer the title of leader, but these people are acting as managers. A key difference between a manager and a leader is that you cannot legitimately appoint a leader, but you can appoint a manager. Leaders typically emerge and a great deal of the leadership literature is about trying to pin down how they do it. Managers can become leaders within their organisation because of who they are – their personal qualities – and for what they do – how they behave rather than a list of responsibilities they fulfil.

A leader may or may not be a manager and can be defined simply as someone who has followers. In other words, people want to follow leaders; they are not required to do so by virtue of the organisational hierarchy. Leaders can emerge in organisations because, for one reason or another, their colleagues value them. They may be better informed about what is happening on a national or local basis, or more skilled at explaining this kind of information. They may provide helpful counsel to colleagues when choices in practice are complicated or causing anxiety. They may have expertise in an area in which their colleagues are motivated to learn more. This kind of leader is not necessarily senior to the colleagues they support.

So, leadership and management may co-exist in the same person or the skills may be demonstrated in different ways by more than one staff member. The skills of management and leadership need to be equally respected. They do overlap, but are different in a number of ways. We do not think it is at all useful for early years practice, or any other sector, to opt for blurring the differences, nor to relabel management tasks as another type of leadership. This choice tends to portray the feeling that being a manager is humdrum, so important tasks need to be repackaged as something that sounds more exciting, such as administrative leadership, as in Kagan and Bowman (1997).

Make the connection with ... **choice of title**

Early years settings are plagued by this confusion between management and leadership. The more enthusiastic 'everyone can be a leader' approach (page 126) sometimes runs the risk of sidelining the essential tasks of management.

- What range of job titles have you noticed in the early years settings where you have worked or with which you have contact? What seemed to determine the choice of word?
- What views do you hear about being a 'manager' or a 'leader'? Is there a different emotional tone to each term?

The development in the UK of lead practitioners and the EYP status has raised practical considerations about how practitioners exercise leadership in these roles. Telling people that you are a leader does not resolve the important detail of how to ensure that others follow your lead when you may not have the authority to say, 'We are definitely going to...'. (More about authority from page 41.)

Confusion within the literature

A major problem in looking at leadership and management is that the terms are often used interchangeably or for different purposes. This confusion exists in different kinds of work environments and in research; it is not limited to discussions around early years provision.

Over the past 30 years or so, the word 'leader' has increased in popularity as the status of being a 'manager' has declined. Leadership is fashionable; management is not. In the late 1980s an advertisement was taken in the *Wall Street Journal* by United Technologies (reproduced in Bennis and Nanus, 1985, page 22) which began with, 'Let's get rid of management! People do not wish to be managed. They want to be led.' This fashion may have a point about how people feel in their working situation, but it does not help in making clear distinctions between leading and managing.

Another problem is that words like 'style' or 'role ' are used in an effort to clarify understanding of management or leadership, but sometimes simply add to the confusion. *Style* is mostly about how you carry out a task, your most usual demeanour or choice over how to behave. *Role*, meanwhile, is much more about the part you have to play within this organisation or service. To be clear, the role is more about what is done, style is about how it is done. Both terms have been applied to leadership and management. These can imply that leaders and managers act in a manner which may be consistent, or not, with their preferred pattern of behaviour as if no outside pressure were being applied to them. For example, your role may be as a manager of an early years setting. The style in which you execute this role could be autocratic and controlling, or highly participative and open to influence. Everyone has preferences about how they normally like to behave.

The other confusion arises from the two main sources of ideas about leadership in the literature. After years of looking at leaders in terms of the characteristics they display, most recent leadership research has emerged from the disciplines of social psychology or organisational behaviour. Studies from organisational behaviour typically looked at leadership as a potential way to improve the effectiveness of organisations, so much of this work has revolved around trying to improve corporate productivity and profitability. So theorists from within organisational behaviour looked to find or develop leadership within the managerial hierarchy that already existed in the organisation. An unwarranted conclusion was that leadership was first bolted on to management in corporate settings and then to some extent used to supplant management. In contrast, social psychologists looked at leadership in experimental groups – often in a university psychological laboratory – created for the purpose of study to see how leadership emerged and what it might look like in these temporary groups.

Different kinds of power

Physical power is relevant to life in general, but organisations have gone to great lengths to eliminate this from practical consideration, other than in jobs where height or physical strength are needed. So this section focuses on other kinds of power, as the power given by the organisation to perform your role is at the root of management.

Take another **perspective**

Nothing works without power. Children cannot stand without enough power to their legs. Without food and the energy (power) it brings to the brain we cannot think. Without power, your cooker, your television or your car fails to function. Power is necessary for us to do things. Without it, nothing works.

This concept also applies to working with children. You are bigger and stronger than them; you have more experience and knowledge; you can provide rewards and, as appropriate, reprimand them. Of course, you should use your adult power and greater strength wisely. However, you cannot make a conscious choice over how to exercise power if you are reluctant to admit that you have it.

Power is often a troublesome concept in the early years sector because it seems to be associated with throwing your weight around and being bossy. Yet power is central to any discussion around leadership and we are not convinced that it is at all helpful to relabel it as influence or something similar. Without power of some kind, you have no influence over others.

Discussing different sources of power contributes to understanding the difference between management and leadership. The *Shorter Oxford English Dictionary* sees 'power' as a 'possession of control or command over others, dominion, … sway'. At another level, power can be defined as the 'ability to do something or anything, or to act on a person or thing'. As such this could apply to anyone in the organisation who is skilled in an area, has a strong character, or loads of energy. Other concepts relevant to power include influence – a term that is preferred by some early years specialists – and either personal or social superiority. We use the word 'power' as an accurate, neutral term which should not be seen as negative.

The approach of distributed leadership, which is a model favoured by some early childhood specialists (discussed in Chapter 5), makes no sense without an honest acknowledgement of power in its positive sense. It is impossible to talk about distributing leadership unless the existence of power is acknowledged. Distribution of leadership inevitably involves a distribution of the power that would otherwise rest with one person. You cannot share power if you are reluctant to admit you have it in the first place. This also links to 'empowerment' (page 171).

Consider these different types of power.

Legitimate or positional power is given to the individual by the organisation by virtue of their position in the hierarchy. Basically this means that, unless there are compelling reasons to the contrary, you do what you are asked to do by superiors. The higher your place in the hierarchy, the fewer people there are who can tell you what to do.

Expert power emerges from skill and knowledge – your expertise. Expert power may be a reason for individuals to be promoted and given legitimate power. Equally, colleagues may value someone because of their expertise and informed ability to help, yet the individual has limited or no positional power.

Information is a source of power when individuals know more than colleagues who do not have access to such information. This source is typically strongly associated with expert power; however, a librarian, for example, may have information power without expertise in a particular topic.

Coercive power is the power of punishment. At its most extreme, this may mean the power to fire people. In other ways coercive power may be used by peers to give a colleague the cold shoulder, reprimand them, or deny them information that they may need. In general, organisations attempt to reduce the formal use of coercive power by making tasks and jobs as clear as possible through job descriptions and contracts. The logic is that if you have the skills, know what the rules are and do not break them, there should be no need for disciplinary action.

Reward is a power held to some extent by everyone within an organisation, although some elements are within the gift of the manager only. A reward is anything that someone wants. Within a supportive early years team, colleagues will be generous with spoken praise for a job well done by another individual or to appreciate a helping hand. Unlike the commercial world, reward within early years provision is unlikely to be monetary. A strong sense of commitment to an interesting job can be rewarding in itself, as can working with friendly colleagues (Lindon, 1980). Within early years provision, choices within continued professional development may be rewarding, such as being able to go on a training course you want. Some managers are also keen to organise enjoyable events or treats for the team.

Referent power is given to you by other people because of who you are and what you do. A person who is good at organising social events outside work might be given referent power by her colleagues. In other words, others are prepared to follow this person and hence give her leadership in this area. Similarly, individuals who are valued, perhaps, for their candour and commitment to colleagues may be given referent power. Referent power may also be given on the basis of simple liking, which might be linked with an individual's enthusiasm or what is sometimes called 'charisma'. This concept is rather elusive, but generally combines observable personal qualities and talents which draw others to this person. There are parallels with being seen as inspirational (pages 56 and 132).

Take another **perspective**

Managers can be completely unaware that some staff are being given referent power by colleagues.

For example, we had contact with a small consulting firm, with eight consultants, where there had been no staff turnover for four years. One individual consultant left the team and within three months five others had resigned. Clearly, the person who left first had a high level of referent power. If he decided it was sensible to leave, others quickly followed. As can sometimes happen with referent power, the consultant who first chose to leave had no idea that he had been given referent power until colleagues left in quick succession after him. Other sources of power are usually clear to the individual holding them.

Referent power is an important concept for senior people in any organisation to understand. The dynamics of the group may only be clear when the manager becomes aware that many staff look towards one individual for guidance on how to behave day by day. Such a person can be a positive influence in terms of best early years practice. However, a practitioner with strong referent power could be leading the mutiny about use of personal mobile phones in work time.

Independence is also a possible source of power. Most simply, the power of independence in the work situation is that people do not need the job. They are more able to ignore instructions they do not like or to resist changing their practice than those who need the work to support their own family.

Legitimate and expert power are the two sources most of use – and of interest – to organisations. Both are always present and necessary. However, organisations vary in terms of whether they place more emphasis on legitimate or expert power. Organisations which most value legitimate power will usually reward people for their length of service, their age, performing their jobs adequately and respecting superiors. Progress for individuals through levels of seniority will typically be formalised, and there may be a minimum time to be spent in one post before it is feasible to be considered for promotion. More status is given as of right to people higher up the hierarchy. In contrast, organisations that stress expert power will typically reward people more for performing well, developing their skills and coming up with useful new ways of meeting the requirements of the job. Promotion will be on merit and as available; neither being older nor in post for longer are relevant criteria.

Make the connection with ... **early years practice**

In your experience of different early years settings, how do you judge that legitimate and reward power operate? If possible, compare experiences within a course group.

- Have you spent time in early years settings where legitimate, positional power was a key issue? Perhaps staff meetings were dominated by the more senior staff members, who sought to close any discussion with words such as, 'When you've been in the job as long as I have ... '.

- Have you experienced settings where you realise now that expert power was highly valued? What kind of expertise or knowledge built that expert power? Did this come from extensive understanding of a single provision, or from work in other settings or sectors?

- Commercial organisations may reward staff with increased salary or perks associated with a higher position in the company. Early years provision does not operate in that way, so what rewards do staff seek?

- What happens in a setting where the main or only reward is not to be criticised, because 'you should all be doing that anyway!'? Why is affirmation of a job well done so important?

Management and managers are largely dependent upon legitimate or positional power to carry out their work. Managers prosper in formal organisations with rules, roles and responsibilities. Leadership is not based on legitimate power and will typically draw on other sources such as reward, referent and expert power. Leadership more easily thrives in the informal organisation in which there are no organisation charts or fixed job descriptions to limit flexibility. Leadership is more likely to emerge in organisations with fewer levels in the hierarchy – and hence where status differences are lower.

Exploring leaders and managers

There has been a considerable amount of research into and theorising about leadership. The amount of information is in itself something of a problem.

Nearly 30 years ago, Warren Bennis and Burt Nanus wrote: 'Decades of academic analysis have given us more than 350 definitions of leadership. Literally thousands of empirical investigations of leadership have been conducted in the last 75 years alone … Never have so many laboured so long to say so little' (1985, page 4). Rather more recently Kenneth Leithwood *et al.*, writing specifically about leadership within schools, expressed the view that 'leadership by adjective is a growth industry' and went on to list seven versions of leadership that they had found to be prominent in the literature about school leadership. The review team continued with: 'A few of these qualify as leadership theories and several are actually tested theories. But most are actually just slogans' (2008, page 7). Leithwood *et al.*, like Bennis and Nanus (and us, too), acknowledge the frustration and confusion, but continue to believe that there are very good reasons to develop our understanding of leadership and management.

Leaders and managers are different and this difference is not one of better–worse. Consider the following list of contrasts, based on discussion within the literature about the differences.

- Leaders act so as to innovate – developing new ideas and ways of working – whereas managers administer what has already been established as the way to run the organisation.
- Leaders are originals; they develop brand new ideas and ways of working. Managers are copies of what has worked well in the past; they imitate tried-and-tested ways of working. Leaders develop ideas, people and fresh ways of working; managers maintain existing systems.
- Leaders focus on people whereas managers focus on systems and structures. This is not saying that individual nursery managers do not care about people. They could combine a manager's role of attention to robust systems, which means the nursery does not grind to a halt, with a leader's role, which focuses on how to develop staff so that new ideas fall on fertile ground.
- Leaders inspire trust – they cannot work without it – whereas managers rely on structure and control – expressed through 'this is the way we do it'. This approach does not have to be heavy-handed.
- A big difference is the time frame. Leaders think long term and so they keep their eyes on the horizon – what is in the future. Managers think short term and keep focused on the day-to-day details. Consider this difference for a moment, especially if your continued professional development has included programmes implying that the best, most whizzy thing to be is a leader. What will happen in any early years settings if there is nobody acting like a manager?

- Leaders and managers both need to ask questions. But a leader tends to reflect on 'what' and 'why', whereas a manager considers more answers to 'how' and 'when'.
- Leaders are ready to challenge the status quo, hold true to what they believe and do what they are sure is the right thing. Managers, meanwhile, are keen not to rock the boat, to be consistent with agreed systems and to ensure that things are done correctly. Leaders hence focus on effectiveness, managers on efficiency.

So, leadership is essentially emotional and about relationships, whereas management is rational and about systems and control. Overall, management serves organisations well when the environment in which they are working is relatively unchanging and stable. In other words, management is most useful when you know what you are doing and have learned how to deal with the predictable issues that arise. In such a situation questions such as 'what do I do?' and 'when do I do it?' are completely appropriate and relevant. Having someone ask 'why?' can feel irritating when that question was asked and answered a long time ago. In such a stable environment, employees are typically asked to perform defined jobs and are not invited to 'think outside the box' as this just wastes time. However, when circumstances change and previous certainties ebb away, then organisations need to tolerate – even welcome – the 'why?' question. There is a need to use the entire range of talent from the workforce. Once it is no longer certain what is needed or most effective, the usual repertoire of managerial skills is not sufficient.

The need for leadership is much greater when change is a feature of work and past experience is not such a good guide as to what to do now. When facing an uncertain future, challenging the status quo may be exactly what is required in order for an organisation to adjust and to face unexpected challenges. Original thinking and innovation may be crucial for the organisation to survive in changing times, because tried-and-tested ground rules and established control systems do not apply any more.

Make the connection with ... **use of words**

For a long time, the concept of positive change was usually called 'progress'. This word carries the sense of change towards a better state, a positive move forward. Doubters would sometimes say, 'Well, that's progress, isn't it?' as a way to reconcile themselves to changes with which they were not entirely content. Now it is very common to hear the word 'change', which carries negative as well as positive associations – hence there is sometimes discussion around enabling people to see change 'as an opportunity rather than a threat'.

- What do you think about the associations of 'progress' and 'change'?

Times of change bring leaders to the fore, but not always to support the direction being taken. It is equally possible that leaders emerge in an organisation as a focus for colleagues trying to block changes to the familiar patterns. In early years provision, as with other organisations, these leaders of resistance may be 'old hands' who have 'seen it all before'. They may be experienced in using existing organisational systems – and their colleagues' feelings of insecurity generated by the threat of change – to undermine change attempts.

The changing world of work

The world of employment changed a great deal over the last decades of the 20th century. By the mid-1990s, Carole Pemberton (1995) described the shift in what was offered by employers and what was generally expected of employees. Consider how far this contrast makes sense for your knowledge of working in the early years sector in particular.

- Historically organisations offered security and care. In return the workforce offered to conform to what was asked. Today few if any jobs are secure, even those in sectors which used to be safe. Nowadays employees are more likely to offer flexibility because the expectations of the organisation will change – insecurity is everywhere. Hence whereas roles were clear and unchanging, they are now less clear and subject to change.
- Organisations used to offer a clear career path forward; now there are opportunities to develop but no promises as to future progression. As such the individual's commitment to the organisation itself – often helped by these career paths – has been replaced by the individual's desire to develop themselves, so that they are more generally employable.
- Previously many – perhaps most – jobs offered predictable rewards for service (staying with the organisation); now the pattern of rewards is more related to how well you perform than with length of service (emphasising expert, rather than legitimate, power). Whereas employees previously offered their loyalty to an organisation, and to do the job, now they offer a good standard of performance – often beyond what is specifically part of their job.
- Work is typically more stressful. Workers are asked to deal with this stress – and the possibility of work–life imbalance – by working long hours.
- A previously high level of trust in the employing organisation has been steadily replaced with distrust and scepticism.

The early years workforce has undoubtedly experienced considerable change, but it is not alone. Across different sectors changes have meant that everyone has to work harder, use more of their capabilities in their job than historically, and people are confronted by considerably more uncertainty in their daily work. In early years provision, as elsewhere, there used to be a clear hierarchy and a general assumption that you learned the skills needed for the job and got on with it. There is far less clarity now, added to by waves of external change affecting early years and related sectors such as education or social care.

Leadership for times of change

The argument is that change is now the normal state of affairs. Rather than being a cause for alarm, it is the best way to make real progress. It is very hard to find any organisation that does not experience some degree of change, such as staff turnover, on a continual basis, even in a mainly stable setting. However, there is a difference between intentional change and imposed change. On balance, people are usually positive about change they have personally chosen to undertake and more negative when that change has been launched by an external force.

- *Intentional change*, such as giving up smoking or improving your diet, may still feel challenging and carry the threat of possible failure. Yet the change is anticipated and planned for, at least to some extent. You can choose the pace that suits you: opting for making significant and immediate changes to your lifestyle or going for a more gradual approach. You can anticipate the upside if you succeed: you hope to feel more healthy, save money or be able to participate in new activities.
- By contrast, *imposed change* is not your decision, yet in different ways you are asked, perhaps expected, to implement the change. You may know that some kinds of imposed change are on the way but you are less able to anticipate or plan in advance. In early years provision, for instance, you know a new framework or important guidance document is on the way but you are thin on details until it is in front of you. Often imposed change – or a series of unrelenting changes – appears abrupt, even wilful, on the part of those insisting on change, and neither gradual nor properly paced. Rather than being a change to your life which you have planned, imposed change disrupts routine and often seems to create more problems than it solves.

Make the connection with ... **your own experience**

Thinking back over recent years, what kinds of changes have you experienced in your work?

- What kinds of changes were intentional and fully under your control?
- Were some changes anticipated and planned? What did you and your colleagues see coming and how did you prepare?
- Were some changes imposed from the outside? How did you deal with them?

Feel free to return to this reflection after reading more about change in Chapters 3 and 7.

With imposed change, individuals who cannot tolerate the new circumstances will leave if they are able to find alternative work. Equally disgruntled colleagues, who feel they have no option but to stay, are confused when they no longer see what is expected of them or what will please the more senior staff. If senior people are unable to deal with the fallout from change, then staff motivation and morale will plummet. People will look to someone to blame: internally by blaming the management, externally by blaming the government or the inspectorate. It is difficult to manage your way out of this conundrum, precisely because there are no longer the old certainties. You might, however, be able to lead, and be led, out of the period of uncertainty.

For many people change is scary; they wish to hold on to what they have because it is what they know: old habits die hard. A personal sense of security in your skills, talents, even your employability, can be challenged by change or the threat of change. When there are few certainties to point the way, two-way trust is crucial: trust in employees from the organisation and not just employees trusting that the organisation will do right by them. Rather than established procedures and controls, mutual trust becomes the glue which holds an organisation together.

Even in times of uncertainty and change, organisations still need to be effective in what they do and management will always be required to ensure that this happens. Over the major changes of recent times for early years provision, somebody has still had to keep track of fees from parents, ensuring that staff are paid (as is the supplier who delivers food for lunch) and that nobody is getting lax over the children's health, safety and well being. Some details do not change, even if over time the systems vary: increasingly you take money through direct debit and not cheques, or you improve the physical security of your setting with a higher level of technology.

In early years provision major changes have been made to the context in which daily practice operates – the children have not changed. So what has happened within and around early years provision that had made leadership such a central issue?

Leadership as a key issue for early years

The history of the study of leadership and what it means spreads over many decades in the theory and practice of making organisations better. A huge number of books and articles have been published about leadership in the commercial sphere and the list is steadily increasing in health, social care and education. Ideas and models have evolved in very diverse ways, with much of value for the early years profession to learn (Chapter 2). In contrast to business organisations, in early years provision there has been a long delay before leadership has become central as a professional issue.

A new focus on early years leadership

The sector has experienced a sustained period of strong pressure towards change, so the skills of leadership have become necessary. Similar pressures have also affected Australia and New Zealand and, to an extent, some other European countries and the USA. This common ground further supported the international links already established within early childhood studies in the UK from the 1980s (Nivala and Hujala, 2002; Siraj-Blatchford and Manni, 2007).

Several broad and interrelated changes affecting early years have supported a focus on the need for leadership in and for early years provision.

- An increased concern to challenge the low status of working within early childhood and to establish an appropriate confidence and professionalism. Leadership was needed to raise the profile of the sector as a whole and to nurture the potential for leadership within settings.
- Over the second half of the 1990s, there was a significantly heightened profile for early years in policy and government agendas. This change brought an unprecedented degree of government intervention into a sector more familiar with highlighting the problems of being overlooked as a crucial stage in children's development. 'Be careful what you wish for' – allegedly an ancient Chinese proverb – is relevant here.
- The focus on the childcare needs of the economy, and concerns about improving children's life chances, led to a significant expansion of early years provision, especially of the private and voluntary sectors. This development raised concerns about quality of provision. Leadership was needed to address best practice and bring about improvements where necessary.
- Confident leadership has included advocating on behalf of young children as well as their families. The imposition of targets and shifting government expectations have highlighted the need to establish an early years sector that does not exist solely to meet the childcare needs of the economy, nor to prepare children for primary school in the narrowest sense.
- A significant increase has been seen in the number of early years centres aiming to combine services for children and families and specifically the growth of children's centres. Such centres require the ability to lead across professional boundaries and to cope with multi-agency working.

Since the 1980s there has been no shortage of detailed guidance about best practice with young children; materials have been produced in the UK, the USA, Australia and New Zealand. There was definitely an awareness of the role for a manager, but its importance was often left unspoken. Managers were responsible for establishing a clear policy about partnership with families or ensuring systems that valued a key person approach (Bredekamp and Copple, 1997; Post and Hohmann, 2000). It became clearer that the best drafted guidance would not get established alone, even in the fertile ground of nurturing and well-intentioned teams.

Even motivated practitioners need guidance and specific coaching, not just telling. Munton and Mooney (2001) reported how practitioners well disposed to completing self-assessment formats still struggled with their next steps to changing practice without effective guidance from a leader (more in Chapter 7). Manning-Morton and Thorp (2001) represent the change towards explaining what else needs to happen with their subsection running throughout the *Key times* resource which is headed up, 'When there are high quality opportunities for … The management of the setting ensures that …'.

Dunlop (2008) points to the increased mention in statements from the Scottish Executive about the importance of leadership in schools as the 3–18 Curriculum for Excellence was developed and launched. Changes over school inspection in England from 2005 onwards meant that heads had to consider Teaching and Learning Responsibilities (TLRs) that applied specifically to the early years part of any primary school. Best practice should always have fully recognised the importance of the nursery and reception class – but respect was not a given in all schools. The TLRs for early years raised the issues of leadership for quality for the youngest children on the school site. Also, the growing literature on educational leadership was affected by the drive to ensure enhanced achievement for children and young people in schools.

Pause for reflection

This section presents the main themes that provoked this heightened focus on leadership within the early years sector.

- Are there other strands which you would be inclined to put more to the fore of any explanation of this broad social change for early years?

Many readers will be involved in a leadership module or programme.

- For what reason(s) did you decide that a focus on leadership was an important step in your continued professional development?
- What was the rationale from anyone who directly encouraged you in this direction?
- To what extent do these more individual reasons connect with the broader social explanation which we have offered here?

Searching for the model for early years leadership

So from the 1990s onwards there has been an increasing focus on the need for clear leadership within the early years sector, and much discussion about what kind of leadership is best suited to early years provision. Muijs *et al.* (2004) and Dunlop (2008) undertook significant literature reviews and reported that there were only a very small number of research studies that provided documentation of early years leadership in action. Dunlop explains how she extended her review to include any books, articles and unpublished papers which had discussed this subject since 2000. This decision produced a more extensive bibliography to the review and she summarised the considerable exchange of views and development of concepts.

Much of this food for thought is potentially very valuable. However, we agree with Dunlop and Muijs *et al.* that the balance of the literature about early years leadership is biased towards firm opinions about what is appropriate or likely to work best rather than towards informed research data. There is nothing the matter with expressing clear-cut views; you will read ours throughout this book. There is, however, a problem when assertions are backed by limited research showing what early years leaders actually do day by day. There are a lot of opinions, yet limited observational evidence to show what kinds of leadership behaviour actually work best against appropriate criteria.

A frequent line of argument is that 'traditional models of leadership don't work for early years'. This assertion runs through many of the academic papers in the International Leadership Project (Nivala and Hujala, 2002); also in Kagan and Bowman (1997), Ebbeck and Waniganayake (2003), Thornton (2007), Garvey and Lancaster (2010) and Dickins (2010). The closely linked argument is that the sector needs a different model that fits the ethos and working practices of professionals within early childhood. In the background reading for this book, we would read yet again about allegedly 'traditional' views on leadership and the choice of word became increasingly odd. To what time span are writers referring and who holds this, or even which, view as traditional? We agree with the conclusion of Muijs *et al.* (2004) that much discussion around early years leadership is not well informed about the broader field of leadership studies, encompassing business, social care and education.

There are exceptions. For example, Hard (2005) and Rodd (2006) consider the genuine diversity of models for leadership while focusing on the specific issues of the early years sector.

There seem to be several themes behind the stance that traditional models have nothing to offer: we will take each one in turn. There is a question mark against each heading because we want to flag that these proposals need to be carefully considered. They are not proven statements simply to be accepted on the basis of continual repetition. Some regular proposals have a small nugget of truth, but there is good reason to challenge that they offer the full picture for a serious consideration of early years leadership.

All about traits of a leader?

Some firm statements that 'traditional models don't work for early years' appear to rest on scanty reviews of the huge leadership literature. Existing theories of leadership are said to be all about trying to establish leadership traits that will apply in any situation. The search for persistent traits shown by effective leaders was one, early strand of leadership theory but a small part of leadership knowledge today (as shown in Chapter 2).

Intriguingly, some of the literature about early years leadership is strongly focused on identifying important traits, although they are labelled as characteristics, qualities or attributes. The words vary, but there is a continuing effort to describe what it is personally that makes a leader effective (Moyles, 2006; Pound, 2008; Rodd, 2006).

All about the hero-leader?

Early years leadership is often pitched as incompatible with what is claimed to be a focus elsewhere on the individual, charismatic, heroic style of leader. The argument is, then, that the early years sector needs what Garvey and Lancaster (2010) call a post-heroic style, characterised by features of social sensitivity, inclusiveness and collaboration. However, it is untrue that the available leadership literature is dominated by a superhero model.

Furthermore, we would argue that some discussion around early years leadership gets very close indeed to promoting a new heroism (super-heroines in fact) with high expectations and a long list of required qualities. Inspirational hero-leaders are criticised as an alleged problem in the general literature on leadership. Yet, being an inspiration is a key feature of some discussion around early years leaders (page 130).

Only about the overall leader?

Most, or all, theories outside early childhood are said to be focused only on the person in overall charge of any organisation, not allowing for any kind of power sharing. This conclusion is not justified. Undoubtedly some studies have been especially interested in the behaviour of chief executives and the highest echelons in business organisations. However, a considerable amount of exploration has gone beyond the top of the hierarchy, looking at kinds of leadership that work for middle management, or for individual employees, or for leading a small team – even for being an effective follower.

Models suited only to the commercial world?

Apparently, leadership theories are all about the commercial sphere of business and therefore cannot offer any relevant ideas to the primarily public early years sector. It is true to say that a considerable amount of the leadership literature was generated within the world of business (and in the USA), but the models discussed in Chapter 2 are about interpersonal relations and choices over how to lead. They are about people working with, relating to and leading other people.

A related argument for dismissing alternative leadership models is the claim that they ignore context. This criticism is sometimes linked to the belief that leadership is discussed only, or mainly, with the assumption that the goal is profit. Yes, some applications of ideas around leadership are tied to the goal of making money, but not all by any means. Further, it is increasingly shown that making money has little to do with being an effective leader; it is but one of a host of outcomes.

Many interesting theoretical perspectives are all about context: that there is no single approach for a leader that is appropriate for every place, time and team. There has also been a growing literature about leadership in schools. That sector has produced a considerable amount of discussion about distributed leadership – frequently promoted as the ideal model for early years leadership (page 119) – so it is unwise to ignore this body of information.

What do practitioners believe about leadership?

Some authors seem to be referring to beliefs about leadership held within the early years workforce itself: that leaders can only ever be the people in charge or that they have to be autocratic (for example, Rosemary and Puroila, 2002 and other papers from the International Leadership Project). Yet within the same article, authors explicitly promote the view that, outside the early years professional arena, any theoretical models view leadership in this narrow way.

It is possible that many early years practitioners have a limited view of how a leader should or could behave. Maybe they are uneasy because of a belief that leaders have to provide quick, right answers – even with some of the complex dilemmas that are part of early years practice. So, the early years workforce needs accurate information about what they can gain from the broader literature on leadership.

Autocratic rather than democratic?

Leadership as discussed other than in early years, or possibly education, is allegedly all about exercising power (and often coercive power at that) over people and behaving in an autocratic way. This will not work in early years provision, which is claimed to be by nature democratic. The largely female workforce is said to prefer exercising friendly influence towards colleagues rather than wielding power over them.

Yet available models of leadership address the serious limitations to an autocratic style and explore how collaboration and confident leadership needs to co-exist. Studies of early years practitioners and their leaders, and careful consideration of anecdotal information, highlight that a preference for consensus and a democratic style sometimes hides a struggle with being authoritative when it is necessary. Assertiveness, and understanding how this is different from aggression, is sometimes a learning challenge for early years leaders (page 93) to escape a potential default setting of passivity.

Competition rather than collaboration?

An alternative model for leadership is claimed to be necessary because the early years workforce is characterised by high levels of collaboration rather than competition, and by generous support rather than jostling for position. Available studies, and our own professional experience, would support this viewpoint as a fair description of a proportion of settings, but it is certainly not the whole picture.

Traditional models of leadership are also supposedly all about hierarchy and so have nothing to say to the early years sector because provision is (allegedly) non-hierarchical and unconcerned about status and power. First, there are influential models that see a flat hierarchy as supportive of emerging leaders in any organisation. Second, many early years settings have a clear hierarchy which does not necessarily bring an oppressive use of power. There is most usually someone in overall charge of any provision, often with a deputy or two deputies in large settings. Again in larger settings there can be (and, you could argue, should be) clear lines of responsibility for practitioners who are room or unit leaders.

Rational with no place for emotions?

The early years provision is presented as a sector in which nurturance should be highly valued as it is crucial for the well being of children and their families. We support this view, but we disagree with the implication that early years professionals will not find any useful theories elsewhere because they are all founded on a rational model of a (usually male) leader, for whom emotions interfere and are avoided. Today's leaders need to use their emotions; the broader literature on leadership is very clear on this issue.

A very female workforce

The early years workforce is overwhelmingly female and the argument is made that existing models of leadership are mainly or entirely about men in the role of leaders. So a new and alternative model is needed for early years leadership.

A model to apply to women?

Some early childhood specialists propose that women – as a whole and in particular in early years provision – are considerably more communicative and nurturant than men. Some feminist analysis of leadership offers the most forceful rejection of any existing theories of leadership. All models are claimed to be underpinned with masculine traits, wholly negative and tainted by an aggressive outlook. Therefore, they say these models of leadership are not only inappropriate for the nature of early years work but should be actively rejected along with the oppressive patriarchy they represent.

Not all writers who would happily say they take a feminist perspective go up the conceptual gears of rejection in this way. Some useful ideas are included in the written materials underpinned by this particular strand of academic feminism. However, in company with some other early childhood specialists, we take serious issue with an analysis which depends on sweeping stereotypes about men, who as a small minority in the early years workforce are not really in a position to protest. You can read more about this theoretical approach on page 24. First of all, we want to address the possible existence of sex differences: the assertion upon which this approach rests.

Generally speaking, the phrase *sex differences* is used to mean the existence, or not, of significant variation between people on the basis of their being male or female: basic biology. The word *gender* flags up the importance of social learning and the extent to which being male or female has elements of a social role. Many people would argue that a considerable amount of the apparent male–female difference is caused less by inherent differentiation between the sexes than by social and cultural pressures that direct girls and boys from a very young age (see, for example, Eliot, 2009).

Discussion about gender and children within early childhood studies is often led by the perspective of social learning. By contrast, it strikes us that much of the discussion about the very female early years workforce is expressed in terms that this is how women are, rather than how they have learned to behave. Those writers who criticise models of leadership for being too imbued with masculine features give the predominant message that this is how men are, rather than this is how society has shaped them to behave.

In the end, the question about exactly how much is biology and how much is social learning is a largely irresolvable puzzle. The best way forward is to focus on the prevailing situation in the early years workforce, which has a very small minority of male practitioners. The patterns of behaviour which are said by some early childhood specialists to be typical of this overwhelming female workforce could be interpreted as the consequence of social learning. But it is then necessary to explore the implications, rather than implying that the female pattern is an unrelieved positive, or that the socially learned male pattern has no redeeming features. Also, nobody writing or talking about early years provision should forget that there are some male practitioners and managers in group settings and the childminding service.

How different are the sexes?

The large research literature on sex differences points to some consistent, although not always large, differences between how adult women and men behave. It is crucial to note that *research cannot predict that an individual woman, or man, will behave in a given direction shown by group statistics.* The information, although reliably obtained, speaks of trends, a situation of 'more or less likely to …'. However, when a workforce is dominated by one sex, it is very likely that the overall pattern of behaviour preferences will be affected.

Sex differences research has findings that are relevant to how women and men may behave at work. We have drawn here from an impressive research review by Ellis *et al.* (2008). On balance:

- Females are more likely to conform than males.
- Men are more likely to resist changing their behaviour towards what is viewed as a female pattern than females who are more likely to adjust towards acting in a more male fashion.
- Women are more nurturing, more inclusive of others and provide more emotional support to others – on average. Just keep remembering these are not 'everyone' statements about either sex.
- Females are better than males at reading the messages of body language. They also typically make and maintain eye contact more.
- Women seek more help than men when facing unfamiliar tasks and in resolving interpersonal disputes.
- Males devote more time and energy to raise their dominance or social status. They negotiate more for higher wages. The higher the proportion of men in an occupation, the higher the average salary in that occupation.
- Men interrupt more in communication with others.
- Men use more assertive speech that makes statements unqualified by 'maybes'. Females use more additional comments which qualify what they have just said, with a sense of 'perhaps' or it 'depends'.

So what?

To some extent, the sex differences research supports views about the more collaborative and nurturant atmosphere of early years provision, and attributing this balance to the large number of women involved in the sector. The practical implications of this research for work are that (on average!) females tend to be more social and less dominant. They are less likely to push themselves forward and more likely to seek harmonious working relationships. As such they are less likely to want or to seek advancement. Even when forming friendships, men are more likely than women to seek to achieve specific goals as a result. The implication is that it will be harder for women to take tough decisions which may cause distress because they will be more aware than men of the painful emotions that this decision may bring in its wake. By contrast, males may not be clued in enough, or willing enough, to be able to offer as high a level of social and emotional support, when this is needed, as females are likely to do.

Women as leaders

It has taken time for the organisational behaviour literature to draw on research about women in senior positions in the workplace – largely because there were proportionally few women in top positions. Social pressures, and active discrimination against women in work or being promoted to higher positions, meant that for decades men were the ones occupying the more senior roles. However, as significantly more women became involved in workforces in the western world, researchers began to address issues of gender and leadership. So as women became more senior, the research accurately reflected this change. Research is now readily available on women in senior positions exercising authority and leadership.

Many studies have now accurately reflected the sex bias at the upper sections of organisational hierarchies, and have noted the existence of the 'glass ceiling' which seems to prevent women reaching the very top in some enterprises. The research on patterns of male and female behaviour does suggest some broad between-the-sexes differences, as well as considerable within-sex diversity. There are some implications that women in senior positions, or as leaders, may behave differently from men. But yet again, there is much common ground between men and women.

A substantial review and discussion by Alvesson and Billing (2009) illustrates that studies of male–female patterns in senior positions across different work sectors show broad areas of agreement. There is reasonable consensus that compared with men, women are worse off in terms of income, they are underrepresented in the higher-level positions in many professions and hold proportionately more lower-level jobs. They experience a greater frequency of reported sexual harassment. Women also take more responsibility than their male counterparts for home and family. This situation may go some way to explaining why the authors found that women managers experience more stress than their male colleagues.

A broad swathe of the research literature reports that women and men are not very different in how they operate as managers. The requirements of the job necessitate a high level of consistency for any manager to be successful. A smaller, but still substantial, minority view is that female managers are more network-orientated and skilled in dealing with working relationships. Female qualities such as a higher level of verbal communication, and higher needs for affiliation and empathy have been found to be linked to more positive leadership (and management) behaviours in the workplace. Being supportive and considerate – again a difference found sometimes to be weighted towards women – is associated with more effective leadership within some contexts. There is a consistent finding across different workplaces that women lead in a more participative, democratic way than men. This sex difference has meant that women tend to be more effective in middle management positions where interpersonal skills are at a premium. Equally, it has been suggested that men who behave more like the female pattern have a better chance of success in today's organisations.

When the nature of the work requires women to act in a stereotypical male autocratic fashion, they tend to be devalued by their workforce, a finding that appears to operate across workplaces and not only specific areas such as the military. Since the 1990s a still-open debate has continued over whether the style of leadership that women tend to favour is more effective and under what circumstances. One line of argument continues that female–male differences and what appears to be their preferred styles have little or no relationship to effective leadership. In contrast, it is claimed that the style of leadership preferred by many women tends to be more transformational (from page 54) than men's style, and also that women tend to reward staff more for behaviours that they wish to see.

Collaborative?

Muijs *et al.* (2004) refer to the literature about what are judged to be the characteristics of effective early childhood leaders and conclude that this work is most usually 'normative prescriptions that do not refer to empirical studies' (page 163) – in other words, assertions without factual basis. There is a great deal of description and agreement in listing what is needed in terms of knowledge, warm personal qualities and ability to communicate. The preference for a more collaborative way of working is certainly a dominant theme in discussion about early years leadership. This image is often summed up by a theme that women prefer to influence their colleagues than have power over them. This is a bit difficult because influence depends on using power (see page 6). The argument that women, as a whole and as leaders, are more nurturant and prefer a consultative style of leadership also allows for the potential problem that the style may be viewed from the outside as an inability to take a lead, or failing to have a clear viewpoint.

Looking at the sex differences research, it is possible to see that collaboration and communication are likely to be strong characteristics of very female groups. However, some of the early years leadership discussion is simplistic. All male leaders do not take an authoritarian approach and some females in charge of early years provision embrace the role of despot with enthusiasm. There may, of course, be many reasons behind this choice. With hindsight, some early years tyrants of our professional acquaintance were possibly very anxious about unwelcome change in their familiar world. The safest option seemed to be to hold even more tightly to what was familiar and dismiss even minor rebellion from the staff group as evidence of ignorance and inappropriate challenge.

Feminism, equality and inclusion

There is more than one way to offer a feminist analysis of leadership. Dip into the paper from the *Stanford Encyclopaedia of Philosophy* (2011, full details on page 29) and you will see a maze of different positions and disagreements all under the broad banner of a feminist perspective. Some, not all, feminist approaches to gender studies take what Alvesson and Billing (2009) characterise as 'hypercritique', by which they mean 'a one-sided and exaggerated focus on the negative features of a social order'.

We agree that it is neither helpful nor accurate to overstate the presence of coercive norms across the whole range of workplaces and exclusively emphasise the constraints on women. Alvesson and Billing argue that a gender-sensitive, rather than a gender-exclusive, approach is far more likely to improve a situation that is less than optimal for either sex. We have chosen to use their terms within this section.

The gender-exclusive perspective

Scrivens (2002a) offers a particular feminist perspective on leadership within early years settings. She argues that 'the dominant construct of "leadership" in the English-speaking world is bound by a masculinist construct associated with aggressiveness, forcefulness, competitiveness and independence' (page 25). She explores ways to make sense of leadership which, she proposes, arises from women's preferred ways of leading. Scrivens describes a feminist argument that, regardless of specific models of leadership, any discussion arising from organisational theory creates an image of any effective leader as characterised by dominance, emotional control, confidence and self-esteem. These are seen as antithetical to a more female orientation towards relationships, which inclines women towards a more participatory style of leadership characterised by power sharing. Some of these points have an appeal, but in overall terms this approach has serious problems.

For instance, the earliest history of leadership study occurred when social conditions were such that women were not welcomed in, and sometimes actively excluded from, leadership positions. Times have changed, and things have moved on significantly. It takes a huge conceptual mis-leap to categorise all models of leadership (see Chapter 2) as examples of aggressive approaches devoid of the attention to relationships, well being and the nurturant outlook that is claimed for the female approach. It is equivalent to the misdirection that would result if material about early years provision in the UK were written as if nothing had changed since the 1970s. The stance is just wrong.

Scrivens (2002a) draws on descriptive studies of women in educational posts and other areas of work to argue that an ethic of caring permeates some educational leadership and that men as well as women in these roles often operate in a similar way. The argument is, then, that men are able to behave in line with a model derived from women's theory. An equally compelling argument could surely be that the context is influential and some men are attracted to this kind of work because a more caring, consultative style sits easily upon them.

It is sometimes argued within this kind of feminist analysis that models such as transformational leadership co-opted women's style without acknowledging that source. We support the alternative possibility (likelihood even) that the developers of transformational leadership embraced the diversity within people and transcended gender stereotypes.

Gender-sensitive approaches

Looking across work sectors, Alvesson and Billing (2009) argue for a more nuanced approach than the bold assertion that men are always the happy beneficiaries of a status quo which disadvantages women. They do not challenge, and nor would we, that some debilitating stereotyping continues to bedevil aspects of working life. However, men are sometimes constrained by stereotypes and beliefs about their 'normal' patterns of behaviour. Where it exists, the stereotypical macho approach within an organisation can sideline men who would prefer not to work in this way.

Aubrey (2007) comments on the positive aspects of a feminist perspective on leadership for a sector like early years. She also points out the inherent risks of linking specific characteristics of leadership with values or qualities that are proposed to be masculine or feminine. We agree with Aubrey's concern that this 'leads both to stereotyping women and alienating nurturing men' (page 2). Hard (2005) also raises troublesome features of an analysis that contrasts all women and all men and posits distinctively different styles of leadership around the alleged female preference to operate within an ethic of caring and valuing relationships. The diversity in women is far greater than the gender stereotype: a diversity which challenges the enthusiastic promotion of a 'one-size-fits-all' feminised style of leadership allegedly followed by all women.

Feminist approaches are diverse; only some writers chose a hard-line view in which gender studies are only interested in addressing the perceived concerns of women, with the consequence that men are marginalised. However, this non-inclusive approach has implications for early years provision and genuinely reflective practice. It appears to underlie statements acceptable to parts of the early years sector, that a primary goal of early years provision is specifically to improve the situation of women and children.

Henderson-Kelly and Pamphilon (2000) echo the focus on an early years service developed and run overwhelmingly by women. The childcare directors whom they interviewed were sometimes keen to make clear, 'I'm not a feminist', sometimes with an implied 'but'. Henderson-Kelly and Pamphilon are writing about Australia, but their interpretation of the perspective of the directors is shared by some writers in the UK. Their view is that the directors' model in practice was feminist because it was definitely developed for, by and about women. Korsvik (2011) offers a reminder of the diverse views in the feminist movement. Korsvik outlines major disagreements between different factions of the women's movement over gender equality, childcare and the role of fathers.

Take another **perspective**

There are ethical problems with an outlook on practice that risks sidelining men as fathers, or other family carers, and men working in early years.

- What happens to best practice for partnership with parents: are we back with the word 'parents' meaning only mothers or family carers who are female?

- What kind of commitment to equality – surely another non-negotiable in early years practice – is being offered if men are written out of key aims as if they can be dismissed in terms of social inclusion?
- What effect does all of this have on how boys and girls are treated in the provision?
- What do you think?

Male practitioners in early years

The discussion about gender and organisations is frequently about the underrepresentation of women in some professions or at more senior levels. The discussion is far less often about the possible consequences for men who form a significant minority in a profession: the long-term and prevailing situation within early years and to only a slightly lesser degree in primary education. Men form a very small group within the early years profession, estimated to be about one per cent of the workforce. This percentage of males has scarcely changed over recent decades. It is appropriate to explore both the reasons for this and the consequences of having a workforce that is so close to single-sex.

Alvesson and Billing (2009) talk about gender as an 'organising principle' that significantly shapes the perceptions of young men and women before they start work. By this they mean the directions – implicit or explicit – that young people are given during their years of schooling and careers advice. Certainly, the message is that working in childcare is still presented to secondary school students in the UK as one of the default options for female adolescents, especially those with shaky academic credentials, but not for boys.

Often the first explanation offered for the small number of male practitioners focuses on pay and conditions which are not (comparatively) high. However, an additional complication for men in early years in the UK has been a less than strident challenge from the sector to suspicions raised about the motives of any men who choose to work with young children. Some interpretations of safeguarding have been dominated by a misunderstanding of statistics about abuse and a view of touch as a risk area to be managed (Lindon, 2008). Hence the unease has been able to take root and to counter the equality argument in settings.

Overall, it is probably true that male early years practitioners, rather like women in any sector dominated by men, have to be extra keen to do the job and accept that, even in the most welcoming of environments, they will sometimes be viewed first as a man and then as a colleague. Like other minority groups within a given profession, some male practitioners have welcomed the support offered by male childcare networks.

Take another **perspective**

What about male early years practitioners? What is their standpoint as the minority sex in the profession?

Start by looking at Owen's (2003) paper on men working in early years and accessible online at **www.koordination-maennerinkitas.de/uploads/media/Owen-Charlie-Men_s-Work_02.pdf**

Do a further internet search of any studies of male early years practitioners or leaders – 'men in childcare' brings up quite a few leads.

- What are the main issues that arise for you?
- Ideally, discuss your views and the ideas you have gathered with colleagues.
- Most readers will be female. If you are fortunate to have one, invite the views of your male colleague(s).
- If you are a male practitioner, please be ready to express your views in discussion.

Conclusion

It is valuable to shine a light on what practitioners at different levels of seniority believe about leadership and ways to behave as a leader. However, some of the discussion about 'traditional' models for leadership in books and articles can only be interpreted as a dismissal of anything other than the specific early years model proposed by the author.

The overall aim of this book is to enable experienced early years practitioners to understand leadership: what being a leader entails and the process of leading others, especially colleagues, in different ways. There is considerable scope for individual style within the leadership role; leaders are not all cut from an identical roll of cloth. Yet there are some common themes and challenges across leadership in any sphere. We seek to focus on areas where early years practice can learn from other workplaces and the differences that must be considered. To that end, Chapter 2 now looks at what can be learned from the broad field of leadership research.

Resources

- **Alvesson, M. and Billing, Y.** (2009) *Understanding Gender and Organizations*. London: Sage.
- **Aubrey, C.** (2007) *Leading and Managing in the Early Years*. London: Sage.
- **Bennis, W. and Nanus, B.** (1985) *Leaders: The strategies for taking charge*. New York: Harper and Row.
- **Bredekamp, S. and Copple, C.** (eds) (1997) *Developmentally Appropriate Practice in Early Childhood Programs*. Washington, DC: National Association for the Education of Young Children.
- **Dickins, M.** (2010) *Leadership for Listening*. London: National Children's Bureau.

- **Dunlop, A.-W.** (2008) *A Literature Review on Leadership in Early Years.* Search by title on **www.ltscotland.org.uk**
- **Ebbeck, M. and Waniganayake, M.** (2003) *Early Childhood Professionals: Leading today and tomorrow.* Sydney: MacLennan and Petty.
- **Eliot, L.** (2009) *Pink Brain, Blue Brain: How small differences grow into troublesome gaps and what we can do about it.* New York: Houghton Mifflin Harcourt.
- **Ellis, L., Hershberger, S., Field, E., Wersinger, S., Pellis, S., Geary, D., Palmer, C., Hoyenga, K., Hetsroni, A. and Karadi, K.** (2008) *Sex Differences: Summarizing more than a century of scientific research.* Hove: Psychology Press.
- **Garvey, D. and Lancaster, A.** (2010) *Leadership for Quality in Early Years and Playwork: Supporting your team to achieve better outcomes for children and families.* London: National Children's Bureau.
- **Hard, L.** (2005) *How Is Leadership Understood and Enacted within the Field of Early Childhood Education and Care?* Unpublished doctoral thesis, Center for Learning Innovation, Queensland University of Technology. **http://eprints.qut.edu.au/16213/1/Louise_Hard_Thesis.pdf**
- **Henderson-Kelly, L. and Pamphilon, B.** (2000) 'Women's models of leadership in the child care sector'. *Australian Journal of Early Childhood*, 25, 1, 8–12, March.
- **Hujala, E.** (2002) 'Leadership in a child care context in Finland', in Nivala, V. and Hujala, E. (eds) *Leadership in Early Childhood Education: Cross-cultural perspectives.* Oulu: Oulu University Press, **http://herkules.oulu.fi/isbn9514268539/**
- **Kagan, S. and Bowman, B.** (eds) (1997) *Leadership in Early Care and Education.* Washington, DC: National Association for the Education of Young Children.
- **Korsvik, T.** (2011) 'Childcare policy since the 1970s in the "most gender equal country in the world": a field of controversy and grassroots activism'. *European Journal of Women's Studies,* 18, 2, 135–53.
- **Leithwood, K., Day, C., Sammons, P., Harris, A. and Hopkins, D.** (2008) *Successful School Leadership: What It Is and How It Influences Pupil Learning.* Department for Children Schools and Families with National College for School Leadership. **http://education.gov.uk/publications/eOrderingDownload/RR800.pdf**
- **Lindon, J.** (2008) *Safeguarding Children and Young People: Child protection 0–18 years.* London: Hodder Education.
- **Lindon, L.** (1980) *A Re-conceptualisation of Job Satisfaction: Self-referent or job-referent?* Unpublished Ph.D thesis, University of London.
- **Manning-Morton, J. and Thorp, M.** (2001) *Key Times: A framework for developing high quality provision for children under three years old.* London: Camden Local Education Authority. (The resource was republished in 2006 by Open University Press.)
- **Moyles, J.** (2006) *Effective Leadership and Management in the Early Years.* Maidenhead: Open University Press.
- **Muijs, D., Aubrey, C., Harris, A. and Briggs, M.** (2004) 'How do they manage? A review of the research on leadership in early childhood'. *Journal of Early Childhood Research,* 2, 157–89.

- **Munton, A. and Mooney, A**. (2001) *Integrating Self-assessment into Statutory Inspection Procedures: The impact of the quality of day care provision.* http:// education.gov.uk/publications/standard/publicationDetail/Page1/RR285
- **Nivala, V. and Hujala, E.** (eds) (2002) *Leadership in Early Childhood Education: Cross-cultural perspectives.* Oulu: Oulu University Press. http://herkules.oulu.fi/ isbn9514268539/
- **Owen, C.** (2003) *Men's Work: Changing the gender mix of the childcare and early years workforce.* London: Daycare Trust. www.koordination-maennerinkitas.de/ uploads/media/Owen-Charlie-Men_s-Work_02.pdf
- **Pemberton, C.** (1995) *Strike a New Career Deal: Build a great future in the changing world of work.* London: Pitman Publishing.
- **Post, J. and Hohmann, M.** (2000) *Tender Care and Early Learning: Supporting infants and toddlers in child care settings.* Ypsilanti, MI: High/Scope Press.
- **Pound, L.** (2008) 'Leadership in the early years', in Miller, L. and Cable, C. (eds) *Professionalism in the Early Years.* London: Hodder Education.
- **Rodd, J.** (1997) 'Learning to be leaders: perceptions of early childhood professionals about leadership, roles and responsibilities'. *Early Years,* 18, 1.
- **Rodd, J.** (2006) *Leadership in Early Childhood.* Maidenhead: Open University Press.
- **Rosemary, C. and Puroila, A-M**. (2002) 'Leadership potential in day care settings: using dual analytical methods to explore directors' work in Finland and the USA'. In Nivala, V. and Hujala, E. (eds) *Leadership in Early Childhood Education: Cross-cultural perspectives.* Oulu: Oulu University Press. http:// herkules.oulu.fi/isbn9514268539/
- **Scrivens, C.** (2002a) 'Constructions of leadership: does gender make a difference? Perspectives from an English speaking country'. In Nivala, V. and Hujala, E. (eds) *Leadership in Early Childhood Education: Cross-cultural perspectives.* Oulu: Oulu University Press. http://herkules.oulu.fi/isbn9514268539/
- **Siraj-Blatchford, I. and Manni, L.** (2007) *Effective Leadership in the Early Years Sector.* London: Institute of Education.
- Stanford Encyclopaedia of Philosophy (2011) *Feminist Epistemology and Philosophy of Science.* http://plato.stanford.edu/entries/feminism-epistemology/

Chapter

2

Understanding managers, leaders and leadership

The aim of this chapter is to provide readers with a full picture of the different approaches to explaining management, leadership and how leaders could or should behave. The concept of the leader has been around for millennia, that of the manager for around a century. Given the huge literature on these topics, this review is necessarily concise. However, quality in early years practice will not be supported by an exclusive view that early years is so unique that little or nothing can be learned from other professional disciplines.

It is an important learning journey for actual and potential early years leaders to understand fully the breadth of ideas available. We are prepared to criticise the uninformed 'traditional models don't work' message that is too often conveyed to the early years profession.

The main sections in this chapter are:
- researching the world of work
- seeking effective leaders
- behaving as a leader
- leadership depends on the situation
- leaders as change agents
- leadership through people and teams.

Researching the world of work

Well-rounded explorations of leadership in early years acknowledge that there are several theories to consider, some of which offer different ways of leading than 'traditional' models. Leaders in any sector need to be able, and enabled, to apply potentially good ideas to the details of their practice. This chapter addresses the wide range of ideas available to provoke reflection and application to practice from the significant leadership literature.

The challenge of research

Exploring leadership and management is almost a snapshot of all the work done to develop knowledge about people at work. The research area draws on several disciplines, notably social psychology, organisational behaviour and management theory.

Doing research about people is extremely difficult when you try to do justice to the complexity of human relationships. At the simplest level, you can describe the relationship between just two people as the interaction of person A to B and then person B to A (two interactions). Even this interaction is not necessarily simple; recall the misunderstandings that can occur even between very familiar people. Just add two more people, C and D, to the relationships and understanding the interactions becomes far more complex. You can list the additional interactions, such as A to C and C to A, plus, of course, C to B and in the other direction. But now you also have the possibilities of B and C interacting together with A or pairs like AB with CD and so on. In fact, the total possible interactions of this foursome is now 24. Think about this pattern for your own place of work. If you try to draw out the lines of communication you will soon have a very complicated drawing – even in a small setting. The total interactions you need to study for a full understanding swiftly spiral out of control – certainly if you aim to research organisations beyond very small businesses – and even then you would just find how people are interacting together. You would still have not allowed for the nature of this organisation, the skills of the people, the work that needs to be done, the effect of the hierarchy, the influence of technology and the wider social, political or cultural environment in which this organisation operates. So it is hardly surprising that the development of theory – in order to try to make some order out of this chaos – is fundamental to the study of people in work organisations. Accurately nailing these theories with empirical research is clearly very difficult owing to the complexity of the area being studied.

The basic pattern of research is something like this:

1 Do some theorising, do some research. Good. That seems to be the answer.

2 Someone else does some research and makes a good case that (1) was not actually correct. So that theory gets changed and, for a while, the general view is now we are probably right.

3 Then someone else does some work and makes a persuasive case that (2) is not really correct or is only half the story. It needs additional bits and more work.

4 Repeat stage (3) and continue in the loop – probably for quite a long time and with break-away groups which establish their own circuit.

You can smooth out the messy reality and make an area of study look more coherent. However, such a simplification often removes the food for thought that arises from understanding some of the disagreements and reversals in doing real-life research.

As a result, what seemed to be a simple proposition in the world of work, 'I'm the boss, you do what you're told, and I'll make sure you're paid', has become increasingly complex. The multi-sided nature of working relationships is especially true when trying to understand concepts of leadership, management and what makes for an effective organisation in a rapidly changing world. The concept of performance – what you achieve at work – is key to all of this discussion. Performance matters whether the focus of exploration is leadership or management, style or role. The fundamental issue is that people need to perform at work ultimately to reach the aims of this organisation – its reason for being in existence.

Performance has three components, and it is extremely hard to measure all three effectively. These are:

1 the person who does the work

2 the process by which the work gets done

3 the outcome or result.

A scamper though history

Initially there were very few organisations as we would think of them today. There were religious organisations to help develop faith, and organisations designed to support the will of rulers. There were the army and the navy, some guilds and trading concerns. So it was not surprising that people looked towards these existing structures when the industrial revolution brought the need to form large commercial organisations. Hence, the initial organisational models were of a command-and-control nature.

The big boss was all powerful, modelled on prelates, kings or generals and he – it almost always was he – was surrounded by an inner group of senior and respected helpers – managers – who in turn controlled the next level in the hierarchy until the level of individual workers at the bottom was reached. These were the people who actually did the work. The hierarchy functioned through authority based upon legitimate power: the authority that came from holding this position (see page 6). In this model, the hierarchy was all powerful. Unless you were at the very top, you did what you were told or took the serious consequences of deviation from the rules. Deviation would typically result in punishment (excommunication, being executed, being fired). Loyalty and performing well would often result in rewards being given (parcels of land, a promotion, more money).

Early interest in leadership focused on hero-leaders and quite a lot of the 'evidence' came from biographies of these 'top dogs' at the peak of the pyramid of command and control. The focus of study was on what made these individuals different from 'ordinary' people. This approach began the continuing attempt to identify the qualities that distinguish leaders from everyone else. The preferred term has come to be 'traits' and the area of study has moved well beyond the hero-leader. Research and discussion about leadership continue to circle back to what it is about people that makes them good leaders, because it is impossible to take the individual out of the leadership equation.

Moving quickly on to the early 20th century, much research was done into how to get the best out of people in extreme situations, such as the two world wars, and more normally in work organisations, primarily in the USA. It was a time when the laws of physical science were taken as the model for understanding work and people. Little, if any, account was taken of human motivation and wishes. The objective was to get workers to comply with what was required. At root, if you could accurately define what was needed to do a specific kind of work, you could then determine who to hire because you ensured that they had matching capabilities.

Scientific management and human relations

Frederick Winslow Taylor, in his book *The Principles of Scientific Management* (1911), did just that. He broke jobs into specific tasks and then measured the most efficient ways to do them. As he said, 'It is only through enforced standardisation of methods, enforced adoption of the best implements and working conditions and enforced co-operation that [this] faster work can be assured' (Taylor, 1911, page 83). He even determined the physical characteristics of the person required to work a given machine. The whole aim was efficiency in production. If this 'enforcement' sounds harsh to the 21st-century reader, note that scientific management and the accompanying supervisors wielding stopwatches did not go unchallenged by the workforce of the time.

By the 1920s, problems were beginning to emerge with efficiency through scientific management that viewed the human element as an interference to optimal performance. Humanity would not go away, however. People were affected by their work colleagues and the environment in which they worked. Elton Mayo's work at the Hawthorne works in Chicago in the 1920s and 1930s further emphasised that people were affected by how they were treated, and that contrary to earlier assumptions, payment was not the only factor affecting productivity (Mayo, 1933). The Human Relations movement emerged in the USA to stress the importance of social relationships at work to productivity and job satisfaction. This much more social model was in opposition to the mechanistic models that tried to overlook the 'people factor' and the existence of an informal structure of social relations. It was not possible to explain what happened in work otherwise.

Motivation and needs

Following the work of Henry Murray, who in 1938 first identified psychological needs and motivational processes, Abraham Maslow (1943) contributed his seminal approach to motivation. Maslow's ideas are still discussed and applied to work and more generally today. His 1943 paper is available online (see page 69) and you can read there that Maslow applied his ideas to children as well as to adults. Maslow described five categories of needs. As Figure 2.1 shows, these are arranged from low to high in terms of the extent to which they allow people to rise above a basic level of existence. Thus, physiological and security needs are considered lower-order needs, while self-actualisation needs are of a higher order.

When a lower-order need is basically satisfied, people can choose to move up to the next level of need. When people feel safe and secure, they are able and motivated to spend more time in social interaction. A confident social base can lead to the level of self-esteem, with a focus on advancement, respect, independence and recognition for achievements. It is not the case that you are 'only' in a social need state, for example. While this may best describe your current state, you will be aware of both security and self-esteem issues to some extent.

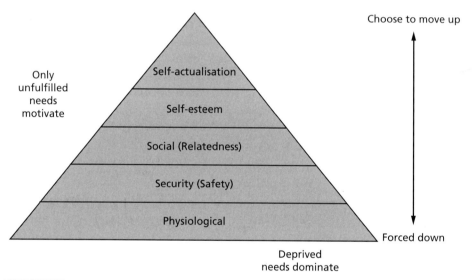

Figure 2.1 Maslow's hierarchy of needs

Make the connection with ... *early years practice*

The concept of a hierarchy of needs is applied to work and raises practical issues that need to be recognised by leaders. Consider these possibilities and add your own or gather ideas in a group of colleagues.

The levels of physiological and social needs might not seem at first to be relevant to work. However, a sense of safety can be easily removed if the very existence of this setting is under threat. Such a threat disrupts the social network at work: will everybody lose their job or just some of us, and who will it be? Alternatively, what if practitioners feel their manager is dismissive about their fears of a parent who easily turns to verbal aggression and confrontational gestures?

That sense of security can also be rocked by changes in the familiar pattern of work, a new head of centre who seems to be brimming with different ideas, or uncertain changes imposed from the outside. Leaders, in early years or elsewhere, need to recognise how anxiety about change can shake basic feelings of security in the workforce.

Many people value the social network provided at work and enjoy interacting as equals. Discussion about leadership in early years settings highlights that some practitioners are very uneasy about taking a leading role that could make them stand out from their colleagues. Some people do not want to place themselves above others, and feel that taking a lead will inevitably be viewed in this way. In Maslow's terms, people do not want to be forced out of their social need state to one focused on self-esteem. Others actively seek additional responsibility and advancement: their motivation to develop new skills is strong and/or the positioning of this new role addresses some concerns about losing the advantages of their current social relationships at work. They are happy to operate in the self-esteem area.

Motivator and hygiene factors

From 1935, job satisfaction – the level of satisfaction that people felt about their job – began to be studied in its own right, rather than the previous, almost total focus on productivity: people's efficiency with the task of their job. Notable among these was the work of Frederick Herzberg (1959). He claimed that job satisfaction was about 'motivators' (which if present at work would make employees satisfied) and 'hygiene factors' (which if not present would cause dissatisfaction). Motivators (or satisfiers) consisted of achievement, recognition and the work itself. The hygiene factors (or dissatisfiers) included salary, working conditions and technical supervision, company policy and administration. Most, if not all, of these dissatisfiers were outside the control of the individual worker.

This two-part view was helpful in getting people to think about job satisfaction as consisting of several distinct elements. However, the division into motivators and hygiene elements was shown not to be correct. The key, and enduring, message from this area of research is that, in general, the more control people feel they have over their work, the more likely they are to feel motivated by that work.

Developments in the second half of the 20th century

Broad social, technological and cultural changes have exerted a huge impact on the world of work. The workforce is increasingly diverse. There have been massive changes to people (better educated and more demanding) and processes (computerisation, total quality management, mobile phones and the internet). Further, the fundamental way in which measurement of people was approached has moved away from the 'hard' physical science model (typifying the approach of Taylor, for example) to a biological model, with its greater flexibility and to allow for emotional realities and broad social and cultural factors. In other words, a less impersonal approach has evolved, which recognises that people are not working only for the salary cheque.

Academics and management consultants had usually kept within their own circles. Yet, from the 1980s, there was the rise of 'superstar' management thinkers. Tom Peters (a former McKinsey consultant), with blisteringly entertaining road shows, promulgated 'In search of Excellence' and publicly challenged the way that most major companies were run. Thinkers such as Rosabeth Moss Kanter from Harvard accepted well-paid lecture tours promoting their books. Businesses were desperately looking for some answers as to how to cope better with change and increasing competitive pressures.

Affluence in general increased, although with a growing awareness of the gap in society between the 'haves' and the 'have nots'. Within the UK, governments from Margaret Thatcher onwards began to run the country more on a commercial model. More 'management thinking' was applied by government, a process continued by Tony Blair's Labour administration. A focus on 'if you can't measure it, you can't do anything about it' and 'performance targets' became increasingly common among politicians. Performance measurement has become more critical during this period as delivering outcomes is increasingly required. Lessons from organisational psychology were being applied to public services, often without enough understanding of their complexity or timeliness.

As a term, 'Management by Objectives' was first used by Peter Drucker in 1954, and developed by people such as Douglas McGregor. The approach was booming across the western corporate world by the late 1970s. Management by Objectives (MBO) was a new way of assessing performance based upon the achievement of agreed objectives for each year. Unlike the previous approaches to appraisal which measured what you did, MBO was designed to measure what you achieved compared with objectives agreed at the beginning of the year.

Make the connection with ... **early years provision**

The individual version of this MBO approach will be familiar to early years settings which have established supervision and appraisal systems. Practitioners will be able to look ahead, in consultation with their manager or other senior member of the team, and set appropriate personal objectives that are consistent with the overall direction and values of the setting.

The total approach to performance objectives, against which whole settings or local authorities are then measured, reached the early years sector towards the end of the 20th century. In the UK, as well as in Australia and New Zealand, early years provision was increasingly faced with imposed targets, relating on the micro level to measurable outcomes for young children by a given age. On the macro scale the targets were about making a measurable difference on broad social problems, getting women back to work, or the poverty gap.

Seeking effective leaders

The earliest explanations of leadership, beginning with the 20th century, were termed 'great man' theories – or sometimes the 'hero-leader'. These aimed to identify and classify traits of great social, military and political leaders, and how they differed from their followers. The vast majority of the people studied were men, reflecting the reality of male dominance in the societies considered in any research.

Traits of a leader

There was a huge amount of research. Ralph Stogdill (1948, 1974), for example, published reviews of more than 100 studies between 1904 and 1947 and then a further 163 studies up to 1970. In 1948, Stogdill concluded that there was no list of traits that was universally associated with being a leader. By 1974 his conclusion was that both personality and situational factors were critical in leadership. The situation had to give people the chance to exercise leadership, otherwise there was nothing and nobody to lead. Stogdill concluded that there was a cluster of leader traits, which was adapted to the work situation in which the leader operated. He identified the following ten individual characteristics and they look as relevant to early years provision as for the business world.

1 Drive for responsibility and task completion – achievement.

2 Vigour and persistence in pursuit of goals.

3 Risk taking and originality in problem solving – insight.

4 Drive to exercise initiative in social situations – initiative.

5 Self-confidence and a sense of personal identity.

6 Willingness to accept the consequences of decisions made and actions taken – responsibility.

7 Readiness to absorb interpersonal stress – cooperativeness.

8 Willingness to tolerate frustration and delay – tolerance.

9 Ability to influence other people's behaviour.

10 Capacity to structure social interaction systems to the purpose in hand – sociability.

Pause for reflection

Think of individual leaders you know, or have known, in the early years sector. If you wish, extend your review to related sectors such as schools or playwork settings.

● Which of the ten characteristics do you think those people showed?

● Think of people who looked as if they were uneasy or reluctant leaders. Which characteristics did they lack, what seemed to be a struggle for them?

● How do you rate yourself as a leader against these ten characteristics? Be honest but not over-modest. It is fine to acknowledge your strengths.

Kirkpatrick and Locke (1991) point out that it is not the traits as such that make an effective leader; it is the actions that the leader is willing and able to take within their organisation. In your experience, what have effective early years leaders been adept at doing? In contrast, what was it that official, but ineffective, leaders seemed unable to do?

By the 1990s the trait approach to leadership was back, although with much more attention to the context. Kirkpatrick and Locke (1991) hold that it is not up for argument: leaders are not like other people. They identified the six differences between leaders and non-leaders as drive, leadership motivation (wanting to lead), honesty/integrity, self-confidence (including emotional stability), cognitive ability and knowledge of the business in which they work. Again, the pattern of leadership traits was not the end of the story. The importance of these traits was that the people with them were more likely to take the necessary actions crucial for effective leadership, such as formulating a vision for their organisation, being a positive role model to their staff and setting goals. Kirkpatrick and Locke reported only weak support in the research for alleged leadership traits such as creativity, originality and flexibility.

Personality – traits grouped together: another way of looking at leaders

Over the last quarter of the 20th century a high level of consensus emerged over the basic factors of personality. These are now established as the 'Big Five' factors of personality. Leadership was associated with being low on one factor – Neuroticism, which is associated with being depressed, anxious, vulnerable and hostile – and high on the four remaining factors:

- Extraversion or Surgency (being outgoing) – you are likely to be assertive and social, having positive energy.
- Openness or Intellect – you are likely to be informed, insightful, curious and creative.
- Agreeableness – you are likely to be accepting, trusting, nurturing and conforming.
- Conscientiousness or Dependability – you are likely to be thorough, organised, controlled, decisive and dependable.

This work establishes Extraversion as the most important trait for a leader. It is therefore hard to be an effective leader if you are introverted, shy and retiring. Extraversion is followed – in order – by Conscientiousness, Openness and (low) Neuroticism. The low score on Neuroticism means leaders are likely to be self-confident, not plagued by too many doubts about their competence and do not worry much about themselves. The weakest leadership link is to Agreeableness (Judge *et al*., 2002).

Effective leaders have to come to terms with the reality that they will not always be seen as agreeable. Sometimes leaders need to be 'disagreeable', in the eyes of other people, to make the tough decisions. It is why in early years and school, like the commercial world, individual leaders sometimes say they feel quite isolated. It can be a lonely position.

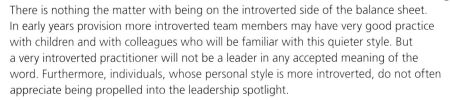

Take another **perspective ... early years provision**

There is nothing the matter with being on the introverted side of the balance sheet. In early years provision more introverted team members may have very good practice with children and with colleagues who will be familiar with this quieter style. But a very introverted practitioner will not be a leader in any accepted meaning of the word. Furthermore, individuals, whose personal style is more introverted, do not often appreciate being propelled into the leadership spotlight.

This is not a problem unless the early years organisational culture becomes infected with a kind of leadership madness that claims everyone can be and should be a leader.

In summary: the person in the role of leader

All in all, more than a century of study has led to some consensus on traits that people might need to have, or be ready to nurture in themselves, if they want to be seen as leaders. From the 1990s these have also included what emerge as, on average, more stereotyped female characteristics such as 'social intelligence' and 'emotional intelligence' (more of this from page 58).

These are the traits that seem to be central to leadership:
- Self-confidence – the ability to be certain (accurate) about your skills and abilities. This includes self-esteem, emotional stability and the belief that you can make a difference.
- Intelligence – particularly in terms of reasoning, verbal fluency and the cognitive ability to 'see the wood for the trees'. Leaders are more conceptually skilled than non-leaders in dealing with the information relevant to their business or service. They are able to solve problems and make decisions. It is sometimes said that the best leaders are intelligent but not brilliant. They need to be able to communicate in words that their team can understand; they are not so different that others find them hard to relate to.
- Sociability – leaders are friendly, outgoing, courteous and tactful, with good interpersonal skills. They seek to have cooperative relationships with others.
- Determination – leaders really want to achieve the goals of their business or service. They have drive, persistence and energy. They have a passion for their work and this is linked with a good knowledge of the sector in which they operate. Leaders are assertive and will take a dominant stance when required. Most important, they want to lead other people and are willing to assume that responsibility.
- Integrity – leaders are honest, being truthful even when this is a tough choice. They avoid deceit, are dependable and loyal to their team. A credible leader is seen as worthy of being trusted and so inspires confidence in their followers.

Studying leadership traits fits well with the common image of leaders as special kinds of people who accomplish admirable things. However, this discussion does not apply only to hero-leaders – current or in past times. Look back over this section – you can surely see possible descriptions of people you know, yourself included.

Changing views of the workforce

In 1960, Douglas McGregor summarised alternative views of people that formed the basis of running organisations. He called these Theory X and Theory Y. Put simply, they offer two polar opposites. In this case, the letters stand for alternatives: 'X' and 'Y' are not shorthand for full words.

Theory X summarised the historical assumptions behind the view of the all-powerful autocratic boss who had little choice but to run a command-and-control structure. The underlying rationale is that people have little ambition and inherently dislike work. Therefore the workforce had to be forced and threatened with punishment to make them achieve the objectives. Theory X as an outlook also argues that people would rather be directed and wish to avoid responsibility (the view of F.W. Taylor, see page 33). Employees, it is argued, have little creativity, except when applied to circumventing the rules. Basically they want only the money and the security of their job.

The alternative view of Theory Y sees work as a natural part of life and something that can be enjoyable. The assumption behind it is that people will exercise self-control in the service of objectives to which they feel committed. Under these circumstances self-imposed discipline is more effective than any imposed threats from a manager. Theory Y states that people's commitment to goals is dependent on the rewards associated with their achievement. Furthermore, that the most important rewards are those that satisfy their needs for self-respect and personal improvement (in line with Maslow on page 34). McGregor contended that people will learn both to seek and to accept responsibility. The assumption is that many people only partially use their capacities at work and that creativity and ingenuity in the workforce are underestimated and grossly under-used.

Make the connection with ... **early years provision**

Think about Theory X and Y – they are posed as two stark alternatives, but the very contrast offers food for thought.

- What patterns have you seen in your working experience – in early years, related sectors or very different jobs within your working career?
- To what extent have you observed colleagues whose outlook is closer to Theory X or to Theory Y?
- What are the implications for leadership within an early years setting if part of the current staff group takes more of a Theory X approach: 'I want an easy life. I do my job, you pay me, I go home. I don't want the responsibility of thinking at all deeply about this job.'

In a nutshell, Theory X says that people have to be coerced into doing what someone else in the hierarchy wants them to do. It emphasises the need for close supervision and firm discipline, coupled with incentives to counteract people's perceived laziness and irresponsibility. Theory Y, meanwhile, sees work as potentially satisfying in itself and seeks opportunities to use people's talents through interesting work and involvement in decision making. Placing Theory Y more central to discussion of work and organisational life ushers in a view of leadership as considerably more subtle than one of the autocratic boss who has to impose authority on an aimless workforce.

Before looking further at leadership behaviour, we think it is important to view work from the followers' perspective. After all, most of us are followers for most of our working life. There is a progression from what is very hard to accept being asked to do, to that which is most acceptable – even welcomed.

Accepting or rejecting requests at work

Most people would agree that *doing something to endanger life* is not a decision that most of us would make freely. We have to believe that this is absolutely necessary. Typically, this is most likely to occur in wartime, when the government will stress the potential collapse of society unless people are prepared to risk their lives. Next probably comes *doing something illegal*, and it is important to remember here that we are speaking about something that you are asked to do. We may all choose to drive too fast or park illegally, but we are likely to resist being urged by our line manager to do so. While it is legal in most countries to sell products with a health risk (cigarettes and cancer, fizzy drinks and obesity), many people choose on ethical grounds not to work for such businesses. Hence, for many of us *doing something unethical* can be as bad, or worse, than doing something illegal.

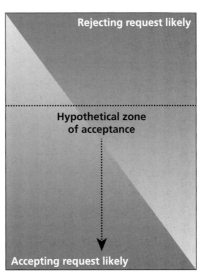

Doing something that would endanger your life

Doing something illegal

Doing something you find unethical

Rejecting request likely

Hypothetical zone of acceptance

Doing something unpleasant

Doing something different to that previously agreed to

Doing something not done normally

Doing something done before

Doing something in your own best interest

Accepting request likely

Figure 2.2 Accepting and rejecting requests from people in authority

In an early years setting the manager may put pressure on you to do out-of-hours evening sitting for parents when you do not want to. Although your colleagues may already do this, it does not mean that the request is an ethical one. In short, it is a favour to help the manager respond to parents' requests. It is not in your job description and hence is outside your manager's legitimate authority.

After *doing something you find unethical* comes being asked to *do something unpleasant* (see Figure 2.2). This is often catered for directly in the way that organisations are managed so that people are paid more for working unsocial hours, doing dirty – or more dangerous – work in recognition that this is unpleasant.

Doing something different to that previously agreed to comes next. In some cases this may be a better job or a promotion. For example, a nursery has decided to offer holiday provision for the over-fives and you are asked whether you want to do this. You may agree or not. Equally, you may need to use and understand a new reporting system. Certainly this is an area where unions often get involved as 'changes to work practice' are regularly cited as a reason why discussions are needed.

Doing something not done normally (which comes next) is different as this would be either temporary or a single occurrence. For example, you may have to 'just this once' arrange sandwiches for a meeting of senior staff. Often our concern when being asked to do something not usually done is that this will set a precedent: 'If I get the sandwiches in now, I'll always be asked to do it.' Having done something once often makes it harder to say no in the future – getting sandwiches now becomes *something that has already been done.*

With this exception, little resistance is generally experienced when asked to do *something you have already done.* People are more likely to resist if they have done things that are not actually part of their job description and tasks that are felt to be beneath their capabilities or status. Finally, very little – if any – resistance is likely when you are *doing something in your own best interest* – why should there be? In this case, you accept the request willingly as it is something you would have done anyway. You want to do it.

In general, the more unwilling the person is to do a particular job, the more management is required and the greater the incentives (or coercion) necessary to get people to do it. We want people to work willingly – moreover, this will take less managerial time and effort to achieve than making the unwilling comply. Therefore a critical objective for any leader or manager is to try to enable or persuade staff that doing what is required at work is in their own best interest. This could be, for example, because it is enjoyable, will make their position more secure or bring them into contact with people they like. As we shall see, getting people to believe that what they do is in their own best interest is a key element of leadership.

Behaving as a leader

By the middle of the 20th century there was serious interest in trying to capture the diversity that was possible within what we would now call leadership behaviour, although the word typically used was 'manager'. The research had moved away from its primary focus on what kind of person was effective in a position of authority. Increasingly, researchers looked more at what managers and leaders did, with whom and in what context. Then, focus began to move away from what managers did to the results of this behaviour. In other words, what people did that worked – resulting in positive outcomes – and what had no demonstrable benefit.

A range of possible leadership behaviours

An early approach to management theory was expressed by Tannenbaum and Schmidt (1958), in which they described a continuum of leadership behaviour. They explored the range of behaviour that could fall between two defined extreme points. The broad message of this model, like many of the examples that follow in this chapter, is that managers, or leaders, do not have to make stark choices of an either–or nature. The cognitive challenge is to understand the possible choices in behaviour and to grasp the circumstances under which different patterns could be appropriate.

> **What does it mean?**
>
> **Continuum**: the broad concept of a range of choices rather than a stark either–or. In terms of leadership, the idea of a continuum highlights awareness that there are subtle gradations in, for instance, how leaders use their authority.

Their continuum from complete managerial control to subordinate freedom offers points along a dimension from freedom to constraint, or from autonomy to control. The triangles indicate greater or lesser authority (or freedom) present. At each point, managerial decisions have to be taken to determine how much or little control needs to be taken.

Figure 2.3 shows the continuum described by Tannenbaum and Schmidt. At the bottom right-hand corner, the manager is using full authority to enforce compliance with no freedom for their subordinates. Along with many writers in the field the authors use the word 'subordinates'. For us, this is not a very positive word – you are not even an 'ordinate', but a 'sub'-ordinate. The very word infers little respect for the employee, let alone for staff to be empowered.

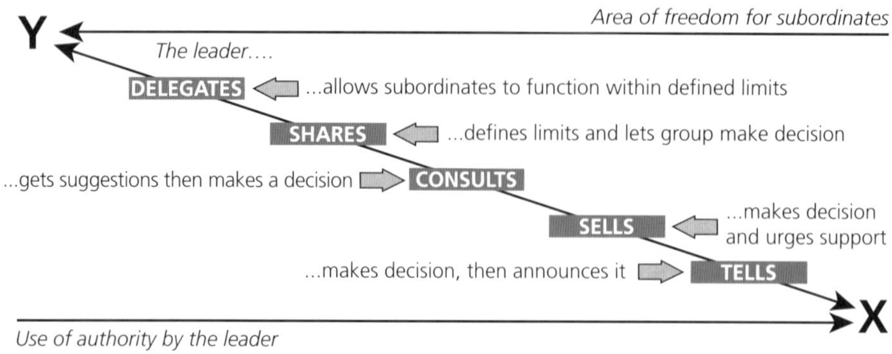

Figure 2.3 The leadership continuum

At the top left-hand corner the continuum reaches the point of maximum freedom for staff to operate as they see fit, trusted to work with minimal need for managerial authority. Look back in this section to Douglas McGregor and his Theory X–Theory Y alternatives (page 40). It makes sense to place Theory X at the 'use of authority by the leader' end and Theory Y at the opposing 'area of freedom for subordinates' end. A view of the workforce as motivated to get involved, rather than needing to be coerced, opens up the possibility that a manager does not always have to 'make a decision and then announce it'. There will be appropriate circumstances for 'gets suggestions and then makes a decision' and to allow staff to undertake clear-cut tasks without being supervised in detail, because there is trust that they understand the limits – the point at which they will need to get back to their manager.

Make the connection with ... **early years practice**

Compared with the models that follow, the approach of Tannenbaum and Schmidt is simple. It offers food for thought about the behaviour of a manager, linked with honesty. Figure 2.3 is close conceptually to authentic and inauthentic consultation within a team.

- The 'tells' option at the bottom right-hand end of the sloping line would be very irritating if the manager of a nursery or school always took that option, perhaps with a sense of 'be grateful I've taken the time to tell you face to face rather than stick up a memo in the staffroom'.

- However, think of some examples of times when outside events and decisions have an impact on the nursery and nobody, including the manager, can do anything to change the situation.

- Authentic consultation within a team rests on the genuine chance that ideas and problem-solving alternatives could be implemented.

- The freedom to operate with minimal supervision from the manager depends on having all the necessary information and relevant skills. It is very demotivating to make errors that could have been avoided with a bit more information or guidance.

Different ways to lead

Social psychologist Kurt Lewin looked at the impact of leadership style by observing 11-year-olds in the psychological laboratory (Lewin *et al.*, 1939). These groups of boys experienced different types of work climate for their group tasks, determined by a leadership style of autocratic, democratic or laissez-faire (no guidance from the leader). Lewin and his colleagues looked at differences in the boys' behaviour under the three different states and concluded that the variation was attributable to the leadership style. They observed more originality, friendliness and working together under democratic leadership. With the change to autocratic leadership the group swiftly became apathetic and showed little initiative in the face of their group task. Hostility and scapegoating increased under autocratic leadership. The boys were also discontented with the lack of any kind of leadership behaviour in the laissez-faire condition.

Blake and Mouton explored group dynamics and leadership through observing experimental groups of adults in the psychological laboratory and then applied their findings to the organisational world. In 1964 they published their *Managerial Grid*, accompanied by a questionnaire which would allow people to assess their own management style. Blake and Mouton identified two dimensions that had been shown in their lab work to be critical for effective group working:

- Concern for Task – provides the necessary direction and structure within which people can work. Leaders communicate what people are to do – where, when and how – and they follow up to ensure satisfactory completion of the task.
- Concern for People – leader gives appreciation and recognition, encourages and rewards good work.

Consistent with the ideas of Tannenbaum and Schmidt, as a manager in the Managerial Grid you could either show a lot of authority or very little. However, other than 'freedom', the issue of Concern for People was not in any sense clear from Tannenbaum and Schmidt's continuum. Whereas this said that the more authority a manager used, the less freedom subordinates had (or vice versa), Blake and Mouton showed, in essence, that this continuum really referred only to their Concern for Task dimension.

The work of Blake and Mouton was significant for distinguishing Concern for People and Concern for the Task as part of management – these had been clear in studies of groups for a while. They, like Kurt Lewin, had come from a background of research into group dynamics and effective teamwork. In this area, the term 'leader' had been regularly used in discussion and interpretation. As a result, 'team leader' entered the management literature.

The Managerial Grid, shown in Figure 2.4, was a more complex view of possible leadership behaviour than the continuum. We have kept the reference to Theory X and Y on the diagram. As you see, not only could you be high or low on Concern for the Task, but equally you could be high or low on Concern for People. The Grid uses numbers from 1 to 9 to indicate movement along the dimensions. Once they had completed the questionnaire, it was possible for managers to place themselves on the Grid and have personal data for reflecting on their style.

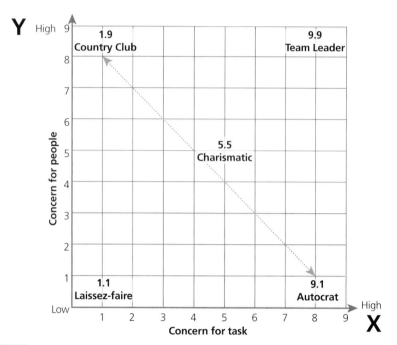

Figure 2.4 The Managerial Grid

Different possible styles

The positions on the Grid give opportunities to talk about options and balance in leadership style. We have made some links below into the world of early years provision.

- The 9.1 Autocrat shows a maximum Concern for the Task (getting the job done) and very little Concern for People. This is the classic 'tell' approach with high levels of managerial control and typically little listening. This style rests on the belief that the manager's responsibility is to plan, direct and control the work. Here we have the early years manager as despot. Such managers exist in some settings, and not only in the past.

- In contrast, the 1.9 Country Club-style manager shows maximum concern for the well being and motivation of people, with little focus on actually ensuring that the job gets done. For early years we would like to call this position the 'coffee morning' style. The work is incidental to ensuring that there is no conflict and that everyone gets along just fine. Think about it: what may happen to the children if the top priority of the manager is always that staff are happy in their job?

- The grid becomes more interesting when the 1.1 and 9.9 points are explored. The Laissez-Faire manager at 1.1 places little emphasis on either doing the job or the well being of people. In essence this style of manager does little that most of us would think of as management, let alone leadership. This leave-well-alone option rests on the belief that people will never do the job much better, because they are lazy and indifferent. It is not possible to improve working relationships because there will always be some conflict, so why bother?

- The 9.9 style, the Team Leader, is all-singing-all-dancing. This style shows high levels of concern for both people and their motivation and for ensuring the work of the organisation gets done well. Being 9.9 ensures that not much can go wrong. However, the style requires an awful lot more work than any other point on the grid; it looks exhausting.

Finally, there is the rather unhelpful term Charismatic, applied to the 5.5 position, right in the middle. We think Chameleon would have been a better and more accurate description. In fact by 1991, Robert Blake, with another colleague, Anne Adams McCanse, renamed this point 'middle of the road management' (amended again in 1999 to 'status quo'). In short, the 5.5 manager does not show enough Concern for the Task when things get tough, deadlines are tight or there are issues in doing the task properly. Additionally, the 5.5 manager does not show the high levels of Concern for People that may be required when their motivation is very low, or there are interpersonal issues getting in the way of doing the job properly. The 5.5 style gets by in normal situations, but cannot cope when anything out of the ordinary happens.

Make the connection with ... **early years practice**

Look back over this section and think in more detail about your own work and your experience in different settings.

- What do you see as the advantages of the five broad styles of the Managerial Grid? What are the disadvantages?
- What style would you prefer in the manager of a setting where you work?
- What kind of profile would you like to show as a manager? How close is this to the way that you think you usually behave?

Are you already thinking 'But surely the best style rather depends on the situation. What is my team like? How experienced are they? If I'm new to this setting, what style of manager has been their previous experience?' Well done – the research literature did move on to look at the situation in which people had to lead.

Leadership depends on the situation

By the 1970s, the focus of leadership research had broadened significantly from both the search to find definitive traits that fit any leader and the search to identify behaviour that was definitive for a leader. The theoretical developments now could be summed up as 'it all depends…'.

Contingency theories

Despite its popularity as a tool, serious questions were being asked as to whether the Managerial Grid (and particularly the 'best' 9.9 Team Leader style) was as useful as it initially appeared. One challenge was to question whether, if your people were experienced, talented and committed – that is, very motivated – to do their jobs, then why not mainly leave them to get on with it (as in the 1.1 Laissez-Faire approach)? However, suppose people did not want to do a particular job, yet they were able to and the job had to be done? Under those circumstances the comment was surely that the 9.1 Autocrat approach was the most efficient and appropriate. The Autocrat may not be warm and cuddly, but sometimes situations at work call for the 9.1 approach – it is quickest of all.

The Managerial Grid was criticised for the failure to address two key questions:

1 What about the quality of the manager's staff subordinate to them? Surely it mattered whether they were capable and motivated – or not?

2 In what kind of situation was the manager working? Surely it would make a difference if this task came with tight deadlines or there was plenty of time? The other work-situation question related to information: were the details of the job in hand well known or not? What did the organisation want or value from its employees – rapid decisions or calm evaluations?

The result of attempts to answer these questions was the development of what were called contingency theories of leadership. The common concept is that the best style of leadership is contingent (dependent) on a number of other issues and not mainly, or exclusively, the style of the leader. The key idea was that there was no leadership style that would be the right approach in any circumstance – it all depends.

What does it mean?

Contingency theories of leadership: the study of leadership style which seeks to identify the circumstances under which different patterns of behaviour are more appropriate to the working situation.

House and his colleagues developed the Path–Goal Theory of leadership, which aimed to enhance employees' performance and satisfaction by focusing on their motivation. House's (1971) Path–Goal Theory saw leadership effectiveness as an interaction between leadership behaviours and situational characteristics. He identified four leadership behaviours: directive, achievement-orientated, supportive and participative. House also identified two situational variables: employees' personal characteristics, and environmental demands such as the organisation's rules and procedures, which were proposed to contribute most strongly to leader effectiveness.

Fiedler (1967) based leader effectiveness on what he called 'situational contingency'. In other words, effective leadership was contingent on the situation in which it was placed. He looked at two kinds of leaders – those who sought good relationships with the group to get the work done (relationship-orientated) and those who focused on the task itself (task-orientated). He claimed that there was no ideal leader but that both could be effective depending on the situation.

Leadership decision styles

Vroom and his colleagues (Vroom and Yetton, 1973) developed a prescriptive theory of leadership decision making based upon three key factors:

- *The technical quality of the decision.* This means that the decision made should lead to the best outcome and therefore should include all the relevant information to make it so. Hence if a leader does not have all the information, they should not make the decision alone. Getting the 'best' decision is critical to this model.
- *The support of followers.* If followers are not prepared to accept the decision, then, with other things being equal, the leader should involve them in making the decision. This will enable explanations to be made and anxieties addressed so that implementation can go ahead more smoothly.
- *Time.* If the decision has to be made today or now, this can make the first two points irrelevant. For example, you do not have an open discussion with staff or children about what to do when the fire alarm sounds: you all leave as quickly as possible. Any discussion will have happened at other times, so that everyone knows what to do in a crisis.

Vroom and Yetton combined these three factors to develop the decision chart – Figure 2.5 – which outlines all possible decisions to be made and how to make them. Like situational leadership (page 50), Leadership Decision Styles underscores the point that if followers do not share organisational goals, they cannot be allowed to make decisions alone. If they do, no organisational benefit is likely to result. Vroom and Yetton specify five ways of making decisions:

1 The leader decides alone, involving no one. This style was called L1.

2 With the L2 decision mode, the leader involves individuals from the group, one on one, and then makes the decision. Basically, the leader gathers the necessary information from key people in order to make the best decision.

3 In the LF1 mode, the leader involves some of the followers as a group and then makes the decision.

4 In LF2 the leader involves the entire group of followers and then makes the decision.

5 The M mode is where the leader allows the group to make the decision alone.

The figure shows the yes (Y) and no (N) choices at each point.

This model for decision making highlights the influence of the two critical dimensions of task – in this case technical quality – and people. Outstanding questions remain, such as how do you necessarily know what information you need and, if so, how can you obtain that knowledge? However, the model extended the understanding of leadership into the area of making decisions based on the best technical information and explicitly recognising the importance of time.

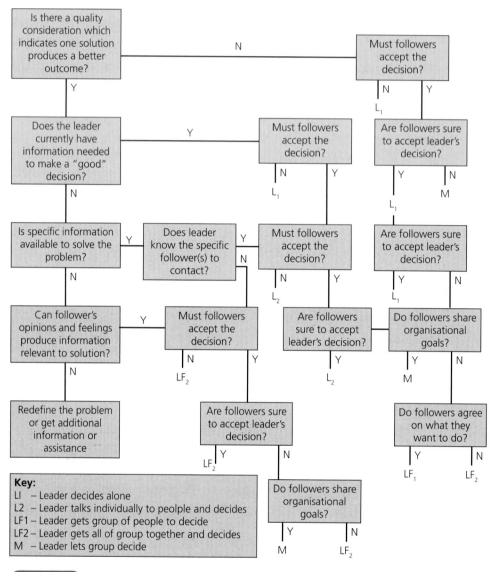

Figure 2.5 Leadership decision styles

Situational leadership

The quality of people and the need for urgency were at the heart of Hersey and Blanchard's situational leadership (1974). They used the term 'situational' to describe the need for flexibility of approach. Leadership style had to be responsive either to the overall situation – leaders cannot afford to take lots of time over issues that are very urgent – or to the competence and motivation of staff. Like Blake and his colleagues (page 45), Hersey and Blanchard developed questionnaires to enable people to measure their own leadership style. These self-evaluation measures are widely used.

Unlike the Managerial Grid, the model for situational leadership is explicitly interactive; the authors chose deliberately to use the term 'behaviours' to describe the two dimensions. The model has more emphasis on 'what you do' rather than Blake and Mouton's greater emphasis on 'what you are'. The situational leadership concept is straightforward to understand. The disadvantage is that there is a limited amount of academic research to justify the underlying theory and it is based primarily on simple questionnaires. See what you think about their ideas.

The situational leadership graphic in Figure 2.6 is very similar to the Managerial Grid (page 46), with some changes in terminology. 'Management' has now become 'leadership', 'Concern for People' becomes 'supportive behaviours', 'Concern for the Task' becomes 'directive behaviours'. Basically, however, these are the same dimensions. Blake and Mouton's confusing 5.5 'Charismatic' style has (thankfully) been lost. The Hersey and Blanchard leadership style S1 (Directing) is broadly the same as 9.1; S2 (Coaching) is very similar to 9.9.; S3 (Encouraging) is close to 1.9; and S4 (Delegating) is basically Blake and Mouton's 1.1. So what is different? First is the notion of subordinate development level, shown in Figure 2.6 as D1 through to D4.

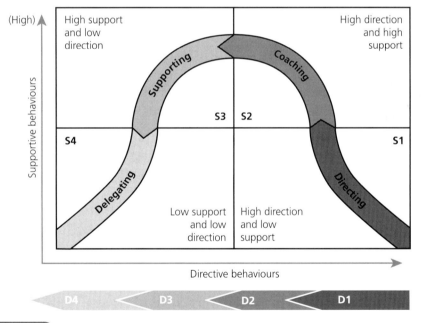

Figure 2.6 The situational leadership model

Hersey and Blanchard developed a model that is progressive, prescriptive and situational. Look at the arrow in Figure 2.6 and how it travels through from Directing through Coaching and Encouraging to Delegating from S1 through to S4. The movement, and appropriate leadership style, is dependent on the developmental level of the staff: the levels that move from D1 to D4 at the bottom of the graphic. The logic applies just as much to leadership within early years settings as to commercial organisations.

Basically, development level is assessed by looking at the subordinate's ability and motivation. If motivation is high, there is little need for encouragement or support (S1 or S4). If ability is high, there is little need for instruction in how to do the work, and little direction is required (S3 or S4). Only when ability needs to be channelled into performance does the manager need to focus on the task elements of direction (S1 or S2). Only if performance is not up to standard, or may decline, is high support required (S2 or S3). S4 (Delegating) is required only when staff are highly able, motivated and take responsibility for performing well.

Finally, if staff are unwilling to do a particular task that must be done, Hersey and Blanchard say that the S1 style is mandatory. It is the best way to ensure that the task is done. Similarly, if time pressures are extremely tight, the S1 style is preferred because it is quickest. Motivation of staff must take a back seat if a job needs to be done now. S1 is not cold; its focus is on giving staff the knowledge and skills to do the job adequately. There is little, but not nothing, in the way of support and encouragement.

S1 is typically used for new staff, who can be assumed to be motivated and need to know what to do (D1). However, the Structuring Style (S1) will be demotivating if it goes on too long. So as performance improves the manager should begin to reward and recognise this, while still giving further instruction as needed and checking that performance levels are ok. This is the Coaching Style of S2. As this continues, the subordinate (now at Development Level 2) should achieve or exceed the performance standard required. This is the time for the superior to move to the Encouraging S3 style.

The manager moves into the S3 style when the subordinate no longer needs to be reminded what to do or to be closely monitored. Staff at Development Level D3 need support and encouragement to develop still further. It is time to see whether they are able to act effectively without much supervision. The manager needs to back away somewhat and to test whether the person they have guided so closely can now complete this task or fulfil this responsibility without the levels of checking and supervision that typify either S1 or S2 styles.

The Delegating Style S4 can be used when the member of staff is seen to be at Development Level D4. They are fully competent in this area of work, perform above the standard required, can be trusted and are motivated. D4 staff will be likely to resent being asked unnecessary questions as to their well being or being checked up on when doing things everyone knows they do extremely well.

Some people will not move through developmental levels, and S2 is often called the 'safe' style as the leader is doing a great deal of management – high on both support and direction – to ensure that work is done adequately at least. However, managers who are stuck in S2 find it hard to delegate to those staff willing and able to take on more responsibility. Not only does this reduce the chance of staff reaching their full potential, it also keeps the interactive part of the manager's work high, leaving less time to do their non-managerial tasks.

The model of situational leadership seeks to enable all staff to reach the Developmental Level D4. It also recognises that this may not always be possible. In D4, individuals will need far less managerial time (as the S4 shows less of both directive and supportive behaviours) and, if they perform well independently, are ready for a new challenge or promotion. Of course, once you are promoted, or the details of your current job change significantly, you will revert to Developmental Level 1. We return to situational leadership in practice in Chapter 6.

Make the connection with ... **your own practice**

Please think about the range of practitioners in your setting whom you now lead and also, if you wish, reflect back on your own needs when you were the team member with minimal experience and knowledge.

A direct application in early years provision can be made to early years professionals who are tasked with being agents of change within their settings. The insights from situational leadership could be of value to EYPs. This possibility raises the crucial issue of being given the authority to direct and guide colleagues. Without clear authority EYPs could be seen by their colleagues as presuming to have a leadership role which has not been given: what right do you have to tell me how to change my practice? You will find more about the role of EYPs from page 128.

Hersey and Blanchard advanced understanding of the need for flexibility as a manager: to respond to changing situations and the differing requirements of individuals in the staff group. Additionally, their approach gave leaders a model for giving staff what they needed to progress and find satisfaction in their work. So situational leadership provides the conditions where people would be likely to wish to follow the senior people in their team – remember the acceptance of authority discussion on page 41 – and having followers is a key requirement for anyone to be termed a leader.

Situational leadership rests within the existing organisational hierarchy and in some ways is practicable only if the leader already has positional or legitimate power (page 6). It therefore seems to us that a necessary condition for Hersey and Blanchard's model is that the situational leader is already a line manager. They are therefore mandated, and able, to help develop those staff who are their direct reports. It would be presumptuous for anyone else to do this.

Make the connection with ... **your own practice**

Finally, a fair question is what happens when individuals at different development levels are all together with you in a meeting: what style should you use?

A productive team meeting requires structure and a clear focus. So you would typically run it in a Coaching S2 style. The exception would be when the meeting must now reach a decision on a tough issue or this item on the agenda is urgent. Under these circumstances, you need the S1 style.

Think back over recent team meetings. Can you identify those different situations? What happens if critical decisions are not made because the person chairing the meeting is reluctant to bring general discussion to a halt? Or the team leader lets therapeutic expression of feelings become more important than reaching a decision?

Therefore, we see situational leadership as being based fundamentally on the legitimate power granted to management. The logical structure of the model and the focus on staff development are likely to be experienced as rewarding by staff and to encourage them to commit to their manager's vision for the setting. However, the 'perfect' situational leader is basically responding to the needs of their people. Leaders do not only react to what they judge to be the developmental requirements from their staff; leaders are proactive, they set new directions. At root, they lead. We look in more detail at the practical applications of situational leadership in Chapter 6.

Leaders as change agents

The model of situational leadership basically describes a stable organisation facing the normal day-to-day pressures of any work organisation, in which the appropriate focus was on getting the best performance from people and aiding them to develop. The model did not consider leadership within the context of major organisational or environmental change, where completely new ways of working – and staff behaviour – may need to be developed.

Transformational leadership

Transformational leadership was first identified as 'transforming leadership' by James McGregor Burns (1978) in his descriptive research on political leaders. The ideas were then adopted by organisational behaviour researchers. Burns' view was that transforming leadership was a *process* in which leaders and followers helped each other to advance to higher levels of motivation for work. Burns described managers as 'transactors' and leaders as 'transformers'. The transforming leader creates significant change in the life of both people and organisations and acts as the exemplar of the new way.

Situational leadership therefore falls into the transactional category as leaders respond to the situation as it presents itself; they are not changing what is given. In this sense the situational leader is a manager. Furthermore, the situational leader is responding to their staff's needs and is not really leading in the way most people would understand the term. As such, situational leadership is transactional: it is about ways of relating to people to get the best out of them, about interpersonal transactions. It is in no sense transformational, in which all current practices may need to be revised.

In contrast, the process of transforming/transformational leadership is dependent on the leader's ability to create change through developing a motivating vision of the future. The personality of the transformational leader is far more important for success than that of the transactional leader. Transformational leadership encourages passion and commitment from all staff and encourages everyone to work harder to achieve that powerful vision of what this organisation could be.

What does it mean?

Transactional (or situational) leaders: managers who help to get the best out of their people, through planned interaction with them. Transactional leadership is often most useful in relatively stable parts of the organisation.

Transformational leaders: seek to create significant change in the life of both organisations and the people in them through developing a vision for the future, to which all can enthusiastically commit. Transformational leadership is needed when rapid and radical organisational change is being experienced.

Warren Bennis (Bennis and Nanus, 1985) developed the concept of the leader with his revealing interviews with leaders in a wide range of organisations in the USA. Bernard Bass (Bass and Bass, 2008) contributed to the development of the concept, calling it transformational leadership. Bass and his associates developed a measure, the Multi-factor Leadership Questionnaire (MLQ), to enable people to assess their own style. This measure has been refined constantly since its launch in 1985. Whereas Burns felt strongly that transactional and transforming leadership were mutually exclusive, Bass took the view that leaders could simultaneously show both transformational and transactional behaviours – and we agree with this position.

The degree to which leaders are transformational is measured primarily by the influence they have over followers. Ideally, the transformational process is one designed to turn followers into leaders. Followers are crucial for the transformational leader and they typically feel admiration, loyalty, respect and trust for their leader. Consequently, transformational leaders have people who work harder than the minimum; they are inspired by the mission of the enterprise. Working is not just about the pay or other benefits; the team feel committed to the purpose set and are proud of their joint achievements. It is possible to see why the concept of transformational leadership has much appeal in sectors such as early years provision and education. This model is the source of concepts that will be familiar to readers, such as creating a vision for an organisation that needs to be shared and embraced by everyone.

The mission – to create a vision of the future
In practice, transformational leaders have a clear statement of the mission of the organisation in order to provide an unambiguous and unified direction for the entire concern. The vision is typically focused closely on one critical aspect of

operation and is accompanied by a strategy to enable successful implementation. The mission or vision statement – often arrived at through debate with at least the senior team and sometimes with the whole staff group – is then written up as a public document for everyone. Typical focus areas include:

- Clarity about what quality or excellence means in this organisation.
- How do we develop and innovate here?
- Whose satisfaction or well being is at the core of what we do?
- 'If we did not do this (for example, care for children well) … we would not exist?'

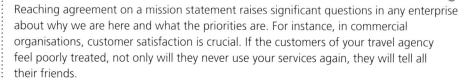

Take another **perspective**

Reaching agreement on a mission statement raises significant questions in any enterprise about why we are here and what the priorities are. For instance, in commercial organisations, customer satisfaction is crucial. If the customers of your travel agency feel poorly treated, not only will they never use your services again, they will tell all their friends.

Early years settings have had to address who exactly is the customer and what kind of service is on offer. Is our customer the parents and, if so, what happens if they clearly want something that our professional knowledge tells us is not beneficial for this baby or child?

It is not enough to create the vision and sit back; that vision must be communicated well. The statement is shared with everyone inside the organisation and often to users of the service and other professionals as well. Excellent communication is key to successful transformational processes. Yukl (1994) identifies the importance of expressing confidence, decisiveness and optimism about achieving the goals. Leadership is active and interactional; a shared vision fails to come alive, to be meaningful, if it is communicated just by posting notices. The details of the shared vision need to make sense and to be motivational for staff. The vision will fail if people cannot relate to the details or do not feel that 'yes, this is why we are here; we can and will make a difference'.

Bass and Bass (2008) called this process 'inspirational motivation'. Their full model is based on what is known as the 'four Is'.

Idealised influence or charisma describes leaders who are a strong model for others to follow: people want to emulate these leaders. They have high moral and ethical standards, and are followed as they can usually be counted on to do the right thing – rather than do things right. They provide a sense of mission to this organisation.

Inspirational motivation describes leaders who have high expectations of their people to achieve the shared vision of the future. They use motivational tools such as encouragement, emotional appeals and appropriate use of symbols (what do we stand for?) to get people to pull together. These leaders publicise successes widely, both about the organisation and about individuals.

Recognition and celebratory events typically occur as small planned steps to achieving the mission are realised. The leader wants to show everyone how their work contributes directly to the success of the organisation. They make what is being done meaningful – and personally relevant – to all.

Intellectual stimulation supports followers in being creative and challenging accepted ways of doing things in order to improve operations. Innovation and questioning are not only accepted, they are welcomed. Staff members are also encouraged and enabled to question their personal values and beliefs, as well as those of the leader and organisation. There are strong links here with the focus on the reflective practitioner in early years provision.

Individualised consideration is about listening to the needs of individual followers and coaching them to develop themselves further. This may involve taking on new challenges (perhaps as a 'team leader'), or the full range of transactional leadership behaviours (from page 173). Individualised consideration provides a supportive climate in which people feel that they are being helped to fulfil their needs. This support may also help to reduce the stresses and strains of the leadership role discussed from page 201.

Kouzes and Posner (1993) add that the transformational leader both enables others to act and supports their decisions, and, in their phrase, 'encourages the heart' by appreciating jobs well done, listening and helping when required. What else do transformational leaders do?

- They create high levels of trust: they do what they say, they deliver on their promises.
- Leaders focus on learning – intellectual stimulation – and on people trying things to continuously learn and develop. 'What is done' is not sufficient for them, 'how it is done' is equally as important. This may result in challenging the status quo and changing the organisational environment to reward success better.
- They focus on both processes and results. Such leaders challenge assumptions, take risks and positively solicit other people's ideas. They nurture those who think independently.
- Transformational leaders develop strong corporate values. They explicitly build values, in which staff believe, that are directly relevant to ways of operating that help the organisation to do better.
- Bass and Bass (2008) point out that 'idealised influence' focuses on the leader as role model for the high standards of ethical behaviour, gaining respect and instilling pride in the process. Their organisations reward staff for acting in accord with these values. Transformational leaders have the ability to harness and channel the collective ambitions and aspirations of the workforce.

Research has demonstrated that transformational leadership moves followers to achieve more than was previously expected of them, as well as resulting in higher levels of job satisfaction. There is some evidence, too, that transformational leadership is directly and positively related to organisational innovation. It therefore appears to be more effective than transactional leadership alone. Other researchers see transformational leadership as going beyond individual needs and focusing on a common purpose by addressing intrinsic rewards and higher psychological needs such as self-actualisation (remember Maslow on page 34), and developing commitment with and in their followers (for example, Coleman and LaRoque, 1990; Kirby *et al.*, 1992; Leithwood, 1992; Leithwood and Steinbach, 1991; Sergiovanni and Moore, 1989; Sergiovanni, 1990).

There are some practical issues with the concept of transformational leadership:
- There is some overlap between the four 'I's; does it matter?
- Transformational leadership covers such a wide range of activities that it is legitimate to ask 'where does it really end?'.
- What comes first? Does the organisation itself need to be in a constant state of flux and change (i.e. transformational) for transformational leaders to emerge? Or can transformational leaders alone transform a stable – even hide-bound – organisation?

Finally, recalling the earlier work on traits and personality (page 38), it is useful to look at the personal characteristics of people who are associated with transformational leadership. Transformational leaders believe in participation and involvement, and seem to share the following characteristics:
- An ability to accept people as they are – not how the leader would like them to be. Transformational leaders work with a realistic assessment of people's strengths and scope for improvement.
- A capacity to approach relationships in terms of the present rather than harking on about the past. Today is what counts, not yesterday's mistakes or what went wrong during last year's parents' evening. Learn from errors and move on.
- Transformational leaders seem to trust others, even when the risk seems great. They almost overdose the team with trust, engendering an even greater capacity for others to take responsibility. Few people in transformational-led organisations complain of 'never having had the chance to fail'.
- They function without the constant approval of others. They recognise – and accept – that leadership is often lonely.
- Most transformational leaders appear to be able to treat those people close to them with the respect and attention they give to total strangers. This attention is applied consistently so that people know it is not merely a ploy.

We return to the practical applications of transformational leadership in Chapter 7.

Emotionally intelligent leaders

The concept of emotional intelligence was first developed by John Mayer and Peter Salovey in the late 1980s. Emotional intelligence (EI) was then brought to a much wider readership with the first edition of Daniel Goleman's *Emotional Intelligence* in 1996. A considerable amount has been written about EI since the beginning, some with well-grounded claims, others not. It is useful to return to the core of the ideas and to see how, or if, they link with the emotional elements of transformational leadership

Caruso and Salovey (2004) argue for the importance of the emotional dimension in the commercial world. They make the business case for understanding and applying how feelings affect thinking and therefore behaviour. Feelings are often viewed as the enemy of rational thought, the disrupter of a smooth intellectual process. As feelings inform thinking, leaders and the organisation lose vital information if emotions are sidelined as inconvenient. It is sensible to look at things both emotionally and logically.

Daniel Goleman, with colleagues Richard Boyatzis and Annie McKee (2002), propose that the fundamental responsibility of leaders is an emotional task: to 'prime' good feeling in those they lead. They use the term 'primal leadership', that driving emotions positively is the prime, original and most important act of leadership. Goleman *et al.* call this 'resonance', as it creates a reservoir of positive feelings which frees up the best in the team. In contrast, when emotions are driven in a negative way, this process is called 'dissonance': a situation which disrupts the positive conditions that enable people to flourish.

A central finding of research around emotional intelligence was that emotions are contagious. A leader's attitude, shown visibly through behaviour and words, can infect a workplace for better or worse (Goleman *et al.*, 2002). Effective leaders are emotionally intelligent: able to perceive and influence the flow of emotions between themselves and others at work. This ability in turn rests upon the leader's skill in empathic listening and a high level of self-awareness. The underlying assumption is that emotionally intelligent leaders use their alertness to emotions in others to benefit the work, and not as fuel for power plays.

Goleman *et al.* propose that the emotionally intelligent leader has competencies within four broad domains, which include 18 leadership competencies. No leader will be highly and equally effective in everything. Self-aware leaders recognise their less secure areas of competence and draw on the skills of their team.

There are two domains of personal competence: leaders' capabilities here will determine their ability to manage themselves.
- Self-awareness: emotional self-awareness, accurate self-assessment in terms of strengths and weaknesses, self-confidence based on realism.
- Self-management – emotional self-control, transparency and honesty, adaptability to circumstances and overcoming obstacles, achievement in terms of wanting to improve personal standards, initiative and optimism.

They identify two domains of social competence, which is the leader's capability to manage relationships at work:
- Social awareness: empathy with individuals, awareness of the currents in the organisation, awareness to the needs of the service and customer.
- Relationship management: inspirational leadership that guides and motivates with a compelling vision, influence supported by a range of tactics for persuasion, developing others, a catalyst and leader for change, able to deal

with conflict resolution, building and maintaining a web of relationships, teamwork and collaboration.

We return to emotional intelligence on page 198.

Authentic Leadership

The focus on Authentic Leadership has developed over the past ten years or so and has responded, in part, to national and international events. The attacks of terrorist groups, the collapse of the banking sector through inappropriate loaning (and, many would say, personal aggrandisement) and the near (or actual) bankrupting of nations have critically raised the issue of 'can we trust our leaders? Are they authentic and real, or is everything just a manipulative sham?'. Key figures in this newest area of investigation include Bruce Avolio and his colleagues (Avolio and Gardner, 2005; Luthans and Avolio, 2003; Walumbwa, Avolio *et al.*, 2008).

Concepts of idealised influence or charisma (page 56) are part of the ideas, but at one level, the concept of authentic leadership is about leaders being true to themselves. Do their actions fit their words? Is their current behaviour consistent with their personal history? Some writers within the area believe that authentic leadership is something that can be developed and nurtured over a lifetime – certainly, genuine trust in the leader would surely need some basis for that commitment. Key elements of authentic leadership include self-awareness, an internalised moral and ethical perspective, and that the leader acts in a transparent and honest way, with no hidden agendas. Authentic leadership additionally involves the interactions between leader and follower, a reciprocal effect of mutual influence.

At the early stage of this research area, it appears that there are four underlying psychological capacities behind authentic leadership:

1 *Confidence* – that you can accomplish the tasks set, and persistence in the face of setbacks.

2 *Hope* – this is really about goal setting and planning, and knowing your aims can be achieved.

3 *Optimism* – seeing the situation in a positive light and having good expectations as to the future.

4 *Resilience* – to be able to adapt to difficult situations, to recover from setbacks and gain strength by so doing.

These capacities are shaped by critical life events – experiences which allegedly enable people to develop themselves in four ways:

1 *Self-awareness* – understanding strengths and weaknesses, your impact on others and a grasp of 'who you are' at a deep level.

2 *Internalised moral perspective* – a deeply ethical standpoint which is not influenced by pressures from others, tasks or the demands of change.

3 *Balanced processing* – the capacity to be objective and to involve others appropriately in decision making. This perspective includes being open about your own perspective.

4 *Relational transparency* – this is about being open and honest in the way you present yourself to others, sharing truthfully.

These components of authentic leadership imply a complex process: an emphasis on the development of capacities, over a lifespan, that helps leaders to be seen as both believable and trustworthy by their people. Much detail in the approach is consistent with other work on leadership: the moral dimension, self-confidence, the need to have self-awareness and excellent influencing skills in working with followers.

Authentic leadership approaches describe a daunting array of qualities to show what is required to be an authentic leader (George, 2003; Klenke, 2007; Terry, 1993). Some of the descriptions provoke a sense of almost a return to the hero-leader, although with strong spiritual overtones in some papers. Some commentaries about the idea raise the dilemmas that can arise in applying openness and honesty to the myriad situations which leaders face. At a more ordinary, and achievable, level we see the details of authentic leadership as possibly creating someone we would value as a friend and as such may influence us and be given a leadership role. If you do an internet search on authentic leadership, you will find a great deal of discussion but, as yet, limited research to validate the claims, however appealing the concept of authenticity may be. Nor is there any evidence so far that authentic leadership in practice brings benefit to the organisation.

Leadership through people and teams

We now return to the world of social psychology and research into effective groups. Robert Freed Bales, based at Harvard, worked in this area consistently from the 1950s onwards. At the end of the 1970s he published his work on 'a system for the multiple level observation of groups' (SYMLOG) in Bales and Cohen (1979). The SYMLOG approach has a long history of consistent research. One of Bales' last works, *Social Interaction Systems*, was published in 1999. Bales and his colleagues developed questionnaires which enable people to evaluate themselves against the dimensions of the SYMLOG field. This model is complicated but it really does capture the complexity of organisational life. SYMLOG links with key concepts discussed earlier in this chapter. Blake and Mouton's Concern for the Task (Hersey and Blanchard's Directive behaviours) becomes, in Bales' approach, Values for Accepting the Task Orientation of Accepted Authority. This is a bit of a mouthful, we know, so we have stuck to Task Orientation from here on. Blake and Mouton's Concern for People (Hersey and Blanchard's Supportive behaviours) becomes Friendly in SYMLOG.

Bales' analysis went much, much further than either the Managerial Grid or situational leadership. The following set of figures goes through the ideas step by step. Take your time and go back and forth if that helps your understanding.

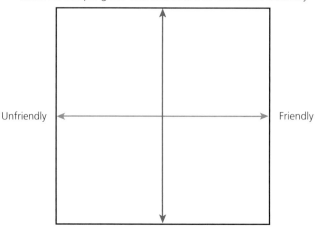

Values for *accepting* the Task orientation of established authority

Unfriendly — Friendly

Values for *opposing* the Task orientation of established authority

Figure 2.7 SYMLOG field diagram

Figure 2.7 shows that, unlike either the Managerial Grid or situational leadership, SYMLOG goes into negative territory. People can be unfriendly as well as friendly. They can oppose the direction of the organisation. So SYMLOG is not a model in which leaders are ranged from neutral to positive on the task dimension: here leaders can oppose what the practice is trying to do. Similarly, the manager/leader does not vary only from neutral to positive on supporting behaviours (concern for people) towards staff: they may actually be unfriendly, even hostile. So SYMLOG gives a more diverse and realistic picture of leadership, summarised in Figure 2.8.

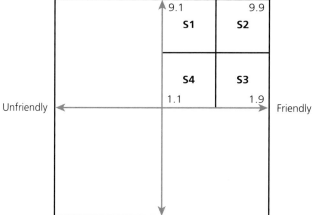

Values for *accepting* the Task orientation of established authority

9.1 S1   9.9 S2

S4   S3
1.1   1.9

Unfriendly — Friendly

Values for *opposing* the Task orientation of established authority

Figure 2.8 The SYMLOG field diagram and situational leadership styles

Observant readers will notice that we have rotated the S1–S4 from situational leadership options (page 51), in order to fit the placement of the core SYMLOG dimensions. This model locates the people dimension along the base rather than the vertical. So, as we see it, both the Managerial Grid and situational leadership fit into the top right-hand box of SYMLOG.

Think about your own experience: have you encountered people at work who were unfriendly, but accepted the details of their job in the setting? Or colleagues who were friendly but resistant to what they were asked to do, in line with the overall goals? If so, SYMLOG can tap this diversity, but the Managerial Grid and situational leadership cannot. Figure 2.9 goes one step further: to show how SYMLOG describes the zones of the space. The diagram is adapted from Bales (1999, page 61).

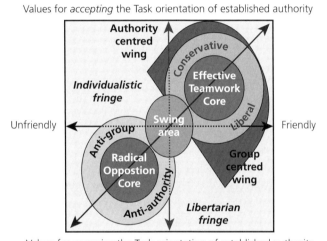

Values for *accepting* the Task orientation of established authority

Values for *opposing* the Task orientation of established authority

Figure 2.9 The areas of the SYMLOG field diagram

- Those leaders who are very high on the Friendly dimension and neutral on the Task dimension are the Group Centred wing in the lower right-hand side of the figure. These individuals tend to be more interested in the group and good relationships than doing the task. Remember Blake and Mouton's description of the 1.9 Country Club style on page 46?
- Leaders who are high on Task and neutral on Friendly form the core of the Authority-centred wing in the upper half of the figure in the middle. They are the 9.1 Autocrat from Blake and Mouton.
- The Swing Area – in the middle of the figure – represents those people who have yet to be convinced that they are right for the organisation, or vice versa. If any readers are *Star Wars* fans, like us, Luke Skywalker (a hard-pressed potential leader) was in this undecided swing area during *The Empire Strikes Back,* the second film made.
- Then there are those who are loners, rebels and turned off in the bottom left-hand corner. Elements of opposition are present to some degree in all organisations. Perhaps they remain for the salary, they may be set in their ways

and are not motivated to exchange 'the evil you know' for one that has unknown risks. They may have tried to leave, but literally cannot get another job. These people are a potential liability unless a leader can bring them around.

● The Effective Teamwork core in the middle right upper describes those who are reasonably high on both Task and Friendly dimensions. This is not as extreme as the 9.9. Team Leader from the Managerial Grid, but is clearly in the centre of the Coaching S2 style from Hersey and Blanchard.

We have given time and space to SYMLOG because the model does more than just expand the arena for exploring the dimensions of leadership and management. An innovative feature for the discussion is that SYMLOG also looks at a further dimension: Dominance. This dimension directly addresses and integrates a key component of leadership that has really been seen only in biographies of leaders. The significance of dominance for leadership does not feature much in academic research on the subject. Dominance is about assertiveness and self-confidence, and in the full 3D diagram (Figure 2.10) is at the opposite end of the dimension to Submissiveness.

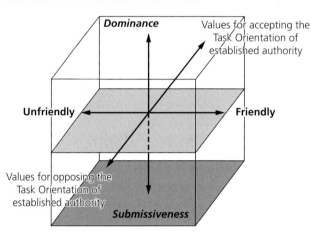

Figure 2.10   The 3D SYMLOG field diagram

For us, this three-dimensional image is about the best picture from the literature of the individual within a broad leadership space. So, for example, you can be very *friendly* but *submissive* and in *opposition to the tasks* the organisation wishes you to perform. It is likely that no one other than close friends will be aware of this orientation. In contrast, the very *dominant* person, supporting the organisation's direction, who is *unfriendly* is the anchor-point autocrat, for whom friendliness may well be seen as weakness.

The detailed research of Bales and his colleagues over decades has shown what seems to be the most effective position for either a leader or a follower and in the present or the future. That place is directly underneath the 'e' in the word 'established' in the upper right of the figure.

- This Most Effective Position (MEP) is reasonably, but not too, *dominant*.
- It is *friendly* but not so much as to blur the work boundaries.
- The MEP is supportive of the *task orientation of accepted authority* but not uncritically.

The MEP sits right in the middle of the Effective Teamwork Core, shown in Figure 2.9.

In summary, the MEP describes people someone who are friendly and approachable, are not afraid to speak their minds and support the organisation in general. They may still have questions or concerns, which will be likely to be raised at an opportune moment. They seek to improve the operation. MEP people do not sit on their concerns, they voice them, so issues can be resolved. In other words, the MEP position represents both the kind of leader and follower that most of us wish for. Leaders need to strive and create the working environment in which it is possible for people to gravitate towards the MEP position.

Make the connection with … **your practice**

Consider the SYMLOG Consulting Group's definition of leadership: 'Leadership is the ability to unify a diverse group of people to work effectively as a team toward a common purpose under varied and often difficult circumstances, through the elimination of scapegoating, the maximisation of mediation, and the judicious use of power.'

- Which parts of this fit with your own experience?
- Are there elements that you would challenge?
- Is there anything missing?

Research supports the capacity of SYMLOG to measure interactions within groups very well. It is less certain whether the three dimensions are quite as independent from each other as is claimed (for example, people higher on *dominance* tend to come out higher on *friendly* and *task orientation*, too). Neither does SYMLOG really address what effects external influences have on the group. Hence the organisational and environmental context does need to be kept in mind when using the interpersonal dynamics of SYMLOG. We will return to SYMLOG in the context of change on page 89.

Conclusion

The literature is detailed and complex, ranging from research on individuals, group dynamics, teams, management and leadership itself to organisational effectiveness and performance. In some ways, the history can be seen to move from a focus on physical labour, designed to get most productivity out of those manual jobs not mechanised. As time progressed and more processes were automated, or then taken over by computers, people were rewarded more for their intellectual horsepower. Levels of educational attainment continually rose and specific courses (such as degrees and other higher qualifications) were developed to further raise our intellectual level. The focus shifted towards logic, brainpower and ways to form strategy and make decisions better.

Today the arena is defined by what could be called emotional work. This understands that, for example, people of all ages and roles are largely driven by what they want rather than by detached logic. This is not to say that the needs for both physical work or intellectual work are no longer present, it is just that the emphasis has shifted to emotional work – an area which had been noticeably absent from the literature until late in the last century. Previously the emphasis was on the need to know; increasingly, it is now on the need to care. (A focus which can be overstated, as in those irritating corporate slogans about 'we care'.) The key issues for leaders are as follows.

The person will continue to matter

We will never be able to detach the person from the role of leader. The individual will always play a part – for good or ill – in the leadership arena. The individual characteristics (traits, personality) of the person, whether they are sociable or not, dominant or not, motivated to achievement or not, seeking power or not, male or female will all influence leadership style. In essence, people who wish to lead need to manage themselves to be more effective, using what makes them unique.

Personal, social and emotional

Work in emotional intelligence and authentic leadership has re-emphasised the need for leaders to have high levels of self-awareness and the capacity to listen empathically. They are honest and trustworthy. Whatever the nature of the organisation and the goals, those aims need to be achieved through people: the human factor. So the skills of influencing others are vital, as is the ability to apply those skills in a variety of contexts: within a group of peers, one-to-one, within a hierarchy.

Leaders use power

Leaders are aware of their own sources of power and will use these judiciously to achieve the results sought.

Balance the task and the people

The critical dimensions of task orientation and people orientation (however they are presented though in different terminology) are firmly established as crucial to the success of any cooperative enterprise. If the scales tip too much towards concern for people, then everything will take ages to accomplish and there will be an awful lot of largely unproductive chat. On the other side, tip the scales too much towards delivering the task and working life can become emotionally cold, demotivating, unrelieved tough work.

Leaders are different from managers

To emphasise: leaders have followers; that is what makes them leaders. Managers are appointed to post by the hierarchy and may or may not be leaders. Transactional leadership is, in our view, *not* leadership as it is typically designed for managers to develop their staff. Apart from being a decent people manager, these individuals do not obviously lead. Transformational leaders do lead and are committed to change.

Value followers

There is considerable evidence that the skills of effective followers provide the bedrock upon which to build the developments indicated by transactional and transformational leadership. We find it hard to see how distributed leadership (a favoured model for some early years writers – from page 119) is more than a different term for formalising effective follower roles within a work group context.

Leaders can stand alone

Our conclusion is that the distinguishing factor for leadership, rather than just being an effective person or follower, is the capacity to take tough decisions and to stick to them in the face of opposition. This requires courage, self-confidence and assertiveness – a belief that you are right. Effective leaders still take into account what their staff want to communicate, including their feelings. Leaders gather as much valid information as they can. But once the decision is made, the leader explains and sticks to that decision. Leaders need to be able to stand on their own feet, and sometimes to be alone.

The key question is, how can all this be done? How can I learn to embrace and value change? What skills do I need to be a more effective follower, group leader, transformational or transactional leader? What more do I need to know? And how can I manage my anxieties better? We will look at these points in detail in the subsequent chapters.

Resources

- **Avolio, B. and Gardner, W.** (2005) 'Authentic leadership development: Getting to the root of positive forms of leadership'. *Leadership Quarterly*, 16, 315–38.
- **Bales, R.** (1950) *Interaction Process Analysis: A method for the study of small groups.* Cambridge: Addison-Wesley. Reprinted 1976, University of Chicago Press.
- **Bales, R.** (1999) *Social Interaction Systems: Theory and Measurement.* New Brunswick: Transaction Publishers.
- **Bales, R. and Cohen, S.** (1979) *SYMLOG: A system for the multiple level observation of groups.* New York: Free Press.
- **Bass, B. and Bass, R.** (2008) *The Bass Handbook of Leadership: Theory, research, and managerial applications,* 4th edition. New York: Free Press.
- **Bennis, W. and Nanus, B.** (1985) *Leaders: The strategies for taking charge.* New York: Harper and Row.
- **Blake, R. and McCanse, A.** (1991) *Leadership Dilemmas: Grid Solutions.* Houston, TX: Gulf Publishing Co.
- **Blake, R. and Mouton, J.** (1964) *The Managerial Grid: The key to leadership excellence.* Houston, TX: Gulf Publishing Co.
- **Burns, J.** (1978) *Leadership.* New York: Harper & Row.

- **Caruso, D. and Salovey, P.** (2004) *The Emotionally Intelligent Manager: How to develop and use the four key emotional skills of leadership.* San Francisco, CA: Jossey-Bass.
- **Catalyst (2006).** *2005 Catalyst Census of Women Board Directors of the Fortune 500.* New York: Catalyst.
- **Coleman, P. and LaRoque, L.** (1990) *Struggling to be 'Good Enough': Administrative practices and school district ethos.* New York: The Falmer Press.
- **Fiedler, F.** (1967) *A theory of leadership effectiveness.* New York: McGraw-Hill Book Company.
- **George, B.** (2003) *Authentic Leadership: Rediscovering the secrets to creating lasting value.* San Francisco, CA: Jossey-Bass.
- **Goleman, D.** (1996) *Emotional Intelligence: Why it can matter more than IQ.* London: Bloomsbury.
- **Goleman, D., Boyatzis, R. and McKee, A.** (2002) *Primal Leadership.* Harvard Business School Press.
- **Hersey, P. and Blanchard, K.H.** (1969) *Management of Organizational Behavior – Utilizing Human Resources.* Upper Saddle River, NJ: Prentice Hall.
- **Hersey, P. and Blanchard, K.H.** (1974) 'So you want to know your leadership style?'. *Training and Development Journal,* American Society for Training and Development, February.
- **Herzberg, F.** (1959) *Work and the Nature of Man.* Cleveland: World Publishing.
- **House, R.** (1971) 'A path-goal theory of leadership effectiveness'. *Administration Science Quarterly,* 16, 3, 321–39.
- **Judge, T., Bono, J., Ilies, R. and Gerhard, W.** (2002) 'Personality and leadership: A qualitiative and quantitative review'. *Journal of Applied Psychology,* 87, 765–80.
- **Kanter, R.M.** (1983) *The Change Masters: Corporate entrepreneurs at work.* London: Unwin Paperbacks.
- **Kirby, P., Paradise, L. and King, M.** (1992) 'Extraordinary leaders in education: Understanding transformational leadership'. *Journal of Educational Research,* 85, 5, 303–11.
- **Kirkpatrick, S. and Locke, E.** (1991) 'Leadership: Do traits matter?' *Academy of Management Executive,* 5, 2, 48–60. http://sbuweb.tcu.edu/jmathis/Org_Mgmt_Materials/Leadership%20-%20Do%20Traits%20Matgter.pdf
- **Klenke, K.** (2007) 'Authentic leadership: a self, leader, and spiritual identity perspective'. *International Journal of Leadership Studies,* 3, 68–97. www.regent.edu/acad/global/publications/ijls/new/vol3iss1/klenke/Klenke_IJLS_V3Is1.pdf
- **Kouzes, J. and Posner, B.** (1993) *Credibility.* San Francisco: Jossey-Bass.
- **Leithwood, K.** (1992) 'The move toward transformational leadership'. *Educational Leadership,* 49, 5, 8–12.
- **Leithwood, K. and Steinbach, R.** (1991) 'Indicators of transformational leadership in the everyday problem solving of school administrators'. *Journal of Personnel Evaluation in Education,* 4, 3, 221–44.
- **Lewin, K., Lippitt, R. and White, R.** (1939) 'Patterns of aggressive behavior in experimentally created "social climates"'. *Journal of Social Psychology,* 10, 271–301.

- **Lindon, J.** (2010a) *Understanding Child Development: Linking theory and practice.* London: Hodder Education.
- **Luthans, F. and Avolio, B.** (2003) 'Authentic leadership development'. In Cameron, K., Dutton, S. and Quinn, R. (eds) *Positive Organizational Scholarship.* San Francisco, CA: Berrett-Koehler.
- **Maslow, A.** (1943) 'A theory of human motivation'. *Psychological Review,* 50, 370–96. **http://psychclassics.yorku.ca/Maslow/motivation.htm**
- **Mayo, E.** (1933) *The Human Problem of an Industrial Civilization.* Boston, MA: Harvard Business School.
- **McGregor, D.** (1960) *The Human Side of Enterprise.* New York: McGraw-Hill.
- **McKee, R. and Carlson, B.** (1999) *The Power to Change.* Austin, TX: Grid International Inc.
- **Northouse, P.** (2010) *Leadership Theory and Practice.* London: Sage.
- **Peters, T. and Waterman, R.** (1980) *In Search of Excellence: Lessons from America's best-run companies.* New York: Harper Business.
- **Schein, E.H.** (1987) *Process Consultation Volume 1: Its role in organizational development.* Boston, MA: Addison-Wesley.
- **Sergiovanni, T.** (1990) 'Adding value to leadership gets extraordinary results'. *Educational Leadership,* 47, 8, 23–7.
- **Sergiovanni, T. and Moore, J.** (eds) (1989) *Schooling for Tomorrow: Directing reforms to issues that count.* Boston, MA: Allyn and Bacon.
- **Stogdill, R.** (1948) 'Personal factors associated with leadership: A survey of the literature'. *Journal of Psychology,* 25, 35–71.
- **Stogdill, R.** (1974) *Handbook of Leadership: A survey of theory and research.* New York: The Free Press.
- **Tannenbaum, A. and Schmidt, W.** (1958) 'How to choose a leadership pattern'. *Harvard Business Review,* 36, 95–101.
- **Taylor, F.W.** (1911) *The Principles of Scientific Management.* New York: Harper Row. Online information at **www.marxists.org/reference/subject/economics/taylor/principles/index.htm**
- **Terry, R.** (1993) *Authentic Leadership: Courage in action.* San Francisco, CA: Jossey-Bass.
- The SYMLOG Consulting Group (1993) *SYMLOG Practitioner Training Materials.* San Diego: The SYMLOG Consulting Group.
- **Vroom, V. and Yetton, P.** (1973) *Leadership and Decision-Making.* Pittsburgh, PA: University of Pittsburgh Press.
- **Walumbwa, F., Avolio, B., Gardner, W., Wernsing, T. and Peterson, S.** (2008) 'Authentic leadership: Development and validation of a theory-based measure'. *Journal of Management,* 34, 1, 89–126.
- **Yukl, G.** (1994) Leadership in Organizations. Englewood Cliffs, NJ: Prentice Hall.

Leadership in times of change

Leadership and management are equally important and this chapter explores when the respective skills are needed for effective practice. Dealing with some change has always been part of the job for early years managers, and daily life with children and families is full of unpredicted events. However, the pace and significance of change have increased. The early years sector requires confident leadership to recognise the need for change and the processes involved.

Leadership is not a simple list of what to do in order to be a leader. Effective leaders seek to reach a thorough understanding of what they face and the kind of change that is required. The best approach will vary according to the situation – past, present and future. It all depends … so the aim of this chapter is to explore those details.

The main sections of this chapter are:
- the context of change
- integrating leadership and management
- managing and leading change.

The context of change

This section focuses on understanding the process of change within the context of a leadership or management role. Elsewhere we have dealt with predictable aspects of change from the perspective of individuals' experience and personal development (Lindon, 2010b). While there is inevitable overlap, our focus here is more upon the organisation.

The impetus for change

While change can come from any point in the endeavour, it is typically the role of those in authority to ensure that changes introduced by external factors, such as government regulations or firm recommendations from the inspectorate, are effectively implemented in a setting. In these situations the manager's motivation to change may be low; perhaps this is yet another official change of position or the inspector's judgement seems unjust. Personal discipline and emotional energy may be needed to do what is required and to help bolster the morale of the team. Also, managers should not feel they have to soldier on with no extra support. A valuable message from the early years leaders, with whom we spoke for this book, was the importance of seeking advice, specific consultancy input and tapping any local sources of impartial support, including professional networking (page 200).

Take another **perspective**

An initial thought.

Change **CHANGE** change

Does just how it is written make the word feel different?

The International Leadership Project (ILP) reported by Nivala and Hujala (2002) offers an international perspective on leadership, with particular attention to day-care settings. The ILP brought together reports which highlighted shared issues as early years provision in different countries became increasingly required to meet objectives (outputs) that did not always co-exist easily with the existing organisational culture. Cushla Scrivens (2002a, 2002b) expressed serious concern about the system of New Public Management (NPM) which was established in New Zealand during the 1990s and aimed to make early childhood provision operate more like a business. Scrivens describes how the advisory teachers working with the New Zealand kindergartens experienced tensions between, on the one hand, wanting to support staff and, on the other, being an agent of accountability and compliance with plans and regulations.

There are parallels with the market forces rhetoric in the UK, which was especially applied to private and voluntary provision. Over a similar period in the UK, a focus on judging early years provision by measurable outcomes for children and targets stirred considerable challenge. If you look ahead at Figure 3.2, it is possible to envisage the points of strain in that organisational model when external pressures are in opposition to the established culture, mission and sources of what motivates the team in their work.

Types of change

It is useful to consider three types of change: everyday, enhancement and radical. Sometimes these overlap.

Everyday

Everyday changes are regular and necessary adjustments to work practices and procedures. Some are so minor you do not even think of them as a change. For example, Katy, the manager of FineStart nursery, has to reorganise her day slightly to allow for a changed meeting time. More significantly, Katy has purchased new outdoor resources and needs to consider where they go best in the garden. She also needs to make time to read her emails and to respond to the attached revised pro forma for information gathered on families when they join the nursery.

Typically these changes fall into the category of 'not done usually' in the options discussed on page 41 about acceptance and rejection of authority, and do not cause too many problems. However, sometimes routine changes may trigger a recognition that other changes are also involved. For example, the revised pro forma for creating the family record includes new questions and a different way of tracking children's progress. A closer look raises ethical issues for Katy and calls into question whether the revised system is really a routine change. It looks more like the beginning of significant changes to practice expected by her local authority.

Enhancement

These changes are designed to improve and change current practices and procedures, perhaps because they have drifted away from what was originally agreed. For instance, in theory Princes children's centre has a regular supervision system. However, over recent weeks many scheduled times have been cancelled at short notice. Brigid, the head, needs to understand what is happening in order to decide how to re-establish supervision of staff. She does not want to lose the benefits that supervision brings to practice: for the well being of children and the continued professional development of staff.

Another example of an enhancement change would be that Meerkats day nursery wants to respond to the comment in their inspection report that they could improve their communication with parents. Corinne, the deputy, takes the responsibility for exploring how much and what kind of communication is sought by parents. Maybe one clear message is that parents want to be updated about events as a whole in the nursery. Could the best approach be an email newsletter, texting, or a new section on the website? If so, then who will take responsibility to develop this?

As we see it, the area of enhancement change is the primary focus of the early years professionals, particularly those who are not managers of a setting. Their role is not to deliver innovative change. We talk more about the role of EYPs from page 128.

Radical

This kind of change will profoundly influence the way that a provision operates. Significant change may be imposed by external forces such as changes in legislation or government initiatives. Yet radical change could come from an internal source.

For instance, the AtoZ day nursery has many parents who work in very demanding jobs with long and unpredictable hours. Leila, the manager, feels the nursery already offers a flexible service, but there is a clear demand for longer hours, weekends and maybe even with the facility for children to stay overnight. If such a change is implemented, it will radically overhaul how the nursery operates: different staffing patterns, procedures that ensure continuity of care, not to mention a new registration to permit children to stay overnight.

This kind of significant change raises practical questions (such as would any of the current AtoZ staff be willing to work a night shift?). However, Leila is sure that such a change also raises issues around the core values of the nursery, their vision of what they do and what makes the team proud. Look at Figure 3.2 to consider the two elements that Leila and her team need to balance. There may be a clear preference from sufficient parents to justify the overnight facility. However, will the consequence be that some children scarcely live in their own home? Is this consequence in children's best interests?

The Early Years Foundation Stage brought the requirement that every setting in England had to establish a key person approach to enable personal, sustained relationships between the named practitioner and key children, with their family. Many settings had developed a full key person system when this approach was still a recommendation. Those teams continue to consider how the system works and any improvements. However, managers who previously chose to ignore the clear advice, or found reasons why it was not possible, were then faced with a non-negotiable requirement, but equally important, with changes in attitudes (Lindon, 2010c). For these settings this radical change was also an example of an *enforced* change, which is usually much harder to implement than when there is a choice as staff feel less committed. In terms of implementing the key person system, a great deal depended on whether the manager, and staff group, had let minor difficulties get in the way or they had entrenched objections.

Pause for reflection

Think about changes in which you have been directly involved. What kind of change was proposed or required? For example, have you been closely involved in the changes that follow, when provision extends the age group of children to which the service is offered?

What kind of rethinking has to follow if a playgroup or nursery reduces the age of its youngest children from rising 3s to very young 2s? A small reduction in the youngest age could be addressed through improvement changes. However, best practice will require innovative change around routines, personal care, equipment and adult habits of communication across the provision.

Integrating leadership and management

In Chapter 1 we looked briefly at the distinction between being a leader and a manager (page 3). The detailed discussion in Chapter 2 of the history of leadership and management research takes us to the key distinctions that need to be drawn.

The relationship between leadership and management

Our consistent message is that leadership and management are both essential; it is profoundly unhelpful if beliefs develop that one is more important than the other, or that one is good and the other bad. However, it is extremely helpful – we would say necessary – that the different context for leadership and management is fully understood. In order to define and understand the relationship between leadership and management, it is crucial to introduce the notion of time frame. The key ideas are represented in Figure 3.1.

	Currency	Focus	Utilises
Transformational leadership* *is long-term*	BELIEFS	FUTURE Possibilities and direction	Innovation and commitment
Transactional (situational) leadership* *is mid-term*	INTERACTION	PRESENT/FUTURE Opportunities and threats	Capability and flexibility ** Both of these have followers*
Management *is short-term*	FACTS	PRESENT/PAST Monitors and controls	Knowledge and systems *Management has subordinates*

Figure 3.1 Integrating leadership and management

Figure 3.1 distinguishes between the short term, medium term and long term. It illustrates that Transformational Leadership (discussed from page 54) primarily operates in the long term. No organisation will achieve challenging and visionary objectives within a short space of time. Even experienced and committed leaders cannot work miracles overnight. The focus is therefore very much on the future; objectives which are likely to be achieved over years, if not decades. Furthermore, to be honest, no one really knows whether the vision for significant change can be achieved in reality. People had better believe in the possibility because their commitment is central to achieving the vision. Much innovative change may be necessary and in areas about which they have not yet thought much at all.

We believe that the term *transactional leadership* may be a misnomer. No element within transactional leadership (see page 50) is really about leading; it is the people side of management. The focus of transactional leadership is medium term: a time span of weeks and months. The activity of the transactional leader is designed to develop staff over the present and immediate future, so that these followers are better able to take on more senior roles. Hersey and Blanchard's model of situational leadership (page 51) is ideally suited to this important task.

Finally, management focuses on learning from the past and applying this knowledge to the present. Hence the managerial focus is short term: this week's activities, this week's fees from families, this week's supplier to contact. The key currency that management uses is facts: the library outing went well and should become a regular event, these overdue fees are now paid, the local supplier for fish is now sending the correct quantities. Management focuses on what happened or did not happen. This needs accurate and current data from a constant flow of up-to-date information so that timely and appropriate actions can be taken. So what management uses is the current and historical knowledge of the organisation in conducting its business – the predictable issues that have been faced before and dealt with. There was a greater emphasis (and status) for the managerial role when the pace of change was much slower than it is today.

Make the connection with … **early years practice**

In contrast with the manager, the transactional leader should be more focused on what may happen in the near future: what may go wrong, what opportunities may arise and how to work with staff to ensure that they are well prepared. Consequently, a critical part of the transactional leader's job is to build the capability in the existing team to respond flexibly to events that are likely to occur in the near future, but for which the past is not a good guide.

For example, a children's centre has positive relationships with families who currently attend. The centre outreach worker has established friendly contact with a small local community of Korean families, who are considering the centre's Stay and Play facility. The team need to consider what adjustments would be appropriate to welcome the families, without overreacting on the basis of assumptions about difference, or losing the core values within Stay and Play.

Leadership and management in practice

Look further at the time frame in Figure 3.1. The divisions are neither stark nor absolute; the key difference is in the area of emphasis. Hence the managerial and the transactional jobs are both focused on the present. The tools of the trade, however, can clearly be distinguished.

- Managers focus on the facts and figures.
- The transactional leader focuses on continual communication.
- The transformational leader focuses on beliefs about the kind of operation that will build pride and commitment in staff and customers of the service.

These distinctions do not mean that the transformational leader has no interest in or any grasp of facts, or that the manager is incapable of communicating. In order to get anything done, interaction with other people is essential – so everyone needs some transactional capability. We agree with Bernard Bass (Bass and Bass, 2008) that transformational and transactional leadership are not mutually exclusive. If you think about it, how can transformational leadership affect practice if not through the transactional process? Similarly, everyone needs some management skills to deal with regular events: team meetings, conversations with other agencies, making adjustments because a practitioner will be away attending a training course. In early years provision it will often be the same person who is, at different times, acting as a manager, a transactional leader and a transformational leader.

It is important that someone – ideally the manager, supported by skilled team members – monitors and controls those elements of daily operations which are known and predictable. It would be foolish to make the same, avoidable mistakes over and over, particularly as these would also demotivate staff and pose risks for children. A key objective has been to improve the qualifications of the early years practitioners. A likely, positive consequence of this change is that an increasing proportion of the workforce will look towards a sense of personal satisfaction or fulfilment and not the stark view of 'I work – you pay me'. This is the core arena of transactional leadership: a focus on the continued professional development of staff and helping them to use their knowledge and abilities.

Transformational leadership is most essential when the world is changing rapidly and there are few certainties to point the way. Nowadays the past is a less reliable guide to the future than ever before. As no one knows exactly what is likely to be required, you need everyone on board to achieve what they believe will be best: both for them personally and for the setting. The level of uncertainty is scary for many people, although most of us are learning to accept this better.

One person as transformational leader cannot be successful alone; such leaders need active support from their staff to develop the confidence to help reform what needs reforming, to change what is not working and to commit to ideals and aims in which they all believe. Early years provision, like any enterprise, needs people with leadership qualities and skills throughout the organisation.

Can there be more than one leader?

The evidence certainly suggests that the organisation in which leadership thrives is flat. It has few levels in the hierarchy; no more than four steps from the most senior person to the lowest level is typical, even for large concerns. This reduction in the layers of seniority seems to be crucial if organisations are to create a climate conducive to the emergence of leaders. It means that leaders are able to surface anywhere in the organisation and not wait to do their time in climbing up the pyramid. These potential leaders will, of course, be followers at the moment. Writers such as Robert E. Kelley (1992) focused on the importance to effective organisations of followers who do very good jobs. At the same time, he expressed a heartfelt criticism of the over-emphasis on leadership that led to the topic of followers being largely ignored.

Other researchers suggested that previous theories of leadership were insufficient because they focused more on the idea of a single leader with many followers (Barnes and Kriger, 1986). This alternative view saw leadership as something that was not found within individual traits or skills but was a characteristic of the entire organisation. The alternative situation suggested was one in which leader roles shifted over time, complementing each other and moving from person to person as needed. This perspective certainly implies a more inclusive, organisation-wide view of leadership – more a concept of shared leadership. This recognised that leadership may also be shown by people within a team (Slater and Doig, 1988).

The problem with focusing on the individual leader is that it ignores this 'invisible' leadership of people at lower levels of seniority across the entire organisation (Murphy, 1988). Raelin (2003, 2010) reached the concept of 'leaderful' organisations from observing teams within the business world which appeared to operate very effectively without any clear overall leader. These work teams had sometimes been described as 'self-managed' or as 'leaderless'. But Raelin took the view that they were far better described as 'leaderful' and that leadership could be viewed as part of a democratic process that operated in effective teams.

We think it is more accurate to look at the situations described as shared or organisational leadership as being more about effective followership – Robert Kelley's term. Active and involved followers support a leader or manager who has the legitimate authority to make final decisions as required. You may call these followers 'leaders' if you wish. However, we think use of that word is unhelpful, other than potentially to bolster the self-esteem of people dubbed as leaders. These issues are integral to the discussion about distributed leadership (page 119) and the role of early years professionals (from page 128).

So, in summary:
- Overall, leadership is a process that harnesses staff motivation to deliver improvement actions for the benefit of their organisation.
- Transactional and transformational leadership are not incompatible – far from it. A significant amount of the activity of an effective transformational leader will be transactional in nature.
- Transformational leadership typically focuses on creating significant change – often to values and the work culture – and is primarily an emotional process.
- Managers are essential to predict the predictable and use existing knowledge well.
- Today's organisations need to be leaderful, not leaderless, hence people with the courage to lead are necessary all over the organisation. No one can do everything, therefore we need to use everyone's talents, both individually and in groups.
- Everyone should have the skills of the transactional leader (more in Chapter 6). However, organisations may be compromised if everyone seeks to be a transformational leader (more in Chapter 7).
- Some commentators on early years provision are uneasy about a business model, but many, if not all, settings have to be business-like. If families do not choose your private nursery or pre-school, sooner or later you will go out of business. Leadership focuses organisational energy and resources to build excellent practice and the credibility that gives added value and advantage over alternative settings in an environment of constant change.
- The leadership process requires self-confident people – that is, potential leaders – to operate effectively (more about personal effectiveness in Chapter 4).

Organisations in context

The need for different types of leadership varies organisationally:

● By level – in general, the higher a person is located in the hierarchy, the greater the need for transformational leadership.
● By extent of change required – in general, the more extensive the change needed, the greater the need for transformational leadership.

In the business world transactional leadership is most suited to mature/declining markets and relatively stable functions such as Finance. Transformational leadership becomes necessary in growth markets or where extreme levels of outside pressure are applied. For decades, the sectors of childcare and education were stable and suited to transactional leadership. Significant shifts in expectations for the service and now massive budget cuts have brought the need for transformational leadership to the fore.

Leaders need to look outwards as well as within their organisation because all organisations exist for a purpose: to serve children, families, customers. Fulfilling their requirements and needs – matched with the capabilities of the organisation – is one of the best guarantees of, at best, success and, at worst, survival. All organisations carry with them their history, the resources they have and the effects of the environment in which they operate. Figure 3.2 brings together these strands in an organisational model, adapted from the concepts of Warner Burke (Burke and Litwin, 1992) and Noel Tichy (1983). It is useful to think about an organisation in terms of the inputs of external environment, history and resources, how these affect every aspect of the work and what happens as a result – the outputs.

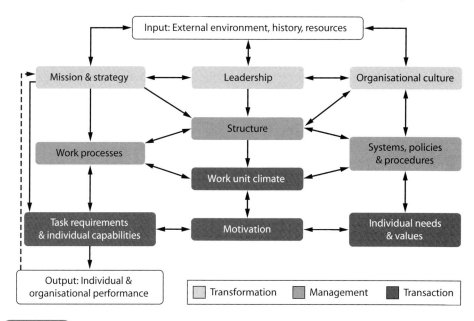

Figure 3.2 The organisational model

The boxes show important elements of how any organisation works but also how the focus for any organisation might be deliberately changed. Adapting Warner Burke's view, we have highlighted each element according to those which our experience shows to be more transformational, more transactional and more managerial. Our aim is to show how experienced practitioners can think more deeply about what they do, whether they are the manager of a setting or a member of the senior team.

Make the connection with ... **early years practice**

Please use the concepts in Figure 3.2 to focus your thinking about leading and managing in your own setting.

- Look at the inputs: what is the broader context in which early years provision operates, in general and in your own setting? How has the history affected how you work now, maybe without even being aware of that influence? What are your resources, including the people?

- A transformational leader will look to the details of the organisational culture (or climate) of this nursery or setting and a clear, shared mission. Even a very positive organisational culture needs to be supported in the 'work unit climate' of each room. Perhaps the transactional early years leader has to find ways to improve the disagreeable atmosphere in the Baby Room.

- Close attention to what is going awry between the staff in the Baby Room lifts the lid on inconsistent implementation of the system established to ensure the key person approach and confusion about the policy on partnership with parents over weaning.

- The same nursery manager, or the senior team, now needs to call on the skills of management. What happened with the routines to which the Baby Room staff apparently agreed? Is the written policy on partnership clear, or does it fail to address the dilemma faced by these practitioners?

- All these details, and the levers for bringing about deliberate change, affect the outputs: in this case the observable well being, or not, of the babies and the closeness of partnership with parents to achieve continuity of care wherever possible.

Change and leadership

In Figure 3.3 we show the relationships between situational leadership theory and the transactional–transformational balance. The greater the need for change, the greater is the need for transformational leadership. In contrast, if the situation is stable there is greater emphasis on management as you know what has to be done; it is predictable. In early years, much of the work is stable – caring for the children and working with parents. The lower section of the diagram gives the options balancing the relative focus on task or on people from Hersey and Blanchard's situational leadership (page 50).

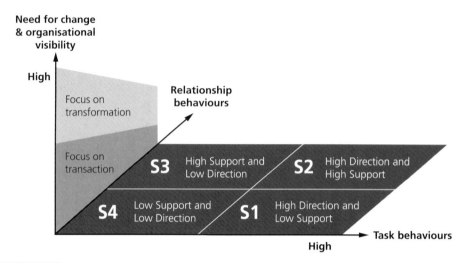

Figure 3.3 Change, situational leadership and the transformational–transactional balance

We stressed on page 66 that it is impossible to take the individual out of the leadership equation. So you will see the presence of the personal leadership globe in the centre of Figure 3.4. You can still see the familiar details of the task and maintenance orientations, with the addition of the need for a reasonable degree of dominance, or self-confidence if you prefer, taken from the SYMLOG model (page 64). It also shows the likely relationship between three types of change from everyday through to radical (pages 71–73) and the leadership types.

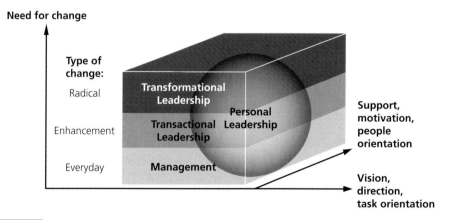

Figure 3.4 Defining leadership in three dimensions

Not everybody is going to be equally at ease in each of the broad options for leadership and management: not everyone is a leader, nor more to the point is everyone able to be any and every kind of leader. Personal preferences are likely to influence whether or not your personal leadership leans more towards the safety of the facts and figures of management, or towards the more visionary, outgoing, 'change-friendly' elements of transformational leadership. Organisations need transformational leaders if there is to be any innovative change or an effective response to external demands for change. However, organisations will cease to function if everyone only wants to be a transformational leader. Followers are most essential to do the work.

Transactional leadership, with its associated links to effective group working, is the way that things get done through people in an organisation. Using transactional skills makes the vision of the transformational leader real and accessible, and the requirements of management clear and comprehensible.

Fortunately, however, much of the repertoire of skills that is required can be learned. Personal values can be defined clearly (for example, from SYMLOG – see page 170) and these are consistent across organisational levels, organisations and national cultures. These skills span transactional leadership, transformational leadership and management. Furthermore, leaders are also followers. The personal requirements for effective leadership are also those of effective followership. For example, good followers give relevant input to their leader and do what they promise to undertake to a high standard. Good followers are reasonably self-confident and will offer suggestions for improvement or actively request feedback (page 100) when appropriate. We look in more detail at the acquisition of personal effectiveness skills in Chapter 4.

Managing and leading change

The roles of both a manager and a leader can be seen as quite distinct when it comes to managing change.

In times of change:
- The role of manager is focused on the present and the short term, so their essential job during change is to ensure that the core work of this setting keeps being done to standard. Young children need to continue to enjoy a happy and safe day, their records need to be up to date and parents' concerns must be dealt with effectively. In addition, the manager's focus should be internal: on the successful running of the setting, whatever else is going on.
- It is the leader's role to focus on the future benefits of the change, with a longer-term perspective, and to build the commitment of the team to this end. The leader's focus should be balanced between internal requirements and ensuring that external forces (such as the inspectorate) are seen accurately, and their influences not blown out of all proportion. In a real sense, the leader should be protecting staff from issues that can be a cause of worry when there is really no need for them to suffer such anxiety.
- The essential meeting point between the leader and manager – particularly during change – is the medium-term arena of transactional leadership (page 74). Here the roles of leader and manager should be working closely together to ensure that staff are fully aware of requirements and supported in

their efforts to achieve them. This is a constant dialogue between two wholly appropriate positions: the need to change as quickly as possible (leader) and the need for stability in best practice for the children and parents who are here on a daily basis (manager).

A question will have struck many readers: is the role of leader and of manager combined in the same person or are we talking about at least two people here? Suppose the roles of leader and manager are spread beyond one person. With a good working relationship between the leader and manager, the essential dialogue need not be full of conflict; it is a question of maintaining an effective balance. Similarly, if the leader and manager is one and the same person, this dilemma needs to be self-managed. Such self-management is a key part of being an effective person and leader (page 201). However, the balancing act – for one person or shared with others – is not necessarily easy.

Make the connection with … **early years practice**

Julian Grenier (2003) makes the point that it is hard, probably impossible, to lead and bring about significant shifts in practice if a setting does not have robust systems and structures in place. (Look back at the organisational model in Figure 3.2.) He also points out that it is all too easy for the head to lose sight of the change process in the day-by-day details of essential management tasks of doing what is necessary to keep a nursery or centre afloat when tasked also with leading improvements.

- Look at Grenier's honest account of his early months in post as a nursery school head (**www.tinyurl.com/slipperymud**). Make connections with the ideas in this chapter and with your own experiences.

- For instance, he highlights the disruptive impact of frequent changes of head – a serial disruption with the consequence that remaining staff were used to change, but not in a constructive way. Practitioners had made their own decisions with resulting inconsistencies in practice.

Three organisational issues and systems

The approach of Noel Tichy (1983) has proved very useful in our consultancy work with organisations. His analysis is that all organisations, however large or small, have three issues to address on a continual basis. We have changed Tichy's terminology to make a better fit with the world of early years, but these remain his 'three issues' and 'three systems'.

The three issues

First of all, we have the *'work itself'*. The organisation has the technical issue of delivering the results that matter here: happy children who progress in their development, parents who feel in partnership with you, positive reports from the inspectorate. Both the people and other resources – experiences for children, personalised care, the learning environment – must be arranged really well to produce the outcomes sought.

Second, we have the '*authority*' issue. The organisation has to decide how to allocate resources and who gets to wield power and authority. The authority issue raises the uses to which the organisation is directed. Do you exist primarily to fit parents' need to work or study? Or should your main focus be what works best for children's development? The rewards for staff in settings – what they are and who receives them – must be sorted out.

Third, we have the '*values*' issue. Organisations are held together by the bond of shared beliefs. As a result, early years settings need to determine what values, beliefs and attitudes need to be held, and acted upon, by staff members. The literature on early years provision often stresses participation and a harmonious working atmosphere. This focus is linked with resistance to concepts such as being powerful and assertive, or to having performance targets. Is this preference best for an effective organisation?

These are 'issues' in the sense that they can never be completely resolved as changes happen continually. The three issues can, however, be addressed and managed. New staff often bring differing beliefs and values and their contribution will subtly change the organisational culture. The presence or absence of particular children, or part-time staff, on a daily basis is an essential feature of everyday life and adjusts the technical elements of your work. Similarly, changes in lines of reporting, or in the leadership of the local authority, will affect politics and the operation of early years provision. All require that the setting adjusts continually to keep on track.

The three systems

Each of these issues to be resolved has a significant part of the organisation devoted to it, whatever the formal organisation charts may look like. We call these *the work itself*, *authority* and *values* systems. To give an example of the difference between these, we are looking just at the human resources (or personnel) function.

When the people management function focuses on the *work itself* system, energy is put into doing this:

- Fitting people to jobs – matching their capabilities, and wishes where possible, with the roles available in your setting.
- Defining performance criteria – being clear in your setting about what makes a person a success in this job, which links to what makes an excellent setting.
- Measuring performance – making sure you know how well individuals, and the entire provision, are doing against criteria from your overall aims.
- Information and planning systems – to gather and collate relevant information so that comparisons can be made or help offered to staff as appropriate.
- Staff selection – choosing the best people for a new role, either from the existing team or from outside. Early years heads, with whom we spoke, had put considerable thought into the recruitment process for job applicants. Job descriptions needed to be accurate, for instance, in that there was explicit reference to working as a key person.

- Training and development in knowledge, skills and abilities for staff – the focus on continued professional development (CPD).

A focus on the *authority* system involves close attention to:
- The appraisal process – how are staff assessed: by the manager alone, through peer observation as well, with input from parents, by everyone?
- Succession policies in the commercial world often define those within the organisation who will replace those currently in senior positions if anything should happen to them. Early years provision, as part of the public sector, has to run an open process of application, interview and appointment. The issue still arises to ensure that less senior staff are able to fulfil more responsible roles. Should a combination of staff be able to perform the role of manager in the manager's temporary absence?
- Reward system components and application – how are staff rewarded? Is it all about the intrinsic satisfaction of a job well done? Is pay a major factor and what happens when circumstances mean it is very difficult to pay staff more? Is training seen as a reward? Can staff choose when to take time off, partially, or not? How is excellent work rewarded if there are no promotion spots? Will additional responsibility or a different role and title be seen as rewards, or the reverse?
- Who makes decisions, plans and controls – is this a team leader or setting manager, or both? If both, where are the lines drawn? What decisions can workers take alone? Where do the EYPs fit? What decisions need to be referred up, and to whom? Who makes final decisions in a setting, one person or more?

A focus on the *values* system brings in all those factors which matter for consistency with the aims and methods of this organisation:
- Selecting people to enhance the organisational culture – a focus on increasing the proportion of qualified staff through recruitment, but also promotion and CPD from within the team.
- The heads with whom we spoke were clear about what they sought as evidence in interviews that this practitioner understood and would commit to the values of their setting. Do you look for practitioners who can be more assertive, or who show skills for managing change? If your team does not reflect the ethnic diversity of the local community or is all-female, how do you address those gaps?
- Development as socialisation – seeing CPD as a way of socialising people into 'our ways of doing things', so that, for instance, being outdoors for much of the day comes to be the normal way of working.
- Recognition for a job well done – how do you celebrate and reward success? In public, in private, or a combination of the two? Is this focused more on individuals, the entire team, or equally? In what ways should parents be involved in the process of recognition?
- Constant clarification of your organisational culture – what it is and how you want it to be. What is the relative focus on being participative and inclusive? Assertive? Mutually supportive? What does involving parents mean here?

- Role modelling – to set a good example consistent with your organisational culture: acting so as to show others how to behave and how to improve.

Approaches to organisational change

Noel Tichy (1983) looked at organisations in terms of three major systems used to get the work done. Earlier, Robert Chin and Kenneth Benne (1976) had identified the prevalent approaches to changing organisations. We think these ideas can be unified by the distinction between 'the mind', 'force' and 'the heart'.

1 The mind
  - Changes are argued logically and rationally as the 'best solution'.
  - Mainly uses the intellect to convince others on objective and logical grounds.
  - Uses primarily expert and information power sources to achieve its ends.

2 Force
  - Is about using coercion – 'we have to' or even 'you have to', there is no choice.
  - 'Might is right' forces changes through against resistance. It typically comes from senior people who have the power to enforce compliance; heads may roll.
  - Uses primarily legitimate and coercive power to succeed.

3 The heart
  - Is about developing ways in which people behave to one another, then established as norms.
  - Focuses on underlying values and beliefs; in that sense it is educational.
  - Typically emphasises social and emotional aspects – 'the heart': we should 'want to'.
  - Uses primarily reward, connection and referent power to work.

Notice particularly the different sorts of power (see page 5 for a refresher) in each of the approaches. Given the organisational culture in much of the early years sector, we would predict that changes which are most accepted are likely to be of *the heart* type. Those likely to be least acceptable will be imposed, top-down driven and showing little regard for the hopes and wishes of practitioners – *force*. Both approaches are likely to be dressed up as logical or rational (*the mind*) – whether they are or not.

These three approaches tend to take different time scales in which to work. Typically, changes made by the force approach will be accomplished quickly, at least on paper. More time is needed to convince people logically that the course of action is right, in the mind approach. Still longer is needed to develop and re-educate staff in the heart option.

Finally, there is a close relationship between these strategies for change and the three big systems. Hence, the heart approach to change is consistent with, and is most likely to have its greatest influence on, the values system. Similarly, the force approach is more likely to affect primarily the authority system and the hierarchy.

Positions typically change, and often staff are moved or remove themselves. Finally, the mind approach is more likely to affect the work itself system. In normal, everyday work, people tend to accept changes that are sensible and logical, as long as they are not painful.

Make the connection with ... **early years practice**

Reflect on a process of change in which you have been closely involved. What combination of approaches did you use? Or do you now realise were used if you were not leading this change?

- Do you think that changes are more likely to be accepted in an appeal through the heart approach? Are there situations in which a more forceful approach would be appropriate?
- Could there be hidden or public resistance to an apparently successful 'you will do this' approach?

Who can lead change?

As a rule, it is possible to effect change only if those responsible for accomplishing the change have an understanding of the process and, critically, are in a position of authority. It is not helpful to call someone a leader and task them with making changes if they do not have the authority to enforce compliance. It is like asking someone to build a sandcastle but giving them neither a bucket nor a spade. Words such as 'compliance' and 'enforce' are not, we know, familiar to – nor often welcome in – the early years sector. However, if something needs to be done, the leader needs the legitimate power to accomplish the goal (page 6).

Practitioners who have achieved EYP status are expected to be change agents. This phrase appears regularly in discussion of the role for EYPs, for instance on the website of the Children's Workforce Development Council. The responsibility for bringing about change is usually focused on continuous improvement in EYPs' own provision, but some of the rhetoric about being 'visionary' gets very close to implying a role in innovative change for EYPs. However, they will not necessarily be the manager of their setting. EYPs are in an impossible position unless they are regarded by colleagues as someone who has the right to lead. They need to have a clear guiding role and be given support from the senior team when individual EYPs are not at that level. You will find more about the role of EYPs from page 128.

What does it mean?

Change agent: an individual with the responsibility to identify the need for change and to manage the process of change towards identified goals.

Approaches to interpersonal relations

Elias Porter (1976) developed an approach called Relationship Awareness Theory® that describes three primary motivations that drive behaviour in our relationships.

These primary motivations, termed Motivational Value Systems (MVS), are key as they affect our choices in influencing others. These motives also work as internal filters that affect our perceptions of others. The three primary motives, colour-coded as red, green and blue in Porter's (1973, 2005) Strength Deployment Inventory®, combine to form seven distinct Motivational Value Systems.

One colour (motive) higher than the other two:
- Blue (Altruistic–Nurturing): Concern for the protection, growth and welfare of others.
- Red (Assertive–Directing): Concern for task accomplishment and leadership.
- Green (Analytic–Autonomising): Concern for meaningful order being established.

Two colours (motives) roughly equal, and higher than the other one:
- Red–Blue (Assertive–Nurturing): Concern for the growth and welfare of others through leadership.
- Red–Green (Judicious–Competing): Concern for intelligent assertiveness, leadership, and fairness in competition.
- Blue–Green (Cautious–Supporting): Concern for developing self-sufficiency in self and others.

All three colours (motives) roughly equal:
- Hub (Flexible–Cohering): Concern for flexibility and the welfare of the group. The Hub is not a colour, but gets its name because it is shown as a circle in the middle of a triangle with blue, red, and green points in Relationship Awareness Theory (Porter, 1996).

Each of the colours are present in each of us to some extent, and these motives work together as an integrated system when things are going well, but in conflict, the motives work in order, which Porter called a Conflict Sequence. If you feel under pressure from someone else, or realise that your favourite approach is not working, you shift to your next option and finally to your least liked. For example, if your order was first for Green, second Red and last Blue, you would first try to resolve an issue in a Green way – logically and rationally. If this fails to persuade the other person you would then shift to Red – saying things like 'we have to do this because the inspectorate requires it. It's not a choice'. If this does not work, your final shift would be to Blue – with an approach such as 'how can I help you to be able to do this? I don't feel it needs to be unpleasant, if we work together'.

The Blue (Altruistic–Nurturing) motivation is of particular relevance to early years provision, given discussion in the literature about the dominant organisational culture, which Hard (2005) calls 'a culture of niceness'. She notes the complications caused for leadership, and what can simmer under the surface of a working atmosphere that presents as cordial (see page 97). So, assuming your strongest motivation is Blue, you will probably work hard to be seen as a nice and caring person. You want to be sure you are not a burden on others, you definitely do not want to be unpleasant and dislike seeing people mistreated. Blue filters may influence your perceptions of others who do not share your values of believing in – and caring for – others. For example, you may look at people preferring Red and think they are aggressive, exploitative, or arrogant. You may see those preferring Green and find them insensitive, unfeeling, or suspicious. Observing Hub MVS people's flexibility may be seen as wishy-washy, or being unable to take a stand.

People with Green (Analytic–Autonomising) motives generally want things to make sense and to be properly thought out. When trying to influence others, they are most likely to use logical arguments and objective criteria. They see this as the way to prevent disagreements and misunderstandings. As they do not respect emotionally-based decisions, they may avoid people whom they judge to be illogical; they 'don't suffer fools gladly'. Think about how someone with Green motives might relate to other colleagues. They may look at someone with Blue purposes and think that they are submissive, or so loyal as to be gullible and blind to the facts. They may see the Red drive for results as aggressive, or may perceive their risk-taking as ill-advised gambling. They may judge the Hub purpose of 'looking for options' as lacking focus, and as not having planned properly.

People with Red (Assertive–Directing) motives want to get things done, to succeed and make progress. When influencing others they typically focus on the results. They want to act quickly and decisively. They don't mind taking risks and confronting challenges head-on. They may dismiss people who move too slowly, or who are 'overly emotional'. When relating to others, their Red filters may cause them to see people differently than those people see themselves. People with Red drives may view the Blue strength of modesty as a lack of confidence, or as giving in without a fight. They may see the methodical, analytical, Green reasons as rigid rule-enforcement to be avoided or worked around. They may see the Hub strength of consensus-building as an inability to argue for their convictions, or as unproductive endless discussions about everything.

People with Hub (Flexible–Cohering) motives want to include everyone – ideally to build consensus within a group. When influencing others, they usually focus on areas of agreement, expanding them gradually to include others' perspectives. They want to be sure everyone has an opportunity to contribute and that all options are considered. They get uncomfortable around people who do not consider alternative views. Their Hub filters may influence their perception of others. They may look at the Blue strength of supportiveness and see it as giving too much, or even sacrificing, oneself. They may experience the Red forcefulness as over-controlling or dictatorial. The strong principles of people with Green motives may look unbending and callous through Hub lenses.

Pause for reflection

Reflect on your approach to interpersonal relations. Of course, the best way to determine your Motivational Value System is to complete the Strength Deployment Inventory® with a certified facilitator. But here, which of the descriptions sounds most like you?

- When you are trying to bring round a colleague with whom you do not see eye to eye, do you generally tend to focus on: feelings, results, logic, or flexibility? For example, do you on balance prefer to have a friendly exchange in which you feel sure that the other person feels you mean well? Or are you most comfortable with a discussion in which you convince your colleague with the reason of your argument?

- The dominant theme in literature about early years organisational culture is that it is collaborative and not interested in power. So what happens when a manager, or a member of staff, shows Red (Assertive–Directing) purposes in their relationships?

Our work in both commercial and public areas has shown us that people's Motivational Value Systems can also influence the way organisations function. This adds to the picture of change in an organisational setting, summarised in Figure 3.5.

Change strategy	Organisational system	Personal motives
• The heart	• Values	• Protect and nurture others (Blue)
• Force	• Authority	• Accomplish results (Red)
• The mind	• Work itself	• Be rational and organised (Green)
• Integrated	• All	• Build consensus (Hub)

Figure 3.5 Change strategies, organisational systems and personal motives

Bringing it all together

For one last piece of the jigsaw, we need to recall the leadership models in Chapter 2 and in particular SYMLOG (page 61). Once more there are very strong links that can be made to the three systems – work itself, authority and values – and the main SYMLOG dimensions. There are definite parallels between dominance, the authority system and the use of force as a change strategy. The use of dominance is needed to effect change using the force approach in changing the authority system, where strength and legitimate authority are required. Similarly, there are strong links between values for accepting the task orientation of established authority, the work itself system and the mind approach. It is logical. Changing the values system is very much about the friendly dimension of SYMLOG;

it approaches the issue in a 'nice' manner and seeks to gain the emotional support of people through the heart. Figure 3.6 provides a summary diagram.

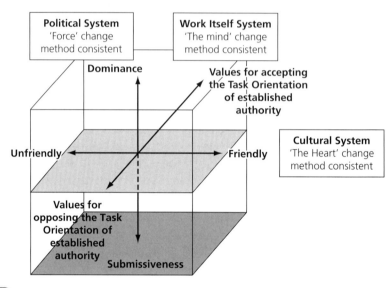

Figure 3.6 SYMLOG and organisational change

Using all of these approaches (the mind, the heart and force) in an integrated manner is the best way to achieve lasting change in any organisation. Unwillingness to use one or other has predictable effects. Failure to use force and the authority system will mean that everything takes much longer, and support from those most senior is likely to be at best fitful and at worst completely lacking. Failure to use the heart will not involve and commit staff to new ways of working; their motivation is likely to be low – and to stay there. Finally, failure to use the mind (this is the most unlikely failing, in our experience) will result in changes which are ill-thought out and poorly planned.

It is undoubtedly easier, in terms of making change happen, to remove those people who do not support change rather than to try to convince them that the change is necessary. If this is not possible – there is no legitimate reason to dismiss people or they do not choose to leave – then changes to structure and performance measurement (a less drastic approach to changing the authority system) will be beneficial. Both of these use both the force and the mind approaches. Further, a great deal of time and effort will need to be spent on the mind and heart change methods to achieve the benefits sought.

It is also clear that being unfriendly, submissive or in opposition to the task orientation of established authority is unlikely to assist in anything, let alone change. From our own observations and work within the early years sector, the potential problem here is about submissiveness (or being passive, if you prefer that word). In most cases, early years managers do not face outright opposition to the key task of commitment to the children, although staff may be confused about the nature of change over concepts such as child-initiated learning. Generally it also seems that provision will be on the friendly side; usually staff get on well with each other. However, there is a strong tendency for staff not to raise concerns for fear of causing unpleasantness and a bad atmosphere. In the worst-case scenario, practitioners may feel intimidated from making a direct challenge to poor practice from a colleague and become unresponsive on the surface and deeply frustrated or distressed underneath.

Assertiveness is a key issue for many early years practitioners as a major way to improve personal effectiveness at work. Greater ease with being assertive will in turn enable views to be shared more readily and then worked through, even though some uncomfortable disagreements may occur in the process. Developing an appropriate level of self-confidence and assertiveness (or dominance) is essential in order to be an effective follower, and is mandatory for an effective leader. These issues are covered in the next chapter.

Resources

- **Barnes, L.B. and Kriger, M.P.** (1986) 'The hidden side of organizational leadership'. *Sloan Management Review*, 28, 1, 15–25.
- **Bass, B. and Bass, R.** (2008) *The Bass Handbook of Leadership: Theory, research, and managerial applications,* 4th edition. New York: Free Press.
- **Burke, W. and Litwin, G.** (1992) 'A causal model of organizational performance and change'. *Journal of Management*, 18, 3, 523–45. http://documents.reflectlearn. org/Offline%20OA%20Models%20and%20Frameworks/BurkeLitwin_ ACausalModelofOrganizationalPerformance.pdf
- **Chinn, R. and Benne, K.O.** (1976) 'General strategies for effecting change in human systems'. In Bennis, W.E.; Benne, K.O.; Chinn, R.; and Carey, K.E. (eds) *The planning of change*, New York: Holt, Rinehart and Winston.
- **Grenier, J.** (2003) *Small Steps, Slippery Mud: 100 days as a nursery school head.* www.tinyurl.com/slipperymud
- **Hard, L.** (2005) *How Is Leadership Understood and Enacted within the Field of Early Childhood Education and Care?* Unpublished doctoral thesis, Center for Learning Innovation, Queensland University of Technology. http://eprints.qut.edu. au/16213/1/Louise_Hard_Thesis.pdf
- **Hujala, E.** (2002) 'Leadership in a child care context in Finland', in Nivala, V. and Hujala, E. (eds) *Leadership in Early Childhood Education: Cross-cultural perspectives.* Oulu: Oulu University Press. http://herkules.oulu.fi/isbn9514268539/
- **Kagan, S. and Bowman, B.** (eds) (1997) *Leadership in Early Care and Education.* Washington, DC: National Association for the Education of Young Children.
- **Kelley, R.E.** (1992) *The Power of Followship.* New York: Doubleday.

- **Lindon, J.** (2010b) *Reflective Practice and Early Years Professionalism.* London: Hodder Education.
- **Lindon, J.** (2010c) *The Key Person Approach: Positive relationships in the early years.* London: Practical Pre-School Books.
- **Murphy, J.T.** (1988) 'The unheroic side to leadership: notes from the swamp'. *Phi Delta Kappan,* 69, 654–9.
- **Nivala, V.** (2002) 'Leadership in general, leadership in theory'. In Nivala, V. and Hujala, E. (eds) (2002) *Leadership in Early Childhood Education: Cross-cultural perspectives.* Oulu: Oulu University Press. http://herkules.oulu.fi/isbn9514268539/
- **Nivala, V. and Hujala, E.** (eds) (2002) *Leadership in Early Childhood Education: Cross-cultural perspectives.* Oulu: Oulu University Press. http://herkules.oulu.fi/isbn9514268539/
- **Porter, E.H.** (1973, 2005) Strength Deployment Inventory. Carlsbad, CA: Personal Strengths Publishing.
- **Porter, E.H.** (1976) 'On the Development of Relationship Awareness Theory: a Personal Note'. *Group Organization Management, 1*(3), 302–309.
- **Porter, E.H.** (1996) *Relationship Awareness Theory.* Carlsbad, CA: Personal Strengths Publishing.
- **Raelin, J.** (2003) *Creating Leaderful Organisations: How to bring out leadership in everyone.* San Francisco, CA: Berrett-Kohler.
- **Raelin, J.** (2010) *The Leaderful Fieldbook: Strategies and activities for developing leadership.* Boston, MA: Nicholas Brealey Publishing.
- **Scrivens, C.** (2002a) 'Constructions of leadership: does gender make a difference? Perspectives from an English speaking country'. In Nivala, V. and Hujala, E. (eds) *Leadership in Early Childhood Education: Cross-cultural perspectives.* Oulu: Oulu University Press. http://herkules.oulu.fi/isbn9514268539/
- **Scrivens, C.** (2002b) 'Tensions and constraints for professional leadership in the kindergarten service in New Zealand'. In Nivala, V. and Hujala, E. (eds) (2002) *Leadership in Early Childhood Education: Cross-cultural perspectives.* Oulu: Oulu University Press. http://herkules.oulu.fi/isbn9514268539/
- **Slater, R.O. and Doig, J.W.** (1988) 'Leadership in education: issues of entrepreneurship'. *Education in Urban Society,* 20, 3, 294–301.
- **Tichy, N.** (1983) *Managing Strategic Change.* New York: John Wiley.

Developing your personal effectiveness

Early years practitioners may recognise the need to be assertive. Yet this concept is sometimes confused with being pushy or aggressive. There seems to be a relatively widespread concern within the early years sector about not behaving, or not being seen by the team, as the Big Boss. The preference is sometimes described by managers as wanting to pull the team along with their cooperation, rather than push them regardless of their feelings. However, the bottom line is that, first, managers need to manage and second, leaders do not exist without followers. The discussion in Chapter 3 about leadership and management brought to the fore that confident use of authority is necessary to bring about change and can be compatible with the organisational culture of early years provision.

This chapter focuses on the leader as a person. We cover elements of personal effectiveness for managers and leaders, but also for effective team members, who will contribute fully to meeting the aims of the service, in ways compatible with the core values.

The main sections of this chapter are:
- reluctant leaders?
- self-confidence and assertiveness
- communication and personal effectiveness.

Reluctant leaders?

Almost every account we read of early years leadership – commentary or research – raised the suggestion that a significant proportion of the workforce faced uncertainties or felt conflicted about the implications of being a leader.

Mixed feelings about leadership

Jillian Rodd (1997, 2006) describes her research into the outlook of managers in early years provision during the 1990s, with studies in Australia and then in the UK. It was not unusual in her sample to have early years practitioners, including senior team members, expressing unease about leadership and what it meant. This research predates the growth of early years leadership programmes in the UK and the much stronger emphasis on the need for early years leaders. Yet Rodd's observations are useful to highlight mixed feelings about the need for leadership in the sector.

At that time it was more usual that early years practitioners reached a senior position in charge of a setting with minimal further training. However, Rodd's (1997) UK study reports that the majority of those interviewed had made an active choice to move into a leadership role. It was only a minority (less than 10 per cent in this sample of 76 early childhood professionals) who had been effectively persuaded to apply by others, or had been the only person available for the role. Managers had been motivated by being able to implement their own ideas and to make a positive difference for children. Of these, it is likely that some, perhaps many, were acting in ways that we would say were leadership.

Manjula Waniganayake (2002) describes a reluctance to think much about leadership within some Australian early childhood centres. Some teams worked with a confidence, or the belief, that things just happened. Waniganayake attributes the success of this outlook to women's sensitivity to the unspoken message of colleagues. This unwillingness or inability to articulate the issues around leadership can be linked with the enhanced profile in the UK for reflective practice, to avoid the hit-or-miss of depending on non-verbal communication (Lindon, 2010b).

Kate Thornton (2006, 2007) describes the early childhood centres established in New Zealand from 2002. These Centres of Innovation (COI) had a specific brief for developing innovations to practice. On the basis of talking with staff and analysing the content of the centres' documents, Thornton identifies different working models for leadership across the six centres. Some had a clear designated overall leader while others had some team members taking a leading role on aspects of practice. Some practitioners were more comfortable than others about taking on a leader role or being viewed as a leader. Those interviewed also varied over how much they had already reflected on anything to do with leadership.

Natural leaders?
Duffy and Marshall (2007) suggest that some of the early years workforce believe that good leaders are born with the qualities to make them effective and the rest are destined to be followers. This is quite consistent with elements of the wider leadership research (Chapter 2). Their counter-argument is that everyone has the potential to be a leader; what is needed are opportunities to take a leading role and develop confidence from this experience. We agree that there is untapped potential in a workforce that is still gaining confidence. However, we would add the proviso that not everyone wants to be a leader in their professional arena and that any discussion has to consider what kind of leadership is meant – transactional, transformational, a whole setting or merely a specific improvement area.

Waniganayake *et al.* (2000) report mixed views from interviews with centre directors, teachers and assistants in Australian centres. At least some of the interviewees believed leadership in early years provision was something into which you could grow so that appropriate experience was definitely part of that development. Leadership did not come as part of holding a position of seniority, because being able to exercise some kind of authority did not mean that someone was necessarily viewed as a leader. This observation links with the key concept that leaders have followers and being in charge of a setting does not mean that a manager automatically becomes a leader as well (page 3).

Different ways of being a leader

Rosemary and Puroila (2002) offer detailed case studies of two leaders of early years centres, one in Finland and one in the USA. The authors show that some of the differences between the two individuals were affected by the prevailing way of organising early childhood centres and of being a centre director in their country. However, the descriptions showed that some differences appeared to arise from the choices made by each director as to how to best be in charge.

Both directors had the administrative responsibilities of running a centre – tasks which fall under the heading of manager. However, the director in the Finnish centre spent more time working directly with the children and also acted as an advocate for early childhood with her local authority. In her working relationship with other staff she was described as 'more like a working mate than a leader' (see also the example on page 96). The director of the US centre had to deal with a higher level of regulation and inspection than her Finnish counterpart. Yet it looked like her personal choice to continue to get staff to ask her permission to make relatively minor decisions about the children. The US director appeared to be less self-confident and less 'hands-on' than her Finnish equivalent.

Issues around confidence and assertiveness

Rodd (1997, 2006) suggests that many early years practitioners have reservations, sometimes serious ones, around personal commitment to leadership in their setting. Part of the problem seems to be the belief that leadership is inevitably autocratic: a style of telling people what to do and not being interested in their views. This style does not fit with a nurturing approach, nor with the strong focus in early years on good two-way communication.

Rodd's discussion about this reservation over leading is a common feature of early years commentaries. This concern has also arisen in our informal conversations with experienced members of the early years workforce. Scrivens (2002a) agrees that perceptions about power are an issue and she makes a distinction between 'power over' and 'power for' others. Scrivens argues that power relations are more equal between the leader who makes plans and practitioners who carry them out in this female-dominated area, compared with those areas with a more equal balance of the sexes.

Waniganayake (2002) argues that the predominantly female profession in early childhood centres is in a difficult position over leadership. The consequence of social learning and gender stereotypes is that most early years practitioners do not think of themselves as having the capacity to lead. However, this reservation is sometimes linked with a suspicion of fellow practitioners who put themselves forward for leadership. This observation gives pause for thought: here is a strong hint that resistance to leadership behaviour can come from within the early years workforce itself.

Take another **perspective**

Stepping up to leadership means no longer being just one more member of the team. This brings practical problems for senior practitioners who feel unable to tolerate that changed relationship. You are no longer equal, but senior. In this the early years is not alone, for in other organisations the shift from worker to supervisor is one of the most difficult to make.

For example, Rosemary and Puroila (2002) describe an incident with the Finnish director in which she asked a practitioner to take responsibility for a student who would soon come on placement at the centre. The practitioner flatly refused this request. The director's response was that the staff could maybe draw lots for who took the student (page 59).

- Does this seem like a wise decision, to take a random approach? What factors should determine the matching of a student to an existing team member?
- Do you experience issues – for yourself or hearing others' concerns – about whether there should be a distance between senior practitioners and the rest of the team?

Niceness as a block

From her interviews with early years practitioners Louise Hard explores what she calls 'niceness as a leadership inhibitor' (2005, page 127). As well as a reluctance to lead, this wish to be viewed as nice creates discomfort with leadership when viewed as a forceful exercise of power. It is worth reflecting on niceness as a possible block. It could also be expressed as the wish to be liked, or at least to avoid being disliked (or seen as 'nasty') for making decisions or directing others.

Leaders may not always be liked

Niceness, as a way never to be disliked, can disrupt effective management and leadership. Overall leaders can be friendly; they do not have to be despots who keep the office door firmly shut. However, all leaders sometimes have to call attention to something that an individual, subgroups or the whole setting would rather not hear about. All interactions at work cannot be unswervingly pleasant. Practitioners with a clear responsibility to improve an area of practice – as in the role of EYPs – will not get very far if they fail to raise the practices that could be improved. They can raise them with respect and attention to constructive comments (page 112). However, early years practitioners in any leading role will fail to lead if their main priority is to ensure that colleagues think they are just like everybody else and not getting above themselves. Wanting to be liked by colleagues, fears that acting as the leader will be disliked or low self-confidence – all these can play havoc with leadership behaviour and hence the effectiveness of the provision.

Hard offers considered insights from analysis of her interviews with practitioners working in Australian early childhood centres. The compromise over leadership that seemed to work in some centres was a kind of 'team-based leadership', in which the manager was 'not too much the boss' (2005, page 132). The leaders, who appeared at ease in their role, had a view of being active in coordinating the team and were confident about communicating their vision for better practice. The interview data show senior practitioners wanting to establish collaboration, build the team and bring everyone on board over decisions.

Make the connection with … **emotional literacy**

The discussion in this section has conceptual links with ideas in at least three other parts of this book. The shared theme is that of emotional literacy: an honesty about your own emotions, an understanding about how other people may be feeling and an awareness of how feelings affect thinking and action.

As you read this section, you could take a moment to look at:

- The discussion about approaches to interpersonal relations from page 87.
- The discussion about leadership, change and heart and mind on page 85.
- The section about emotional intelligence from page 58.

Under the surface

Hard has some thought-provoking ideas about problems arising from a 'culture of niceness'. She highlights the emotional working environment of some of her interviewees and provides a challenge to some of the cosier descriptions in the literature. She describes the past or present experience of some practitioners in which pressure to conform to the prevailing ways of working was very strong.

One interviewee describes the situation as the 'tall poppy syndrome' (2005, page 144), one in which the nursery subculture values neither new ideas nor the person suggesting them. Any change is seen as a threat to established patterns, so other practitioners act to marginalise and block the colleague who questions the established ways. Some practitioners had not only failed to find support from their centre manager over fresh ideas; they had joined in the verbal humiliation in a clear example of scapegoating.

Early years settings can be both nurturing and intellectually lively places; we have been privileged to visit many in the UK. This positive working environment is the direct result of hard, focused work from the manager and other staff members. However, this does not apply to all early years settings. Hard sums it up in this way: 'The notion of niceness emerges as an ironic category. It superficially suggests deference to, and care for others but subversively demands adherence to a … culture of compliance' (2005, page 130).

To explore this working environment, Hard introduces the concept of 'horizontal violence', which she identifies as having roots in nursing. This relates to the pressures exerted on fellow practitioners at the same level, not to intimidation from more senior people. The harassment is psychological (not physical), uses verbal abuse, innuendo and threats to attack colleagues' sense of self-esteem at work and can even exclude individuals. The concept of horizontal violence is also used to explain why, in some early years subcultures, practitioners resist stepping into a leading role or wanting to be the overall leader. Practitioners are virtually coerced by colleagues to remain where they are. If experience so far is a good guide, becoming more senior in the staff group is a very unattractive prospect, which predicts a tough and disheartening ride for efforts to improve practice through leadership.

Alternatives to being an autocratic manager

Some early years managers are keen to distinguish themselves from an image of people who lay down the law and expect staff to be subservient to them. This issue seems to be significant in the sector, even if some people have resolved their unease over leading. Chapter 2 highlights the many alternatives to operating as an autocrat, but here we want to make a connection to styles in parenting: the options of *authoritarian*, *authoritative*, *permissive* or *uninvolved* (Baumrind, 1967; and discussed in Lindon, 2009b).

Some discussion in the literature seems to accept that females' alleged disinclination to step up to leadership is an understandable, and possibly laudable, reluctance to take an authoritarian stand. An *authoritarian* style in early years leadership would be, 'I'm in charge around here and you do what I tell you'. Early years provision, along with the children and families involved, will not benefit from an atmosphere in which practitioners, even senior ones, struggle to speak up or disagree for fear of being considered a dragon or a battleaxe. However, leadership, like parenting, has another option: you can behave in a way that is described as authoritative: self-confident and clear.

Being *authoritative* as an overall leader, just as when the term is used about parenting styles, rests on an honest acceptance of the leadership role. Being a confident leader has common ground with willingness to be the grown-up in positive relationships with children. Early years leaders are not just one of the team, no more than parents are just big kids or the same as their children's friends. Both of these styles show high direction in situational leadership terms (page 51). One is done well (authoritative) and one is done poorly (authoritarian).

A *permissive* style of early years leader – also known in the parenting literature as a laissez-faire (the same term as used in the Managerial Grid, page 46) or an indulgent style – will incline towards giving practitioners considerable scope for making their own decisions. So, is this a form of democracy within the setting or is this a recipe for anarchy? Is it close to a collaborative approach, emphasised by quite a few writers on early years leadership as the option of choice for women? Could this style be a misleading front to disguise an unwillingness to take hard decisions, to say 'no' or 'not that way', when the occasion requires it? This style is clearly that of the S3 Encouraging style in situational leadership, with a focus on support and little direction.

A laissez-faire model may appear appropriate because practitioners are able to organise themselves and will actively seek help if they require it. They are D3s or D4s in situational leadership terms (see the discussion on page 52). However, there is a risk that a mainly laissez-faire approach could be seen by the staff group as abdication of responsibility by the manager, who is accurately judged to be nervous about setting boundaries for best practice. Is the manager overly concerned about niceness? Does an uncomfortable team leader feel obliged to go with what appears to be the group consensus, so as not to appear like a despot? It is not helpful to have a democratically inclined manager who is loath to exert authority when required, particularly if they have better information, or time is pressing.

Finally, reflect upon whether an early years manager could take on a style that risks being *uninvolved*, even neglectful of the staff. For a staff member, having an uninvolved leader basically means, 'I can do what I like'. As with the family comparison, the leader might not aim to ignore the well being of the staff group or their need for positive guidance. It just happens, if the leader fails to lead.

Think about how this situation may arise.

- Maybe the manager of an early years setting has become sidelined by continual worries about making the inspectorate happy. Perhaps they have lost sight of the reality that the inspector, along with everyone else, has to focus on what works best for the children.
- Perhaps the manager, or even a room leader, has accepted – or been persuaded to take on – a list of other responsibilities that squeezes the time available to do anything other than daily tasks. The situation has deteriorated so that the core work of keeping a close eye on practice with children and families and supporting colleagues has been relegated to the bottom of the list of priorities – or has disappeared altogether.
- Perhaps a previously effective team leader has been struggling with overwhelming personal problems. In a setting which prizes nurturance above all, nobody wants to tell the manager or room leader that their effectiveness is desperately compromised.

Make the connection with … **your practice**

These ideas can shed light on styles of leadership in the early years.

- Please reflect on the four broad styles that adults might take in their leadership relationship with fellow adults. What have you experienced over your professional life by watching someone else lead or reflecting on your own inclinations?

- In this section we have deliberately taken ideas that will be familiar about relationships between adults and children and applied them to relations between fellow adults. Can you think of any other concepts from your work with children that can be applied to thinking about the dynamics of working together as adults?

Self-confidence and assertiveness

Self-confidence is a critical element in becoming effective as a person and is linked with self-esteem – look back at Abraham Maslow's needs hierarchy on page 34. Positive, reinforcing experiences are likely to build self-confidence, whereas negative ones tend to undermine it. Less than fully positive experiences can, however, provide opportunities for powerful learning which, if taken, can develop greater self-confidence. The contribution of early experiences and family life is crucial, and it is when negative life experiences outweigh the positives that self-confidence suffers.

At a basic level, self-confidence stems from an accurate understanding of your personal strengths and weaknesses (scope for improvement, if you prefer). The key word here is 'accurate'. If the personal assessment is unrealistically positive, then the outlook is one of arrogance. If the assessment is too negative, then the outlook is dominated by pessimism.

Accurate understanding is supported by three elements:

1 The ability and willingness to look inside yourself: introspection and the part of reflective practice that means looking closely at your own motivations and behaviour.

2 Asking other people for feedback about your behaviour so you can learn about what works, what does not, and how others see you. They know this; you are one who is ignorant about how you come across.

3 Telling others honestly your thoughts and wishes and what you would like from them.

The three elements are underpinned by an understanding of what it means to be assertive. We will deal with each of these in turn.

Self-reflection – learning about yourself

Goleman *et al.* (2002) recommend a five-step process which they describe as learning better leadership skills. For us these are personal effectiveness skills for the workplace and focus primarily on increased self-awareness and gaining detailed feedback from colleagues.

One way of expanding understanding of your own practice is to ask colleagues for feedback. You may gain this information through an established system of peer observation (Lindon, 2010b) and through conversations. You need to be as specific as you can about what you would welcome, listen attentively and be able to summarise what you have heard. Aim to avoid justifying 'why' you did whatever is being commented on; it does not encourage the person to give you more feedback.

For example, suppose Jane has said to her colleague, Geeta, 'What do you think about how I handled the argument between Johnny and Marie this morning – when Marie tipped the paint water?' Geeta replies with, 'I wondered why you cleaned Johnny up first. There was a long gap before you could ask them both,

"What happened?".' Geeta has expressed an opinion – she has been asked – but she is unlikely to say any more if Jane comes back with, 'I only did that because Johnny was crying and he hates being in a mess. He is my key child, after all.' There is no reason to think that Jane is wrong in her judgement about Johnny's feelings, but equally, Geeta is quite likely to think, 'Why did I bother?' She was given little space and an immediate rebuttal of her feedback. She will think twice next time about giving any more feedback other than 'Fine'.

It is important to distinguish between *feedback* and other information that is expressed by colleagues, about how you behave. The key feature about feedback is that you have asked other people to tell you about what they have noticed and to express their opinions. Feedback is therefore focused on your need to learn something, rather than someone else's wish to tell you something. Other comments may be useful – much will depend on the way in which they are expressed (see page 112) – but you have not requested this kind of information.

What does it mean?

Feedback: the process of asking for and receiving information about yourself and your behaviour. The key point about feedback is that you have requested it.

Goleman *et al.* (2002) also focus on empathic listening to others. The skill is to listen attentively, without rushing to interpretation, evaluation or judgement. The aim is to understand exactly how others see the world, and your behaviour in it, and to benefit from feedback when given. Coaching is also central to this pattern of professional development. Goleman *et al.* stress that successful learning of skills depends on a context of trust and encouragement: relationships that provide support during the learning process. The five main steps are as follows:

1. Identify your ideal self – exploring your core values and beliefs to paint the picture of what you would ideally like to be

What is important to you? What are you passionate about? It is hard to progress without a clear personal direction and a goal that is meaningful for you. The SYMLOG questionnaire, for example, asks explicitly about ideal self and actual self. The measure also pulls together extensive feedback from managers and colleagues, to provide a full picture known as 360° feedback. Of course, every organisation does not have the wherewithal to call in an organisational consultant. However, you can use materials developed specifically for early years provision, for example the assessment materials of Moyles (2006), to help.

2. Identify your real self – discovering an accurate picture of how you are seen by others, regardless of how you see yourself

Sometimes these views are startlingly different. Sometimes other people rate you more highly than you do yourself. If you are reasonably honest and self-aware, then you may already have an accurate idea of the difference between how you are and how you would like to be. Perhaps you would like to be a better listener in team meetings but know that you have a strong tendency to jump in with questions and comments. You are not very comfortable with silences, even very short ones.

You will extend your understanding by welcoming, and reflecting on, feedback from colleagues (page 114) and the personal feedback that is possible when you have the regular support of someone coaching you in relevant skills (Lindon, 2010b). Another valuable source of accurate information derives from systems of peer observation set up by managers in the context of the professional development necessary to ensure that this approach works constructively (Lindon, 2010b).

3. Comparing your real self to the ideal

Accurate information, and the self-reflection that lets you benefit from it, allows you to bring together your ideal and current self – as you are at the moment. This step is powerful because it helps identify your strengths – areas of practice in which you are successful and colleagues recognise your skills. It also enables you to focus on gaps in your practice, where you are not as effective as you would like to be, or even as you believed yourself to be. Recognising and then addressing gaps takes time and is often somewhat uncomfortable. Sometimes the source of accurate, and ultimately valuable, information may not come from the most preferred and welcome source. Everyone would probably rather have an excellent report from the inspectorate, but inspectors can sometimes put their finger on a part of practice that is less impressive than the remainder to help you to improve.

We spoke with several managers who had worked hard to see the point of constructive comments from an outside source. One head had been able to use her understanding of the difference between leadership and management to accept that her clear vision for the centre (her leadership) was not effectively backed up with the monitoring systems (her management) to ensure the vision was put fully into practice. This was initially pointed out by the inspectorate. The result was to pay closer attention to ensuring proper follow-through – and subsequently, an outstanding inspection rating.

4. Develop a plan to build on strengths and reduce gaps

Even the best and most experienced managers and practitioners will not be good at everything. The reflection and analysis done in steps 1–3 should help focus on areas that:
- you are motivated to address
- are easier to tackle and
- will bring the most improvement most swiftly.

It may also lead you to know where feedback from your colleagues would help you most to improve your practice. Sometimes this means stopping doing things that you think help but do not, and hence saves you time.

5. Experiment with and practise new skills

With a focus on a detailed plan, you need to follow those steps that will bring about change according to your plan.

This process has to be a personal journey supported by the feedback and suggestions of trusted colleagues. Figure 4.1 offers some thoughts about ways that most of us look at other people. Some of these may feel more central to your own development, or to that of a colleague you support.

POSITIVE	NEGATIVE
Active and assertive	Passive and withdrawn
Seeks challenge and 'stretch'	Does only what they know
Seeks self-knowledge	Avoids self-knowledge
Sees time and energy as valuable resources	Misuses time and energy
In touch with feelings	Out of touch with feelings
Shows concern for others	Does not care for others' feelings
Relaxed – flexible responses	Tense – reacts to things
Open and honest	Manipulative and covert
Clear personal values	Programmed by views of others
Sets high standards	Sets low standards
Welcomes feedback	Avoids and resents feedback – defends self
Sees things through	Opts out
Tolerates and uses opposing views	Intolerant of opposition
Uses conflict to learn	Avoids or smoothes conflict
Gives freedom	Restrains, bureaucratises
Happy about life	Unhappy

Figure 4.1 Positive and negative sides of personal effectiveness

Everyone has to consider and choose the best approach to support their own journey to enhance personal effectiveness in the workplace. These are a few, brief examples of what usually helps. All depend on willingness to put reflective practice into action (more detail in Lindon, 2010b).

- Planning ahead and rehearsing – managers in general, and not only in early years provision, do much less trying out of possible approaches than is ideal. More effective managers think ahead and rehearse how they could approach a practitioner who is known to have a problem with a part of the work. Too often, meetings just happen rather than being properly planned.
- Time management – looking carefully at how you allocate and keep to time. Making sure that your professional development is not scrunched out by the everyday needs of the work.
- Focusing on your CPD. This will include reading relevant books (like now), selecting appropriate training or taking the opportunities from local

professional networks (from page 195) to learn from other settings, maybe through joint projects.

- Coaching is also important: the guided professional development from your leader, manager, between peers or from external consultants.

Developing an assertive approach

A degree of assertiveness is required in order to develop both self-disclosure (talking about yourself) and the confidence to give and receive useful feedback. There is often confusion over the difference between assertive and aggressive behaviour and the key differences are as follows:

> When you talk and act in an *assertive* way, you stand up for your own views and expertise within a conversation, yet you recognise and listen to the contributions of other people: 'We are equal. We both have the right to talk and be listened to.' You communicate your feelings and preferences in a direct and honest way and allow space for the concerns of others. You acknowledge your choices and accept the consequences of those choices. Frustrations are not handled by seeking to find somebody else to blame. However, you do not apologise for problems not of your making merely to have a quiet life. The rule is that the person is OK, it is their behaviour that is not OK.

> People who take an *aggressive* approach are motivated by the desire to win and are unconcerned about other people's rights to speak or their emotional well being. The aggressive outlook is 'me first'. An aggressive approach pushes forward this person's opinions and often includes blaming others for negative consequences as a result of what they do. People who take an aggressive approach may criticise others for being 'oversensitive' and exploit the reluctance of non-assertive peers to seem 'rude' or 'pushy'.

> The third broad option is to behave in a *submissive* or *passive* way. These people fail to stand up for their rights; the usual message is 'you first'. Their aim is to avoid conflict, to please others and to feel liked (or at least not disliked). They typically express opinions apologetically or offer contributions in a self-effacing style that almost invites dismissal. For example, 'this may not be important, but' or 'I may have not been here very long, yet…' Individuals with a submissive style may resist accepting the consequences of their actions; it was not their fault, they only did what they were told.

We compare assertive, aggressive and passive approaches in more detail in Figure 4.2.

Aggressive	Assertive	Passive
• Insecure	• Secure	• Insecure
• Insensitive	• Sensitive	• Over-sensitive
• Domineering	• Respectful	• Submissive
• Impatient	• Patient	• Patient
• Me first	• Both of us equal	• Others first

Aggressive	Assertive	Passive
• Win-lose approach	• Problem-solving, negotiating approach	• No-win or lose-lose approach
• Dishonest	• Honest	• Dishonest
• Decision maker	• Decision maker	• Indecisive
• Unreliable	• Reliable	• Reliable

Figure 4.2 Comparing the three approaches

Issues in becoming more assertive

Given the organisational culture of much of early years provision, there is good reason to predict that assertiveness sometimes becomes bogged down with worries about being autocratic and/or non-collaborative. Effective leadership, teamworking and genuine collaboration between practitioners all depend on using an assertive approach rather than being passive or aggressive.

We want to make links here with Relationship Awareness Theory (Porter, 1996; page 87 this text). A key idea is that strengths can become weaknesses when they are overdone. However, it is not just actually overdoing it that causes trouble in a relationship; it can also cause trouble if other people perceive you to be overdoing your strengths.

Let us take the Blue MVS as an example because it is most similar to the general culture of early years organisations (Hard, 2005). People with a Blue MVS are concerned about the protection, growth, and welfare of others; they may be perceived as the 'nice' people at work. Review Figure 4.3 to see how Blue strengths can be overdone and what people with a Blue MVS might need to watch out for.

Saying 'no'

Being able to be assertive, and hence to use power and influence, is significantly influenced by our experiences, values and beliefs. One of these is an unwillingness to say 'no' and getting snarled up in 'trying to help'. If you really do not want to do something, then say 'no'. Doubts and problems also come from trying to help and are therefore not sure that you *really* want to say no. You can read more about making and dealing with requests from page 109. This difficulty in saying 'no' makes it very hard to be assertive, and even harder to use all the sources of power necessary to achieve your goals. The reverse may be true. If you really do not value the other person and what they have to say, it is easy to say no. If you have found nothing to value in another person, it may be almost impossible to listen to them, let alone attempt to help them. The challenge for the responsible manager and leader is to address these issues: have you really understood this person, do you understand their world?

Assertiveness also gets entangled with emotion. The early years culture purports to be at ease with emotion, but a closer look suggests that it depends on what this emotion is. While it is important to avoid sweeping stereotypes, the overwhelmingly female nature of the sector (from page 19) tends towards a situation in which many practitioners are less troubled by dealing with distress (maybe expressed with tears) than with anger (expressed with raised voices and shaken fists). You may feel that being assertive is more likely to give rise to emotionally charged exchanges – specifically feelings of anger from a colleague or parent – and therefore choose not to try.

Blue (Altruistic–Nurturing) Motivational Value System	
Characteristic strength:	*If overdone can become:*
Trusting – I place my faith in others.	Gullible – Being so trusting I put my faith in people I really shouldn't trust at all.
Loyal – I remain faithful to the commitments made to others.	Blind – I close my eyes to faults in others that should be obvious to me.
Helpful – I give assistance to others who are in need.	Smothering – Being so helpful to others I do too much for them and get in the way of them doing things for themselves.
Modest – I play down what I am really capable of doing.	Self-effacing – Being so modest I hide what I can do really well and then miss out on the chance to do it.
Devoted – I am dedicated to some purpose, person, or activity.	Subservient – Being so devoted to others I put off looking after myself until everyone else is taken care of.
Caring – I concern myself with the well-being of others.	Submissive – Being so caring for others' needs and well being I give them anything they ask for.
Supportive – I give encouragement and help to others.	Self-sacrificing – Being so supportive I put aside my own personal needs in doing so.
Things to watch out for… Wanting so much to maintain harmony that I don't push for what I want Being so quick to believe in others that I don't use good judgement Being so loyal to others that I let them take advantage of me Expecting that everyone is going to be as concerned about how other people feel as I do Wanting to help others so much that I push my help on them and get in their way Being quick to blame myself first for anything that goes wrong Sharing my thoughts and feelings with people I shouldn't trust with them Fearing that if I said what I really feel about others, they would be hurt and not helped Struggling to maintain harmony at the expense of facing issues or of facing the facts Acting to please others just to be likeable.	

Figure 4.3 Strengths and Weaknesses has been reproduced from the Strength Deployment Inventory® (SDI®) (Porter, 1973, 2005) with special permission of the publisher.

Practical influencing through assertiveness

Assertiveness can be characterised by owning your own position honestly, respecting your own rights, yet respecting equally the rights of others. The essence of assertion revolves around the self-confidence necessary to be open about what you want. Of course, it matters how you do it: the manner in which honesty is expressed is crucial. Effective assertiveness recognises the need to be socially skilled: to be able to communicate in such a way that misunderstandings are successfully resolved and that staff understand the reason for a request, including whether this is a choice or not.

An underlying assumption of assertiveness is that others have the right not to be assertive, although you can legitimately continue to operate assertively. A dilemma for managers is how to deal with practitioners who do not wish to say no to a request or who struggle to ask for something. You can look towards coaching individual practitioners towards a more assertive approach, but they need to live with the consequences of their decisions. Being assertive is a choice, and as with any choice, individuals need to accept the consequences of making that choice.

Three aspects are crucial to effective assertion. The senior people in any provision need to set the example, the role model for others to follow:

1 Look and sound self-confident. Maintain regular eye contact, but avoid staring. Aim for a relaxed and attentive body language and a measured, audible tone of voice. Walk with a posture that includes 'standing tall' (not slumping). Walk with purpose rather than any hint of shuffling apologetically.

2 Use assertive language, which typically means using phrases involving the word 'I': 'I think', 'I believe', 'I feel' rather than the less honest 'It's a problem', 'Don't you think…' or 'we all feel that'. Avoid language which invites rebuttal, such as 'If it's not too much trouble' or 'If you don't mind'. You can be courteous without implying that you are not really serious about this request. Statements such as 'I want to reinstate the home-nursery day books' are more constructive than 'You should never have let them lapse'.

3 See any situation as a problem which needs to be resolved by joint agreement. The basic approach of assertiveness is, 'I want to reinstate the day books. What do you think?' There is a chance to explore what has happened, but it is less effective to define the problem immediately in terms of a solution: 'You must restart the day books today.' People are generally much more flexible if they feel that they have a choice. Assertion skills give other people some manoeuvring room, yet they honestly communicate relevant information, so that the limits around the choice are very clear.

Assertion helps to make information public so it can be addressed. With more information, it is likely that any decisions made will be of better quality (look back at the leadership decision styles on page 50). Assertiveness is about asking and telling. Skilled assertion is about doing that in a socially appropriate way, actively and with self-confidence. Undoubtedly this requires effort, and responsible managers are self-aware in considering the reasons why this issue calls for assertion. It also helps to be honest with yourself about any feelings of reluctance to face this person or room team.

- Be clear about your objective in being assertive. Do you want this person to change their behaviour and, if so, how?

- Do you want this room team to start doing something, or stop doing something else? Is it what they do, or more how they do it?
- You need to be clear about what you want them to do in detail. For example, Alicia, manager of the Daleside after-school club, feels that her team are expecting too much from the four-year-olds. Alicia will have be clearer than 'You're expecting too much of the younger ones' and share some specific observations linked with knowledge of child development.

If you have the confidence to tell others what you know, think, value and feel, then their view of you becomes more accurate. This self-disclosure involves taking the risk to surface information which the other person does not know. This issue here is not about telling everyone absolutely everything and having no secrets; the focus is on sharing relevant information that could improve working life. Even so, some people are reluctant to voice their views of preferences because they think far more about what could go wrong, 'if I speak up', than what could go right. This focus on the downside of taking the risk of self-disclosure (or other kinds of risk) is called 'catastrophic expectations'.

Scenario

In Crocus Playgroup Felicity understands the new accounting system better than anyone. Natalie, the manager, regularly asks Felicity to help in sorting out minor problems. Initially, Felicity did not mind, but she is now irritated at what feels like constant interruption to her time with the children.

- Look back at acceptance of requests from someone in authority on page 41. Is Felicity concerned because she is being *asked to do something not done normally* regularly? Also, Natalie does not seem to be trying to understand the new accounting system.
- Felicity is relatively new to the playgroup and is worried that, if she objects, Natalie may think she is uncooperative. Unfortunately, if Felicity says nothing, then Natalie has no idea about the simmering resentment. If Felicity can voice at least some of what she feels, there is a chance that she and Natalie can discuss ways to ensure that the manager learns how to use the system.
- Felicity could say, 'Why do you keep taking me away from the children?' or 'Why don't you do this? It's your job'. This confrontational approach is unlikely to result in anything other than an argument.
- It is preferable that Felicity makes an assertive 'I' statement, such as, 'I'm finding that the children are unsettled when I keep leaving to come into the office' or 'I want to talk about how I can help you learn the new system'. The assertive statements and problem solving that could well follow need to be supported with confident body language.
- Felicity may also be tempted not to be assertive because it seems quicker to help Natalie in short bursts rather than find the time to explain so that her manager will no longer need to ask for the help. But if Felicity is already irritated with Natalie, it is time to assert.

Requests – asking and declining

The skills of assertiveness also apply to making requests of staff or peers and the acceptance or refusal of those requests. It needs to be clear in any team who has the authority to organise who does what within the daily routine and therefore who can legitimately ask, and the boundaries of a reasonable request. This is in addition to the normal requests for help that are a regular part of everyday work.

Be honest and direct so that the other person is clear about what you want. You say to Hattie, 'I would like you to take charge of our rolling snack today' or 'Every observation of a child or a photo needs to have a date'. Initially at least, do not clutter requests with a justification, most of which begin with 'because...'. You can follow up with an explanation if there is an objection to a fair request.

Avoid pleading or emotional blackmail – this is unnecessary and unprofessional. So do not say 'Please do it for me' when it is legitimate to ask a practitioner to take responsibility for this task. You can be courteous: 'Please do the snack with the children this morning' or 'I'd like you to scrub down the climbing frame'. Avoid offering to do something in exchange, as a sweetener. Negotiating a trade is not appropriate for fair requests. It erodes mutual respect, as well as misdirecting the reluctant practitioner over what is, or is not, up for discussion within their job description and role. It is a different situation when a team has sat down to organise how to allocate responsibilities for an area of practice.

In the same vein, *do not apologise as a habit*: avoid softening your request with a 'sorry, but...'. If the request is fair and honest, what is the purpose of apologising if it only invites refusal? If you genuinely want the person to do something, why start by highlighting a possible objection they may have?

Be clear in your own mind when you are making a request to which the other person can legitimately say 'no'. Do not take this kind of refusal as a personal rejection, or lack of professional commitment. You would very much like Gareth to attend the meeting next week but he has booked a day's leave. You ask him to change the day and he says this is not possible: he has promised to help all that day with his daughter's school play. It is acceptable for Gareth to decline the request, as it was acceptable for him to be asked.

Finally, to emphasise, respect *the other person's right to say no*. In Gareth's case, pressure to agree will force him to choose between the competing priorities of his work and a promise to his daughter. It also pushes the boundaries of work into agreed time off. If Hattie chooses to say 'no' to legitimate requests like taking responsibility for the rolling snack time, then the source of her reluctance, or the dynamics in this room, will need to be addressed. Hattie can be assertive about what she views as her rights. However, the room leader, supported by the manager, will need to explore the responsibilities that are an integral part of Hattie's role.

From the other side, here are some points to bear in mind about responding to requests:

Keep your refusal short, if you want and need to decline a request. A simple 'no' in a friendly tone can be followed up – only if necessary – with a brief explanation. You do not need to apologise profusely: 'Not this week, sorry' is often enough. In the organisational culture of early years provision – as in much of the UK – people are reluctant to just say 'no'; there is fear of giving offence or being thought brusque. At work there may be a concern about being judged as uncooperative, not part of the team.

Be honest – the problem with saying or implying 'yes' or 'maybe' when you actually mean 'no' is that the dilemma is simply postponed. Suppose your centre head asks you, the deputy, 'Can you come in over the weekend and get the hall ready for the decorators on Monday?' A straight answer of 'no' may well bring, 'Alright then, I'll ask Jean'. Being assertive is often as painless as that and does much to overcome catastrophic expectations that refusals will have bad consequences. If necessary, give a short reason why you are refusing. In this case it is wise to make this an honest emotional reason rather than a logical one.

Scenarios

Consider these two fictional examples and reflect on the ways the events may parallel your own experience or that of practitioners you support.

The AtoZ nursery

The setting is part of a national chain and Head Office has asked Leila to agree to a six-month secondment with a struggling nursery on the other side of the country. Leila is flattered by the confidence expressed in her skills, but she does not want the disruption to her personal life which this project would entail.

It will be wiser for Leila to communicate the true reason behind her refusal rather than construct a less genuine reason. Suppose Leila focuses her refusal on how much is currently happening in her nursery and this is not a good time for her to leave. Head Office might resolve her problem with practical suggestions about training for her deputy or similar ideas. Alternatively, Head Office might accept Leila's refusal this time, yet assume – reasonably – that she would agree in the future.

Leila and her husband have agreed to avoid significant time apart and he recently turned down a posting in his job because of their agreement. They are also very close to wanting to start a family. Think about how Leila could express these personal reasons. How much does she need to say? Discuss your ideas with colleagues.

Princes Children's Centre

You can set a trap for yourself with an excuse of, 'I can't, because...', as the requester may have an answer to remove the 'because'.

The head of centre, Brigid, has got into the habit of working over the weekend and has started to expect that her deputy, Harriet, will do the same. Today, Harriet has backed up her 'no' with 'because I've got to complete my course paper this weekend'. This statement is true, but really Harriet does not want to work weekends and is actually rather irritated at being asked.

Brigid offers to resolve the objection with, 'No problem, I'll free you up Wednesday afternoon to do your paper, then you can help me over the weekend'. Brigid has removed the objection and hence Harriet has no reason not to work over the weekend. Thus Harriet now has to be more assertive in saying 'no' and is back to the beginning. She needs to begin a further discussion with 'I don't want to come into the centre at weekends'.

Again, think about how Harriet might put her feelings into words and share ideas. What are some of the issues here? For instance, is it easy for committed practitioners, passionate about their work, to lose the boundary between work and personal life?

Offer options when this response is your honest reaction. If you would genuinely like to agree but only if the details were different, then say so and give alternatives. For example, 'I can't get the pallets from the Garden Centre this week. But next week would be fine for me', or 'Usually I could stay late on Wednesdays. It's just that this week we have a do at my partner's work. Would Tuesday be alright?'

Communication and personal effectiveness

The previous section had many examples of what you might say, highlighting the importance of communication. This section looks in more detail at communication between managers and staff, and between colleagues.

Recognition of feelings

Work with young children stresses the importance of the role of emotions and of adults who are emotionally literate in their dealings with colleagues, as well as with the children. Effective communication between adults allows for recognition of feelings and has links with discussion around emotional intelligence (Caruso and Salovey, 2004, and more on pages 58 and 199).

Acknowledgement of emotions matters, but it is inappropriate for practitioners, in meetings or elsewhere, to spend ages and ages musing over emotional reactions or what it all might mean. Reflection and self-awareness are valuable skills, but the point of being sensitive to what you are feeling is to access, share and resolve that information. Recognising and expressing emotions in the workplace is not an end in itself. The potential risks in a nurturing emotional working environment are to encourage expression of feelings – better to get it out – without addressing the questions 'so what?' or 'where does this take us?'.

Early years settings should place a high value on nurture and emotional support for team members, but they are not therapeutic communities for staff, volunteers or students. An alert leader needs to spot, and act, when an emotionally needy practitioner is gaining centre stage in the life of the team or when their emotional life is undermining the quality of their practice with children or families.

Responsible early years managers or room leaders cannot allow a practitioner to put the children to one side, like an unfinished report, until this adult feels more able to cope. There is a generous middle ground between an uncompromising 'Leave your troubles at the door; we don't want to know' and 'Let it all out – regardless of the consequences on the children'.

Anxiety or worry are not inevitably negative emotions that need to be hidden. Bringing these feelings out into the open enables you to address what can make a difference to this anxiety, or to recognise what this high level of anxiety is doing to your practice. Is the anxiety real or just imagined? Are you spending too much time on 'what if' rather than 'what is'? Positive feelings such as enthusiasm or excitement can be energising and help to bring about change. Making even minor adjustments is a seriously uphill task in an emotional environment characterised by glumness: 'it'll never work' and 'what's the point'. However, gung-ho enthusiasm to 'let's just get on and do something!' needs to be tempered with the practical questions: what, how and who along with why.

Making your comments constructive

Here are some key practical points that apply to communication within working relationships, whether someone has specifically asked you for feedback or you, as the manager, are legitimately making an observation about how individual staff behave.

Focus your comments on the behaviour, not the person. This basic rule should be familiar from positive relationships with the children and guiding their behaviour.

- For example, Paula, your deputy, is frequently late and you are irritated because it is impossible to pay attention to parents as you wish in the morning when there is only one of you. However, it will not help to tell Paula she is 'disorganised' or 'thoughtless': a personal criticism which will misdirect the conversation. This is an attack upon the person. Focus on the consequences for you of her lateness, and be clear that, otherwise, you feel the two of you are working well as a senior team.

Implicit in the above comment is the need to *be specific*; it is also more realistic.

- You need to focus your comment on the fact that Paula has arrived at least half an hour late twice a week since she started this role. She is not 'always late'.
- To take a different example, it is not helpful to tell Katie that her presentation at the recent family information evening was 'hard to follow' or 'unclear' – she is being given nothing to help her improve. What can she do differently, surely not everything? Specific description is also more constructive and less threatening. In Katie's presentation, the text was too small to be read by any parents beyond the front row. Katie can do something by changing a font on her presentation slides. This is a small adjustment, much easier to deal with (both practically and emotionally) than 'your presentation was unclear'.

Be clear about what you want, in terms of both your motives and the results you wish to achieve.

- Is it Paula's lateness that most bothers you or that she is not always present to talk with parents within your reception area? If your objective is to have Paula more active in communication with families, do not focus your assertion and the comments on being punctual. Otherwise, she may get into work on time every day and then sit in the office avoiding parents. So, you will have to assert yourself once more.
- Was Katie also unclear in what she said to parents that evening? If she used specialist words and phrases, then a larger font on her slides will not resolve that problem.

Be timely and do not leave important comments so long that your feelings of irritation become dominant. You are then more likely to challenge the whole person rather than the behaviour.

- If your motive is to 'give Paula a piece of my mind', it is unlikely that you will be assertive without some very careful planning. Avoid letting Katie's presentation style puzzle several groups of parents before you say something.
- Be clear but do not overwhelm someone with a long list of points, even if each one is well expressed. It will not feel constructive; it will just feel like criticism and the person will feel the urge to defend, or even stop listening.
- If you are uncomfortable with saying negative things, you may reduce the frequency with which you do this. This leads to 'banking' criticisms over time to be finally communicated in one big 'gotcha' package. The person on the receiving end may well be surprised (and hurt) on the basis that having heard nothing for months, surely things were alright. The ground rule is for short, specific and timely comments.

Balance positives and negatives – whenever possible, balance constructive criticism which implies 'please change' with positives. Assertion is even-handed, but it is also honest.

- Help the person listening to save face: to recognise their strengths as well as weaknesses. The concept here is as she is OK, or even great, as a person, there should be no problem for her to change this bit of behaviour which is getting in the way of fully appreciating her work here.
- However, you need to be authentic – do not pretend something is fine when there is scope for improvement.
- Do you feel uncomfortable in making a criticism which urges the other person to change their behaviour? You need to deal with that sense of pressure without watering down your comments to the point where the other person thinks nothing is actually the matter.

Support is needed when staff members or colleagues accept the truth and relevance of your comments. As people change their habits, initially they may well feel odd, hesitant or uncertain. Managers and colleagues can recognise that this difficulty is likely and be there to help, not least saying, 'Thanks, Paula. It made a real difference to be working together at the beginning of the day all this week. Can you bring me up to speed with Daria's family?'

Receiving comments in a constructive way

The previous section focused on the person expressing the comments rather than on the person receiving this information. Most, probably all, of us would rather our work was always beyond reproach. It is unlikely that anyone will announce happily, 'I feel so much better. I've just been constructively criticised'. However, it is legitimate and appropriate for managers to tell the employees what they need to do to improve. Also, a positive working atmosphere is created when colleagues are able to offer and receive comments in a positive way.

Here are some tips about being on the receiving end:
- If the comment you hear is non-specific, it is appropriate to ask for more information: 'Can you give me an example?' or 'When was this?' or 'Which report should I be looking at?'
- Do not let justifications block your listening to the information. You will often have a good reason why you made the choice that is being criticised. You will not listen properly if your mind is busy with rehearsing your justification, the rebuttal of this criticism. You know your colleague is saying something about Liam's developmental record, but miss exactly what.
- Instead, mentally note what is being said. Make conscious efforts to shut down your inner dialogue so that you hear what the other person is saying. This focus helps to prevent you from overreacting to a minor criticism, or replying at length with information that is irrelevant.
- Maintain friendly eye contact: looking helps listening. But avoid staring and feel free to glance away sometimes. Continually looking down or away can be seen as submissive, or an admission of guilt. However, there are undoubtedly cross-cultural differences in this area.
- Acknowledge the person giving you this constructive criticism; they may be finding this conversation difficult or stressful. Once more, focus on behaviour – what your colleague says and whether it is constructive – and not on them as a person.
- If this criticism really seems unjustified, calmly state your perception of the situation being described. Use assertive language like, 'You see it like this ..., I see it like this ...' Speak up if you are sure the criticism is based on an inaccuracy, for instance that 'I didn't have any conversation yesterday with Ben's father'.

Giving and receiving praise

You will be familiar with the ground rule of guiding children's behaviour: to give at least three positive comments for each negative (or constructively critical) comment. Adults also flourish with active encouragement within their work. In a team, practitioners should not have to go fishing for positive feedback. If the manager decided it was important to make a constructive criticism last month about the use of photos in the children's records, then they have a responsibility to follow up and reward the marked improvements.

Make sure you are generous with positive recognition. Take the time and give the attention to show the other person you mean what you say. Just as with constructive criticism, be specific and detailed. General praise is too vague to be useful. Katie needs to know that she has successfully adjusted her professional language without patronising the parents. They now understand what she is saying and that is why at the end there are now plenty of questions rather than a bemused silence. Be personal and be at ease using 'I' statements: 'I'm very pleased with the way you think about the captions that go with the photos', 'I think you've got the perfect balance for language between professional terms and everyday ones.' Praise should never be grudging; never give the impression that positive comments are unwillingly dragged out of you.

On the receiving end, be appreciative of the complimentary remarks; avoid making the other person uncomfortable for having given them. Avoid dismissing the praise with, 'It was nothing' or 'Ciaran still writes better reports than me'. This reticence can be a habit from childhood and cultural background: that it is impolite to accept praise (rather like eating the last crumpet, it is not done easily), maybe there is an element of false modesty. At the very least, thank the giver for the praise, accept their judgement gladly, agree briefly and smile. If you are grudging in your acceptance, or dismissive of praise, why should someone make the effort to praise you next time?

If necessary, ask the person giving you praise to be specific. If you honestly do not know what it is that you are being praised for, it is in your own interest to find out. After all, if it works, do more of it!

Assertion is positive influence

Assertiveness skills are life skills; they can enrich your professional and personal life. Assertion requires everyone to think before they act, yet not be so pessimistic about the possible consequences of actions that they fail to act. Assertion is about surfacing information that is relevant to decision making, either through telling or by asking, in such a way that the communication is clarified and everyone's rights are respected.

Planning helps to achieve anything; this is particularly true when seeking to influence and persuade others. If you are seeking to influence, then:

- Be absolutely clear on your objective, both for the first meeting or conversation and later if required. Define what an agreement might look like for you.
- Find the right time and place for the conversation or more formal meeting. Given good planning, when the meeting happens, you can focus on the issue as one between you that needs to be jointly resolved. So the format is, first, 'I see it like this, how do you see it?', followed by, 'This is what I'd like, what would you prefer?' Ask for what you want, and seek common ground.
- Think about what the other person might want, need or even fear. If you can overcome their problems or objections, they are more likely to agree with you. Listen and discover what the other person actually wants. Unlike you, she may

be happy to work at weekends. How similar is this to what you want and prefer? Make no assumptions in advance, listen.

- People do not always seek the same things out of work or their life in general. This is equally true for professional development. What excites or worries you may work in reverse for colleagues or members of your team.
- Allow the other person room to save face. In other words, if she changes her mind, seek to ensure that she can do this without feeling put down, trapped or simply indecisive because she cannot easily communicate the reason.
- Know what will need to happen next, whether or not you succeed. Sometimes you can be so surprised when someone actually agrees to something you thought they would refuse that you have forgotten to work out what this actually means in future practice.
- Understand the benefits – what the other person has to gain (perhaps as little as 'not having to have this conversation again') – and not your description of what might happen in general.

Scenario

In the AtoZ nursery, Leila has struggled over how to persuade Eva to be more active outdoors: she will stand out in the garden but does little.

Would Eva be more active if given a specific task? Leila has been patient, listening attentively so that Eva feels her manager understands that she cannot get over feeling like a bit of a twit rushing round in lively games with the children. Leila recognises that Eva is a very organised person; she brought order out of the chaos that used to disrupt the kindergarten room and made a very popular creative workshop. Would she take on the garden shed which is not working at all well as the outdoor storage facility?

Think about your own practice and the ways in which you have adjusted an appropriately assertive line with sensitivity to individual practitioners.

Links between personal effectiveness and leadership
To be personally effective requires many of the skills that show personal leadership. Studies of people seen as peak performers (Garfield, 1987) – those most likely to be seen as leaders or suitable for promotion – showed the following qualities:

- The ability to manage themselves well, having self-confidence and what was called 'bimodal thinking' – in other words, they can see the big picture as well as sort the detail. They regularly rehearsed, they thought and planned ahead.
- Willingness to adapt when changes are needed. They have mental agility, are creative and change their view of things as required. They have stamina, concentration, resilience, and deal well with stress. They learn from their mistakes.

- A focus on results. Individually, they focus on achieving their goals and implementing well. They also collaborate and build on other people's ideas. They innovate and find alternative ways to do things.
- The ability to build the skills required in a changing world. They develop themselves through self-teaching, development activities and feedback from others. They use every opportunity to learn new skills.
- The ability to develop teams to achieve results. They delegate tasks to others who are better at them and do not hold onto tasks at which they are second best. They challenge and support colleagues to stretch and grow, and encourage sensible risk taking.
- Manage change for future success. They map alternative futures and the ways to reach these. They will update the mission in the face of radical change so that the team can still perform well. As they continually learn, they can visualise what success will look like and will expect to reach it.

The key to personal effectiveness is being aware of your own strengths and weaknesses, and being honest about what you want. Furthermore, remaining reflective of what you are doing, rather than just doing what appears to come naturally, benefits your provision as well as your professional skills. The behaviours required to be personally effective are those that form the basis of personal leadership, better performance in your job and the chance to progress in your chosen line of work. Change is both constant and inevitable. Recognising this fact helps develop the motivation to learn continually in order to be more flexible. We will explore change and the additional challenges of management and transformational leadership in the next chapter.

Resources

- **Back, K. and Back, K. with Bates, T.** (1991) *Assertiveness at Work,* 2nd edition. Maidenhead: McGraw-Hill.
- **Baumrind, D.** (1967) 'Child-care practices anteceding three patterns of preschool behaviour'. *Genetic Psychology Monographs,* 75, 43–88.
- **Caruso, D. and Salovey, P.** (2004) *The Emotionally Intelligent Manager: How to develop and use the four key emotional skills of leadership.* San Francisco, CA: Jossey-Bass.
- **Dana, D.** (1990) *Talk It Out: Four steps to managing people problems in your organisation.* London: Kogan Page.
- **Duffy, B. and Marshall, J.** (2007) 'Leadership in multi-agency work'. In Siraj-Blatchford, I. Clarke, K. and Needham, M. (eds) *The Team Around the Child: Multi-agency working in the early years.* Stoke-on-Trent: Trentham Books.
- **Garfield, C.** (1987) *Peak performers: The new heroes of American business.* New York: Harper Paperbacks.
- **Goleman, D., Boyatzis, R. and McKee, A.** (2002) *The New Leaders: Transforming the art of leadership into the science of results.* London: Time Warner.

- **Hard, L.** (2005) *How Is Leadership Understood and Enacted within the Field of Early Childhood Education and Care?* Unpublished doctoral thesis, Center for Learning Innovation, Queensland University of Technology. http://eprints.qut.edu.au/16213/1/Louise_Hard_Thesis.pdf
- **Lindon, J.** (2010b) *Reflective Practice and Early Years Professionalism.* London: Hodder Education.
- **Moyles, J.** (2006) *Effective Leadership and Management in the Early Years.* Maidenhead: Open University Press.
- **Nivala, V. and Hujala, E.** (eds) (2002) *Leadership in Early Childhood Education: Cross-cultural perspectives.* Oulu: Oulu University Press. http://herkules.oulu.fi/isbn9514268539/
- **Porter, E.H.** (1973, 2005) Strength Deployment Inventory. Carlsbad, CA: Personal Strengths Publishing.
- **Porter, E.H.** (1996) *Relationship Awareness Theory.* Carlsbad, CA: Personal Strengths Publishing.
- **Rakos, R.F.** (1991) *Assertive Behaviour: Theory, research and training.* New York: Routledge.
- **Rodd, J.** (1997) 'Learning to be leaders: perceptions of early childhood professionals about leadership, roles and responsibilities'. *Early Years,* 18, 1.
- **Rodd, J.** (2006) *Leadership in Early Childhood.* Maidenhead: Open University Press.
- **Rosemary, C. and Puroila, A-M.** (2002) 'Leadership potential in day care settings: using dual analytical methods to explore directors' work in Finland and the USA'. In Nivala, V. and Hujala, E. (eds) *Leadership in Early Childhood Education: Cross-cultural perspectives.* Oulu: Oulu University Press. http://herkules.oulu.fi/isbn9514268539/
- **Scrivens, C.** (2002a) 'Constructions of leadership: does gender make a difference? Perspectives from an English speaking country'. In Nivala, V. and Hujala, E. (eds) *Leadership in Early Childhood Education: Cross-cultural perspectives.* Oulu: Oulu University Press. http://herkules.oulu.fi/isbn9514268539/
- **Thornton, K.** (2006) 'Notions of leadership in the New Zealand ECE Centres of Innovation Programme'. *New Zealand Annual Review of Education,* 15, 153–67. http://www.victoria.ac.nz/nzaroe/subject-area/.%5C../1996/.%5C../2005/pdf/text-thornton.pdf
- **Thornton, K.** (2007) *Courage, Commitment and Collaboration: Notions of leadership in the NZ ECE Centres of Innovation.* Victoria: University of Wellington. http://researcharchive.vuw.ac.nz/bitstream/handle/10063/124/paper.pdf?sequence=2
- **Waniganayake, M.** (2002) 'Growth of leadership: With training can anyone become a leader?' In Nivala, V. and Hujala, E. (eds) *Leadership in Early Childhood Education: Cross-cultural perspectives.* Oulu: Oulu University Press. http://herkules.oulu.fi/isbn9514268539/
- **Waniganayake, M., Morda, R. and Kapsalakis, A.** (2000) 'Leadership in child care centres: is it just another job?' *Australian Journal of Early Childhood,* 25, 1, 13–20.

Shared responsibility for best practice

The concept of shared leadership arose from the observation that some effective teams appear to operate without an obvious person in overall charge of the work. The concept of distributed leadership has become central to raising achievement in schools and this model is proposed by some writers as the most appropriate for the early years sector.

This chapter explores the practical issues of shared leadership, and who can operate as a leader. Such questions are relevant for the role of Early Years Professionals and any other practitioners who are tasked with taking a lead in best practice and bringing about change. Finally, questions about sharing leadership across professional boundaries and multi-agency working arise in terms of the challenges for heads and teams within complex organisations like children's centres.

The main sections of this chapter are:
- distributed leadership
- the role of early years professionals
- leadership of complex centres.

Distributed leadership

The approach to leadership which looks beyond the overall leadership of one person is often described by the word 'distributed', but sometimes the descriptive term is 'distributive'. We have also encountered 'shared', 'dispersed', 'consultative', 'democratic' and 'inclusive' as the preferred term for discussing what sounds like essentially the same concept. We have chosen to use 'distributed' because that term is the most common within the literature about schools and early years provision.

Distributed leadership and early years provision

In brief, distributed leadership is a deliberate process of sharing leadership behaviour, so that team members other than the head or manager take an active lead. They accept responsibility for some areas of the work and developing best practice. This is a critical point; it is not about being the overall leader of the setting, but of practitioners adopting a leadership role. Certainly, having the capacity to act in a leadership role when required is a key element of being an effective follower. You are not in control of everything, but have strong influence in certain areas at certain times.

> ## What does it mean?
>
> **Distributed leadership**: a deliberate organisational strategy in which aspects of leadership behaviour and actions are shared with some, not necessarily all, staff throughout an organisation.

The rethinking of leadership as a shared enterprise has been a positive for early childhood services, because it has been seen as compatible with the nature of the service and the reported inclinations of the workforce. There are three main lines of argument offered to support the proposal that distributed leadership is ideal for the early years sector, or that this model is already in place:

- The rationale that early years provision, and the mainly female workforce, operates in a collaborative rather than competitive way and so a distributed leadership model is the best fit.
- The related argument is that early years practitioners are more at ease with a democratic rather than autocratic style of leadership and distribution of leadership is democratic in nature.
- An additional rationale has been that leadership has to be distributed out from the position of head or manager, given the complex pattern of services within some large centres. There is a belief that there is no way that one manager or head can take sole responsibility to deliver the high expectations of what such provision will deliver.

There is a considerable amount of discussion about the advisability of the distributed leadership model for early years provision in the UK, Australia and New Zealand, or the assumption that this pattern is an accurate description of how a large number of settings actually operate (Henderson-Kelly and Pamphilon, 2000; Thornton, 2006; Waniganayake, 2002 and Waniganayake *et al.*, 2000). However, there is a very limited amount of observational information about the extent to which distributed leadership has consciously been implemented and how it actually works when the model is fully operational.

There is a continuing problem in some of the early years leadership literature – in the UK as well as abroad – that distributed leadership is presented as the best or the only appropriate model for early years provision. In the background reading for this book we regularly followed up references quoted with the strong implication that they were studies demonstrating that distributed leadership worked in early years provision. We regularly then found unsupported statements about the nature of a female workforce, or how women prefer to act in what is hard for us to describe as other than a non-leading leadership role. It was less common to find discussion of the downsides of a model of distributed leadership, or at least predictable problems that need to be discussed and resolved.

Siraj-Blatchford and Manni (2007) provide welcome honesty in their *Effective Leadership in the Early Years Sector report* (ELEYS). This was partly a re-analysis of the data from the late 1990s *Researching Effective Pedagogy in Early Years* (REPEY) project, along with a literature review and a report from a focus group of early childhood experts. The REPEY project did not study models of leadership directly. The ELEYS report discusses distributed leadership as one possible way to build professionalism and skills with the early years team. But Siraj-Blatchford and Manni conclude that within the available literature the concept is decidedly blurred and there are few concrete examples of distributed early years leadership in action.

Siraj-Blatchford and Manni argue that clear overall leadership is often necessary in order to develop high levels of collaboration and teamwork. Unlike some other commentators, they do not seem to take the collaborative approach as a given in all early years settings. They stress the importance of a head/manager who has high expectations and is able to recognise how staff might progress from their current skills level. Effective leaders set an example of reflection, providing a model with clear purpose and values. Rodd (2006) and Pound (2008) also note that young and/or inexperienced early years practitioners may benefit from a more directive style of leadership, and that a strong overall leader may be necessary when the group is struggling with change. This observation is consistent with the leadership styles described by Hersey and Blanchard – see page 51.

Aubrey (2007) also expresses reservations about the model of distributed leadership in practice. She led a study of 12 different types of early years settings based in Warwickshire. Data were gathered from questionnaires completed by the entire teams of settings and interviews with leaders, plus some group interviews. Two significant themes emerged from this study. One crucial issue is the nature of who takes the final responsibility in any kind of distributed leadership model. The second issue is the importance of regular feedback and monitoring of team members to whom aspects of leadership have been distributed. These two points were also highlighted in their own words by several of the experienced practitioners and leaders with whom we spoke for this book.

Learning from distributed leadership in schools

There is considerable discussion about distributed leadership in the literature about school leadership in the UK, the USA, Canada and Australia. In these reports the model is sometimes described as teacher leadership or the creation of teacher-leaders. Much of this material has been made accessible through literature reviews (Day *et al.*, 2009; Harris, 2002; Harris and Spillane, 2008; Leithwood *et al.*, 2008). Very practical observations have arisen from reports and there is much of direct relevance to early years provision. Yet, as Daniel *et al.* (2004) point out, there is a noticeable absence of reference to this source of information in much of the promotion of distributed leadership for early years provision here.

Until the late 1990s the discussion about leadership and school achievement focused on head teachers and their descriptions of what they did. The emphasis shifted to looking at the reality in some schools, and the possibility in others, that behaviour associated with leadership was spread beyond the head teacher. Distributed leadership is a central concept in much discussion about school leadership and achievement, with a strong focus on improving outcomes for children and young people. Quality of teaching in schools significantly affects children's motivation and achievement. The quality of school leadership is seen as a strong influence on the motivation of the teachers and therefore the quality of what they offer within the classroom.

Kenneth Leithwood *et al.* undertook a substantial review of school leadership and the possible impact on pupils' learning. They comment that, 'both teacher leadership and distributed leadership qualify as movements driven much more by philosophy and democratic values than by evidence that pupils actually learn more if a larger proportion of school leadership comes from non-traditional sources' (2008, page 9). Traditionally, power would rest with the authority of the head teacher. As Leithwood and his colleagues point out, many of the core leadership practices in school have their roots in the transformational model of leadership (from page 54).

There is limited evidence for a strong relationship between distributed patterns of school leadership and improved outcomes for children and young people. The need for caution may be explained by the fact that distributed leadership is a relatively recent concept, although Harris (2002) judges that the evidence of such a relationship is growing. An additional factor will continue to be that the label and similar ones are used to cover a wide range of understandings and misunderstanding of what distribution of leadership activity means. The early years sector has come under increasing pressure, like the school sector, to prove success in terms of outcomes. It is crucial that promoting distributed leadership for early years provision does not move to claim that this model has proven links with improved outcomes for children, because that evidence does not exist.

How might distributed leadership work?

It is important to realise that, even when the same words are used, distributed leadership is not a single, coherent model that means the same to everyone. It is more a collection of ideas, some of which have a longer history in educational or early years practice. The most useful aspects of the research reviews of school leadership are that they highlight essential practical points for anyone taking a serious look at whether the model could work in early years provision.

Distributed leadership does not replace the manager/head

The model of distributed leadership raises the question of what does a designated leader, overall leader, positional leader (all these terms are used) do when aspects of leadership are distributed across the team? There is no reason to say that the overall leader always has to embrace an identical role. Equally, there is good reason to challenge any suggestion that it is a positive move to lose the positional leader (or manager) altogether, or to blur the boundaries to the extent that nobody is willing to own up to being the overall leader.

- The model of distributed leadership – at least in its realistic versions – does not necessitate having no overall leader at all. It is not a case of a positional leader/ manager bad - distributed leadership good.
- Distributed leadership is a feature of how an organisation works: that leadership can develop anywhere in the organisation, not just from the person in overall charge.
- The concept is not the same as delegating some managerial or administrative tasks. The manager may have good reasons to pass over some routine responsibilities which have so far rested only with the person in charge. However, this situation is not the same as distributed leadership.

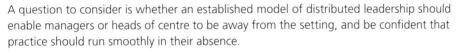

Take another **perspective**

A question to consider is whether an established model of distributed leadership should enable managers or heads of centre to be away from the setting, and be confident that practice should run smoothly in their absence.

- For instance, the introduction of no-notice inspections in England for non-school based early years provision provoked anxiety in some managers that they could therefore never be out of touch with the setting, even to take a holiday.
- Postings on early years websites, and letters pages in magazines, showed an alternative view from some managers who felt that their team, including their deputies, should be fully capable of explaining and showing their best practice.
- Should managers also switch off their mobile phones, BlackBerrys and the like, when they are delegates on a training course? This 'do you-don't you' switch-off can be a contentious issue.

What do you think?

The balanced discussions of distributed leadership do not imply that a suitable aim is to whittle away at the role of manager until there is scarcely an overall leader in the setting.

- There is good reason to argue that, like any organisation, early years settings need someone who is ready and willing to bring the team back to focus on issues that are non-negotiable. What happens if the team is enthusiastically going off on a track which might be inconsistent with core values, fails to help the children or which has overlooked key issues?
- Sometimes these 'hold on' moments may be raised by practitioners. They have the confidence and competence to speak up and take the risk of being seen as someone to pop the balloon of a good idea. But, if this cautionary note of any kind does not emerge swiftly from within the team, the overall leader (or a close working senior group) is responsible for speaking up sooner rather than later.
- There will be times for the manager or head to make the tough decisions. The descriptive accounts provided by research sometimes illuminate how early

years managers and school heads have to speak up, even when they are fairly sure the team may not welcome their words.

- Distributed leadership is about sharing activity, open discussion and jointly reached new directions. Look at page 3 for an initial discussion about the difference between management and leadership.

Make the connection with … **not just another team member**

The avowed aim of establishing a pattern of distributed leadership needs to be part of continued reflection by the manager and senior team. This model could well undermine best practice, if it enables the manager/head of centre to abdicate responsibility for making timely decisions in the name of seeking consensus.

During visits and informal conversations linked with this book, managers and heads of settings expressed a commitment to significant aspects of distributed leadership. However, they were clear that sharing the responsibility of leading on practice did not mean that managers were just another member of the team. It was important to have friendly relationships, yet with the slight distance that enabled managers to offer a firm guide over best practice, or to reiterate the overall direction that was being taken.

The role of room leader, and the role envisaged for EYPs (from page 128), also necessitated that practitioners are comfortable, or become at ease, with stepping away slightly from the existing social group in the room or unit. You do not have to become unfriendly, but it is misleading if discussion around distributed leadership implies that there will be no impact on working relationships. No longer is everyone equal.

- What has been your experience, or that of your colleagues or fellow students?
- To what extend did mentoring support you or, looking back, can you see that more opportunities to discuss the issues would have been beneficial?

Staff need to be ready for distributed leadership

Achieving the aims of distributed leadership depends on the experience and maturity of the existing team and their views on taking a lead or specific responsibility.

- Managers or heads who are new in post have to build their understanding swiftly of the usual way that the setting operates. An overall leader, committed to distributing aspects of leadership, will have to start with the current working atmosphere and habits established in the past.
- Sometimes the previous head may have taken a strongly autocratic line and the staff will not do anything without checking 'Is it all right?', 'Should I...?', 'Can you please talk with ... because I don't know how.'
- It creates uncertainty and anxiety when people are required to work in unfamiliar ways, especially if there is limited support, or they feel unsupported because the leader has not clearly defined how to work differently or explained the reasons why adequately.

Even the most secure team may hit a period of serious uncertainty and need their manager and the most senior practitioners to offer a clear lead. Changes to established work practices, plus clear communication in the time of crisis, will mean that the team welcomes strong leadership: it will be experienced as authoritative (page 98) and neither autocratic nor coercive. It provides a helpful structure in which to progress. Further, it is entirely consistent with the tenets of both transformational and transactional leadership (from page 54).

The distribution of leadership, in contrast with delegation of routine managerial tasks, will not develop if a manager, or senior team, is reluctant to let go of their positions of power. However, managers or heads of school can be confident in the legitimate power assigned by their role (see page 5 for more about kinds of power) but still make a responsible decision that the staff group, or only one or two practitioners, have the confidence and skills to share some elements of leadership.

Distributed leadership is neither a magical solution nor necessarily appropriate for every setting. Leithwood *et al.* (2008) emphasise that distributed leadership is not the sure-fire answer for dealing with struggling schools. It is not a ten-step plan to being a good leader, nor a detailed prescription for leaders' actions within education or early years provision. However, the model is a constructive way of thinking seriously and deeply about leadership.

Siraj-Blatchford and Manni (2007) also take a realistic approach to distributed leadership, avoiding any negative connotations of the manager as clearly in charge. They suggest from their interview data that some settings need appropriate structures before it is feasible to support any responsible distribution of leadership. Although the REPEY data were from the latter part of the 1990s, their point still holds that some of the early years workforce is very young.

Responsible distributed leadership takes great care to establish an environment of teamwork, communication and problem solving that enables the concept to work. Distributed leadership, like transactional leadership, is primarily about interactions and working relationships.

- The viability of the model depends on the confidence and skills in the existing workforce. Sometimes focused professional development for the group is necessary before considering applying distributed leadership.
- Recall that the essence of being a leader is that you have followers. Distributed leadership is essentially about recognising and using the skills of competent followers.
- It is irresponsible to insist on leadership activity from people who lack the confidence to take that lead. Leadership potential may be there but it will have to be nurtured, with individuals fully involved in identifying what kind of leading role they feel able and motivated to take on.
- It is irresponsible to merely inform practitioners that they are leaders and that they should effect change, with no substantive support in understanding the process of bringing about change (page 89).

- Genuine distribution of leadership depends on trusting team members to lead in some areas without constant supervision. Ideally, these would be D3 or D4 level staff in situational leadership terms. Again, well-judged continued professional development is often important before practitioners can lead safely. Distributed leadership is also sometimes described as viewing the structure within an organisation like a school as the way to empower team members, rather than the vehicle for control. This view is helpful.

Not everyone is a leader

Some of the enthusiastic, but rather unreflective, promotion of distributed early years leadership sits under the banner of 'everyone a leader'. This phrase carries no sense at all; it is closer to a slogan. Not everyone can be a leader, nor does everyone everywhere want to be a leader. The more practical explanation that usually follows titles or headings of 'everyone a leader' rhetoric is that there is considerable scope for practitioners to take the lead or accept specific responsibility in development of good practice. Such clarification is constantly required if the phrase 'everyone a leader' continues to be used.

Leithwood *et al.* draw attention to the potential problems of the belief that, 'everyone can be a good leader, that effective leadership is an entirely learnable function, perhaps even that everyone already is a good leader – without any specific preparation! This is an empirical claim almost entirely lacking any supporting evidence' (2008, page 67). This review team base this serious reservation on some of the professional rhetoric about distributed leadership for schools. However, the same reservation equally applies to leadership discussions in early years.

Take another **perspective**

Unreflective sloganising diminishes the importance of the crucial ordinary day-by-day work with young children. The growing implication has to be that only by becoming some kind of 'leader' does a practitioner flourish into significance, rather than being stuck with humdrum routine tasks.

The argument of most users of 'everyone a leader' would probably be that their aim is to boost the professionalism of a workforce that is too prone to modest self-effacement – to empower people. However, an unintended consequence of heavy use of the phrase is the risk of marginalising sections of the workforce.

A consistent theme in our informal conversations with managers and heads has been that not everyone wants to step up in seniority with the associated responsibilities for taking the lead. The best practice shown in these settings was that the manager and senior team were alert to supporting practitioners through continued professional development to move out of their immediate comfort zone. Equally they respected and accepted the situation when practitioners clearly showed that a suggested direction was, for them, a step too far.

They also made a significant effort at the recruitment stage to ensure that any new staff understood the requirements for leadership as appropriate. Some examples also included a thorough application of the key person approach or a strong commitment to the outdoors to enable children to have adventures, supported by a robust system of risk-benefit assessment.

- What do you think? Should everyone lead? What may happen if you choose not to?

Leithwood *et al.* (2008) raise similar serious reservations about schools being full of leaders, that the more leadership there is the better, or that head teachers should aspire to be leaders of leaders. The words become meaningless. As the review team rightly ask, if everyone is a leader, then where are their followers? We agree with this challenge: it is an unwise aspiration to aim that everyone should be 'a' leader. A more appropriate and realistic aspiration is to create a working environment and thorough continued professional development so that team members can show their leadership qualities to be able to take a leading *role* in appropriate areas.

Additionally, it is unrealistic and irresponsible to push leadership upon practitioners who neither want it nor are motivated to develop themselves in the necessary direction. As SYMLOG indicates (page 64), some people are not dominant and will not embrace being given authority. You can enable practitioners to nurture the possibilities in themselves, sometimes by significantly boosting their shaky self-belief about what they can do. You can help by providing opportunities to take the first steps safely and address the factors that make it more likely that a new role will work. Providing a visible, positive role model of how it is possible to be an authoritative (task-orientated) and nurturant (relationship-orientated) early years leader will help. (Look back at Chapter 2 for discussion of these aspects of leadership.) Do not foist leadership upon anyone and everyone.

A balanced conclusion seems to be:
- An egalitarian outlook and respect for all members of the workforce is compatible with the truth that not everyone is a potential leader, unless 'leader' is diluted to the point of losing all meaning.
- Some people are able to take on a leadership role. Yet the social benefits to them of being part of the main staff group may be so important that they do not want the distance that leadership would necessarily entail. As a leader you are no longer 'just one of the team'.
- It seems likely that many (rather than few) people are capable of gaining the skills needed to take leading roles.
- Some people will be more strongly motivated to develop those skills, some will develop capability more easily and to a more sophisticated level.
- Some of the 'everyone a leader' rhetoric is reluctant to consider, and is even hostile to, ideas that effective leaders share some common characteristics.

However, there is a lot of support that some traits and behaviours do distinguish leaders who are successful from others (pages 37–39).

Make the connection with ... **your practice**

The possibility of leaderful organisations is an attractive concept in that it resolves some of the reservations about having or being an overall leader. However, it is not a concept that easily fits established working relationships.

A great deal of Joe Raelin's discussion (2003, 2010) focuses on the details of how to establish good teamworking. Think over some of these practical issues and how they have arisen, and been resolved (or not), in your own setting.

● Effective problem solving so often depends on the willingness of a group of people to participate. In your setting do most people contribute ideas, listen to each other and run with ideas rather than stopping at 'yes, but...'? The existence of a leaderful type of organisation in any line of work depends on people's readiness to speak up.

● Some reluctance or caution can arise from personal style. This may be a result of unpleasant experiences in previous settings when expressing new ideas or even when offering a slight disagreement was met with hostility.

● Shared leadership also requires that people other than the overall leader are willing to accept the risks – even mild ones – that accompany taking a leading role on improving practice.

● How do you get the shared purpose and considerate working atmosphere that is integral to leaderful practice? The equally important consideration is, what will get in the way?

The role of Early Years Professionals

A significant aim of the EYP status pathways has been to offer continued professional development for individual practitioners and to raise the professional status of the early years workforce. However, guidance from the Children's Workforce Development Council (CWDC, 2010) is very clear that the role envisaged for EYPs stretches beyond their individual continued professional development. Key themes, communicated also within local EYP networks material, are that EYPs will be responsible for leading practice within their provision. This section considers the practical issues around expectations of EYPs and the more general issues that apply about giving practitioners clear guidance about what and how to change.

A clear direction for everyone

Munton and Mooney (2001) report a series of linked studies on the process of self-assessment and related action planning in English day nurseries. The research showed that many settings struggled over the next steps after self-assessment. Providing specific materials to guide action planning was still not sufficient to ensure that practice did improve. Munton and Mooney reported that the nurseries which were rated as having successfully introduced change, shared common features. The staff were likely to indicate on their self-report questionnaire that they:

- had a good relationship with their immediate superior in the team
- were satisfied with their job and conditions of employment
- perceived themselves as having a say in the process of decision making in their nursery
- believed that their nursery was keen to introduce new ideas
- felt committed to their employer.

Munton and Mooney point out that these findings are consistent with theories of organisational development about the impact of the working environment on the behaviour and outlook of employees. These are issues that we discuss throughout this book. Even the most enthusiastic practitioners will struggle to determine their next steps without the context of commitment for change and a leader who shares the vision and clarifies the values and goals. Without this, keen practitioners can only focus on their own room or unit. If the organisational climate is unwelcoming to change then practitioners will carry on as normal and be disinclined to make even mild efforts, when the more senior 'they' either do not apparently care, or insist on holding tight to any decision making.

In the decade since Munton and Mooney published their research, there has been a significant development in initiatives aiming to equip more experienced early years practitioners to lever improvements to practice or significant change. There are several different ways that practitioners are invited to take this kind of leading role:

- Practitioners who gain EYP status are expected to take a strong lead within their setting. They are often described as, and exhorted to be, an agent for change.
- The role of Lead Practitioner also exists and has evolved to mean one of two things. The first is that a named individual will take a guiding role on a specific area of practice within their own setting, such as positive ways to guide children's behaviour. The second meaning is that the individual is given the responsibility within a local area to support and improve practice, for instance over communication within the national Every Child A Talker programme (England). This envisages a role more like a consultant or advisor. Both types of 'lead practitioner' share common ground over needing to understand the process of bringing about change in practice.

The next section focuses in particular on the role for EYPs, a group that at the time of writing (summer 2011) is estimated to have reached more than 7,000 practitioners, some of whom are managers. Many, probably all, of the points in this section apply equally to Lead Practitioners.

Can EYPs bring about change?

EYPs are often described as change agents. The CWDC guidance expresses it as 'EYPs are catalysts for change and innovation: they are key to raising the quality of early years provision and exercise leadership in making a positive difference to children's wellbeing, learning and development (2010, page 7). Leadership and support are twin themes in materials about EYPs, along with thorough individual professional development. The guidance links these aspects very closely for EYPs: 'It is through their *personal practice* in teamwork and collaboration that they *lead and support others* to bring about change, and thereby improve provision for, and practice with, children' (italics in original, CWDC, 2010, page 9).

Early Years Professionals are often exhorted to be visionary and promote a vision. These words are often linked with being inspirational: inspiring colleagues towards improvement or significant change – very transformational terms. However, individual practitioners in a setting cannot be visionary on their own, even if they are the manager. They have to connect with a shared vision, and related values for this setting. An EYP may be a central figure in a team's effort to identify, or reconnect, with, 'Why are we here?' and to ask, 'What are the implications for the children of this proposal?'

EYPs have an important role but the details will often be much closer to the transactional leadership model manager (Chapter 6) than the transformational leader (Chapter 7). Many of the practical skills explored within the longer EYP pathways are directly relevant to the transactional role. The ability of EYPs to offer a clear lead is closely linked with an enhanced grasp of the reasons behind choices over practice and their skills in being reflective about their own behaviour. Many EYPs are not managers and continue to work closely with children day by day. The aim is that they set an example of best practice, model ways of behaving with children and families and are able to articulate why they behave in that way.

Being realistic about change

In 2009 the CWDC commissioned a programme of research about EYPs and the first wave was published by Hadfield *et al.* (2010). They report that EYPs varied considerably over what they saw as the barriers to change in their setting. Not surprisingly, this depended most on the setting in which the EYPs applied their skills.

The factors that were mentioned more often as problematic for bringing about change were also those issues on which there was less agreement in the sample. For instance, 52 per cent of the sample agreed, or partially agreed, that individuals' reluctance to change was a barrier in their setting. Yet 38 per cent of the sample disagreed or partially disagreed that this was an issue. A barrier created by colleagues not being receptive to new ideas was seen as a barrier for change by a significant minority in the sample (35 per cent), yet just over half the sample (54 per cent) said this issue did not cause problems for them.

There was a higher level of agreement over which possible factors were not experienced by individual EYPs as a barrier to bringing about change. Only 19 per cent of the sample highlighted lack of staff as a barrier and 14 per cent pointed to the failure of the leaders in their setting to recognise the need for change. It is, however, useful to note that this minority in the EYP survey sample could still mean that roughly one in five EYPs might be struggling in a setting with insufficient staff and (again very roughly) slightly over one in ten EYPs might face an uphill struggle because they do not have the active support of their manager.

The authority to take a leading role

EYPs need the confidence and communication skills to explain possible changes in current practice and provide a convincing rationale. They need to have the time and suitable context for this adult-to-adult conversation, so time and space for staff or room meetings are essential. They need to offer a consistently good example in their own behaviour to model what they mean. However, unless their colleagues are already poised to move in this direction, showing improved practice through their own behaviour is unlikely to be effective without shared reflection and professional conversation away from daily work pressures.

The CWDC guidance (2010) offers a range of suggestions for how EYPs could lead and support improved practice. Viable options include running workshops or other means to share knowledge and ideas, one-to-one working with colleagues, taking on the role of coach or mentor (different roles discussed in Lindon, 2010b), specific projects with colleagues or rewriting policies that relate directly to improvements in practice. None of these practical and feasible strands of activity will work, unless the EYP is afforded respect in the setting and is imbued with the authority to undertake such initiatives. Some EYPs are also managers; equally some managers have not gained EYP status. EYPs who are not part of the senior team need to have the public support of their manager, shown through how the EYP's proposed work is introduced and actively supported in regular team meetings.

The experiences of some EYPs have been very positive. From our informal conversations with managers and EYPs themselves, it is clear that the best use of non-manager EYP status can be made when there is a thorough discussion about a special focus for this EYP within the team. It does seem to help when the practitioner is given the authority to lead on a specific aspect of practice in the setting. One example we heard was how an EYP had taken responsibility for developing a new tracking system. Another example was a focus on communication patterns, linked with an expectation that the EYP would undertake observations and feed back to practitioners.

Make the connection with ... **the working environment**

The challenge for the committed manager is to look at effective ways to use the skills of an EYP, but to avoid being naïve about persistent social patterns in the staff group, with power relations that these imply. Look back at the discussion about referent power on page 7.

Informal conversations with EYPs at training and network days – not linked with any of the settings thanked for this book – have raised the fact that some EYPs face an uphill struggle to lead on good practice. The most negative working environments have been those in which the EYPs find themselves sidelined by existing alliances within a staff group. Here, a group is hostile to any kind of change, which threatens their easy life, and the manager is unwilling or unable to dismantle the established power hierarchy in the staff group.

● What has been your experience and that of other EYPs?

Being inspirational

Discussion about leadership in early years often includes the idea that a leader should be inspirational: that she or he should be able to inspire enthusiasm and involvement in others. Dickins (2010) is not unusual in incorporating this aspect into her working definition of leadership in the context of creating a listening culture in early years settings. So it is not surprising that EYPs are frequently exhorted to be inspirational – a bedrock transformational leadership concept.

A positive interpretation of what it means to be an inspiration to others is that someone in position of leadership has enthusiasm: they set a can-do rather than a just-tick-over emotional tone to the provision. They show optimism that developments and focused change are possible. This kind of sharing emotional energy with others needs to be well seasoned with realism about the task ahead. Free-floating inspiration, like visions that fail to connect with reality, can risk disappointment for practitioners who are then disheartened and pessimistic about being revved up again in the future.

Lee (2009) discusses the observable features that are part of the shorthand of 'being an inspiration'. She highlights the role of EYPs, whose continued professional development has enabled them to guide colleagues. The feedback to the Best Practice Network (BPN) is that practitioners with this enhanced experience do not inspire in a vague way. Their impact, and the appreciation felt by colleagues, arises because of how the EYPs behave day by day. Lee describes the shorthand of REACH: that EYPs extend the 'reach' of their roles by being Reflective, Encouraging, Active, Creative and Holistic.

Take another **perspective**

Leaders who inspire in ways that are likely to make an observable difference are also a walking example that something is possible: that this person did reach these achievements or that here is an observable model of how to behave with children or parents.

Being seen as inspirational in a vague way will not be helpful for practice – just like giving vague feedback. The risk is that this kind of inspiration is a dead-end: that this person is wonderful, someone 'I'd like to be' but never will.

Early years needs passionate advocates and some individual early years leaders are veritable powerhouses of energy. However, effective leadership is compatible with different personal styles and everyone has to discover their own version.

Reflect on what you mean if you say, or write on an evaluation form, that a speaker at a conference is 'inspirational'.

- Recall keynote speakers, trainers or consultants whom you described in that way. What did you do as the direct consequence of what you heard?
- Or did nothing in particular change as the result of your positive experience at the time? Looking back, did you need something more practical than a feeling of being inspired?
- Or, to be honest, did you need to take responsibility for connecting ideas to your practice? The keynote speaker or trainer could not take this step for you.

Pedagogical leadership

The role envisaged for EYPs is mostly that of pedagogical leadership, an aspect of leading colleagues that can also be part of the contribution of a manager who also acts as a leader. There has been a fair amount of discussion in recent years about pedagogy and behaving as a pedagogue: what the terms mean, whether there is a shared understanding of meaning within the early years sector and whether the terminology is useful (Lindon, 2010b).

Pedagogy is sometimes described as the craft of teaching, but that wording only works well when the discussion makes clear that pedagogues are not exclusively teachers, nor are they only located in schools. The values and practice summed up by a specific pedagogical approach are not the same as a curriculum, nor are they restricted to a classroom. Some writers use the term social pedagogy with the aim of extending to a learning-rich approach to children's whole experience. This extension is probably not essential, so long as views of pedagogy do not get bogged down in the artificial care-education division.

What does it mean?

Pedagogy: the details of the individual or team approach about how to support children's learning wherever they spend their day. The core values, principles and chosen strategies create the pedagogical base for your practice.

Pedagogical thinking: an exploration to enable deeper understanding of what informs your practice and the reasons why you work in particular ways.

Pedagogical leadership: active support, guidance, explanation and setting a best practice example to other team members over a developmentally sound approach to supporting children's learning.

Understanding what you do and why

A discussion paper from Learning and Teaching Scotland (2005) uses the phrase 'pedagogical thinking' in ways that are closely related to being a reflective practitioner. The ideas also link with the aim that EYPs should be able to articulate their choices in practice, and the reasons behind those choices, as part of their leadership of colleagues. The LTS paper stresses that 'pedagogy needs explicitly to be seen to encompass a spirit of enquiry and professional dialogue about why we do what we do' (2005, page 3).

Make the connection with ... **a passion for the work**

The managers with whom we spoke in connection with this book all showed a passion for their work and the commitment to make a positive difference to children's experiences. They sought and nurtured a team for whom working in the setting was more than 'just any old job'.

The managers showed conscious pedagogical leadership in that they operated as a source of direct ideas. These suggestions were supported by a clear sense of why this would be a good idea, explaining their thoughts, and making space for practitioners to respond with their views. The atmosphere was such that practitioners could come back after reflection or observation with a, 'That's not working so well, how about if we...?'

The managers, and their senior team, were also visible out and about within the setting. Neither the staff nor the children were surprised to see the manager or deputy, because they were a daily presence, not cloistered in the office for most of the day.

- What have you noticed about the range of behaviour from managers in different early years settings where you worked, or have visited?

Pedagogical leadership is not all about the experience of the children – as important as that is. The children's experiences are highly dependent on adult choices over their own behaviour. Guiding change within practice needs to rest on an understanding of adults as learners and a perspective of lifelong learning. In some teams that outlook may have to be nurtured by the senior team, including the EYPs. Depending on their experience, some practitioners may take the view that they have been trained and that is it. A proportion of early years workforce have had less than positive experiences in their own schooling. A pedagogical leader needs to build up the confidence and view of themselves as a learner, which ideally should have happened over their years in statutory education.

Even confident adult learners need support that rests on an understanding of their current skills. Adults vary in temperament just like children – there will never be a one-size-fits-all for staff development. Even the most resilient team members will struggle if there is too wide a gap between their existing knowledge or skill base and what they are now being asked to tackle. Again, even the most confident of early years practitioners will benefit from being reminded of what they can do and what they have achieved in recent times, as well as clear and sensitive communication about the improvements that are needed.

Timing can be important, along with an accurate assessment of adults' current skills. Some EYPs, like some managers, talk about their leadership over best practice as a process like sowing a seed. Within a team or room meeting, they offer a clear and coherent suggestion. They encourage discussion with the aim that practitioners will understand, think over the idea and come back with their own thoughts. The EYP, or manager, obviously feels very positive about the suggestion, otherwise they would not have made it. They provide a lead, but have worked hard to create the working environment that means other staff feel able to take ownership of this idea and develop their own versions.

Make the connection with … **CPD in your team**

EYPs and members of the senior team of a setting can share the insights from their own continued professional development. However, these ideas will fall on more fertile ground when there is a shared understanding in a team that CPD is everyone's business.

- Do colleagues in your setting bring back ideas from training days and share them with the whole team? How?
- Do you have whole team closure days in which the team is able to explore an area of practice in depth, possibly supported by an external consultant?
- Do you access early years exhibitions, with the range of seminars they offer?

The owners of one private day nursery (thanked in the acknowledgements) took the staff group to one such exhibition and shared out the seminars between them. Everyone was equipped with the same feedback and evaluation forms and used the record to share ideas with the team in a meeting soon afterwards.

Leadership of complex centres

The increased focus on the need for early years leadership has partly arisen from the development of a considerable number of combined centres where the complexity of the work and professional relationships has necessitated a rethink of management and leadership.

There is a decades-long history of early years provision extending the boundaries of the core service offered. Some local authority day nurseries moved towards the family centre model over the late 1970s and 80s. From a similar period, combined centres aimed to bridge the artificial divide between 'care' and 'early education', and often to establish a strong community nursery model. Through the 1990s a series of government initiatives brought different versions of similar aims: neighbourhood nurseries, early years centres and early excellence centres. The first decade of the 21st century brought a significant increase in combined centres as neighbourhood Sure Start centres became Children's Centres. These centres varied in details of what they did but shared common ground in two areas:

- The need to lead across professional boundaries, because the group was not composed of people from a single professional background. This situation used sometimes to be called multi-disciplinary teams.

- The opportunities and challenges of multi-agency working. The aim of the centres was to bring several services to families – a one-stop shop – or to signpost them towards appropriate services.

Leading across professional boundaries

Some centres have been established from scratch, yet many have brought together existing settings or extended the services so far offered by a single setting, like a nursery school. Centres need confident application of management skills with the leadership skills that enable previously independent teams to feel they are a full part of this new group and not sidelined into what feels like an inferior role.

The combined nursery centres of the 1970s found different ways of dealing with the issues of a diverse team. Some heads established two-part provision in which day care ran largely separate from nursery education, with different sets of pay and conditions. Some centres, probably the minority, were established as a single coherent group with the same pay scale and conditions for everyone. These choices, and the necessity of making a decision, have continued into the children's centres, since the UK – unlike some Scandinavian countries – does not have a single early childhood specialist qualification.

More complex centres have a greater need for leadership and management than simpler provisions as more diverse strands of practice need, in some way, to be unified. Children's centres need clear leadership to ensure a consistent, shared vision of why the centre exists and what it aims to do. The head of centre has no option but to have senior colleagues taking significant responsibility for parts of the work. Good communication is even more crucial to ensure that different strands remain true to the overall vision, principles and a shared philosophy about how to work with children and families.

> ### What does it mean?
>
> **Leading across professional boundaries**: the task of effective leadership when a range of different professions are represented within the staff group and unrecognised differences may complicate working as a team.
>
> **Multi-agency working**: the task of drawing on the contribution of different agencies for the well being of children and families, possibly coordinating the work to ensure a coherent response that meets defined needs.

Mutual respect and professional understanding

Even when pay and conditions are put to one side, the challenge faced by the head of centre is to establish mutual respect between practitioners, who may otherwise still continue to uphold old professional barriers.

- The clear message throughout the organisational culture has to be that of teamwork: individuals have different professional backgrounds and they have complementary expertise to contribute positively to the staff group.

- In a large centre with many staff, this message needs to be regularly confirmed through joint, or mixed, team meetings and at least some shared continued professional development through training or in-house days.
- The centre head and the immediate senior team (two deputies are not unusual) have to set a consistently good example of inviting and listening to the views of each part of the centre.
- The senior group need to address any rumblings that the day-care section is 'just care', whereas the nursery school section does the (more important) 'education'.
- If the centre head is teacher-trained – which seems to be more usual – then she or he has a responsibility to extend their knowledge of under-threes to truly understand the underpinning of nurture and what is possible for these children.

Centre managers who effectively lead across professional boundaries could well conclude that they have created a secure bridge across when practitioners feel able to speak up and disagree in team meetings. Grint (2010) distinguishes between 'constructive dissent' rather than 'destructive consent':

- *Constructive dissent* is about expressing reservations in a supported, descriptive way, which acknowledges the other person's perspective and reserves the right to disagree – in other words, assertively. It is the leader's responsibility to create an atmosphere in which it is possible to disagree without being censored, and certainly without having your contribution dismissed on the grounds that your professional status is lower than the person or group with whom you have presumed to disagree.
- On the other hand, *destructive consent* is going along with something you doubt will work, or possibly can be close to certain will fail, because you do not want to risk disagreeing or would actually like this person or sub-group to fail in public. This is submissiveness or passivity.

Either of these situations can, of course, arise in provision that would not be described as a complex centre. However, the potential for destructive consent can increase in any setting where one part of the staff group feels undervalued for their expertise and has their informed views overlooked.

Make the connection with … **your practice**

Consider the ideas of constructive dissent and destructive consent.

- Can you recall situations from your own experience which could be described as an expression of constructive dissent in a team meeting or room discussion?
- On the other hand, can you recall examples of destructive consent? Maybe it is only on reflection that you can highlight now the dynamics of what happened.

You could also look at the discussion about assertiveness from page 100.

The whole centre

Some important issues for leading across professional boundaries have existed long before today's range of children's centres. During many years of nursery visits and early years consultancy we have been struck that settings with very good practice include everyone as part of the team. Roles, along with job descriptions, differ between: the manager and deputy; practitioners who are face to face with children and families; the cook in full day care; and, if required, the grounds person. For instance:

- Reflective managers of settings like day nurseries have long realised that the cook must be seen and treated as a member of the team. Healthy eating and sharing skills of food preparation and cooking with the children cannot be developed in isolation from the person who cooks, and possibly also orders, the food.
- Children are involved in the outdoors and decisions about maintenance. They are also familiar with the person responsible for the garden, larger grounds and maintenance. They talk with this person and ask about outdoor projects, while intriguing spontaneous events such as blocked drains are a joint focus of interest. Children take their lead from practitioners who should behave in ways that show clearly they respect the essential contribution of the cook or the gardener.
- In a large centre, the reception area and staff working there are particularly crucial. They set the tone for first-time and repeat visitors. Also they quite often overhear the informal conversation and opinions as families emerge from daily contact or attendance at special events or services. This can often help to inform the team of potential issues with families that can be addressed before they become a problem.

In recent visits and conversations with leaders of a range of children's centres, it is noticeable to us when the head of centre definitely has a finger on the pulse.

- She or he makes a serious effort to get out and be seen within the centre. Heads may ensure that they stand at the entrance every morning, visible to parents and ready to offer a welcome and chat.
- A head of centre who fully trusts the team may nevertheless decide that she or he will always do the walk-round visit of the setting with a family who wishes their child to join. The objective is that the family realises, for example, that the commitment to outdoor play is shared by the senior group.
- Heads of children's centres fully understand the range of work in the centre. They know, for example, the main issues in the under-threes unit and how the range of families there differs from children who join the centre in the nursery class. Heads know enough about the practical challenges in engaging families from a given part of the catchment area, for example, to be able to offer an opportunity to talk with the parent support officer who does home visits.

Multi-agency working

Duffy and Marshall (2007) highlight that the expectations for measurable outcomes from head teachers or heads of centre have increased significantly. The head still needs to be able to lead the team through example and be credible in terms of pedagogical leadership (page 133). The external pressure to make a measurable difference to children has increased, with a greater accountability that now stretches beyond the immediate experiences of children and families in the centre, to meeting targets related to resolving social problems. Often the watchword is about 'value for money' and how well resources are deployed to specific ends, including complex issues such as closing the gap between vulnerable and more advantaged families. This kind of target setting and attempts at quantitative measurement are a reminder that early years leadership has been affected by a more business-like approach.

Duffy and Marshall discuss the challenges of multi-agency working from the specific experience of the Thomas Coram Centre for Children and Families in London. Multi-agency working often co-exists with multi-professional teams but the two are different. Multi-agency working does not show an identical pattern in all centres, but what is consistent is that:

- a range of different services are offered to families under the same roof;
- the centre is a communications hub, signposting families to local services from different agencies which are not necessarily provided on site;
- the core team works together with other agencies and people from a different professional background.

A continuing issue for children's centres has been to what extent services should be available to all families within the catchment area, and how far it is appropriate to target some services to families who are judged especially to need them. Anning *et al.* (2006) discuss different structures that can exist in different children's centres; they are far from being identical forms of provision. The management and/or leadership task has to be established with clarity over the centre organisation. Some centre heads lead a team in which everyone is directly accountable to the head. Some heads coordinate the work of the centre, yet some team members are line-managed and accountable to a different agency. Sometimes a loose network of professionals may need to be coordinated within the centre because they are working with the same client group.

Heads of children's centres, and also of many extended schools, are unlikely to have direct professional experience of all the services which come together under their roof. So the question arises of how centre heads can effectively lead a service, when there are sections of which they have limited direct knowledge.

Understanding and respect

In a similar way to the point made about leading across professional boundaries (page 135), the centre head needs to set a good and active example of respect for other agencies, and the professionals mainly involved in those services. Drawing on Duffy and Marshall (2007), but equally from our informal conversations with centre heads, these appear to be the main issues:

- Centre heads need to show confidence in their own skills, but never in ways that risk minimising the skills of practitioners from different professional backgrounds. The whole senior team must set a consistently good example of active respect for the services being delivered within their physical boundaries, and those agencies to which they refer families – either an agreed formal referral or the suggestion that parents contact this service.
- People need to establish friendly working relationships which allow space to benefit from different specialisms: a sense of equality of contributions without an undertone of superiority from any one discipline. Multi-agency working can be a large jigsaw in which everybody needs some understanding of the big picture, but nobody stakes a claim to having the most important pieces.
- The whole senior team need to address the tone of discussion in team meetings to prevent staff tending towards habitual criticism of other agencies. The way forward is to problem-solve the specific issues highlighted. If there seems to have been a mis-communication, what happened, who contributed what to this misunderstanding, and what can we do now? Any complaints need to be supported by definite actions for improvement; they should not be accepted and left as generalised and un-actionable moans.

Critical incident analysis or technique

The final bullet point above is a brief version of critical incident analysis: a reflective and analytical approach that has a long history of application in a variety of professions, including social care and education. Anning *et al.* (2006) describe use of the critical incident tool within integrated children's services. The approach has proved useful both for issues around leading across professional boundaries in integrated centres and also for considering the detail of potentially troublesome issues in multi-agency working.

> ### What does it mean?
>
> **Critical incident analysis**: an approach that recognises a significant incident, usually one in which practice has not gone smoothly, in order to understand events fully and identify what can be learned for future improvement.

The head of one children's centre described to us how the technique had been valuable for taking a step back to understand what was happening when multi-agency work became problematic. The point made was that it was professional to avoid the trap of trying to attribute blame for why a joint endeavour had not been successful. It was more positive, and more effective in the long run, to work out why things had gone wrong by describing the actual incidents that occurred, and using these to come up with a solution. There is a definite connection here with the skills of helping children with conflict resolution: skills that thoughtful practitioners share steadily with young children (Lindon, 2009b). The aim is to avoid focusing on 'who started it?' or 'whose fault is it?', but rather to address 'what happened?' and to see the problem as one that 'we' have and hence 'what could we do about it?' Once more, this is consistent with the assertive approach (page 104).

The exact detail of critical incident analysis varies between reports of its use. The main features are that the group (supported by the leader or an external consultant) commits to an analysis, which is as objective as possible, of events that are perceived as problematic. You consider:

- What happened in this incident: when, where, who was involved, what was the context, who said and did what?
- Why does this incident stand out, why is it judged to be critical – at least by one of the involved parties?
- On reflection, did the involved parties bring set expectations or bias to the event? Participants can only be sure about their own view, although they may have opinions about what other people brought to the event.
- If more than one team member was involved, do we need to air these differing views?
- Can some team members, not involved at all in the incident, bring fresh insight using open-ended questions? Are there other ways of looking at it?
- What can be learned: are there alternative interpretations rather than the 'obvious' one? Were there choice points, where it was possible for one of us, for example, to have behaved differently – possibly leading to an alternative outcome?

Undoubtedly, problems can arise when one profession does not fully understand the approach and main aims of another. The centre is responsible for extending the knowledge of other professions with whom they come in contact. It is unprofessional to say, 'They don't understand us; they don't appreciate how much we do' and yet do little to counteract this impression. Likewise, it is responsible to extend your own understanding of the key approaches of other professionals and agencies. A key issue in communication is that approaches are often subtly different. For example, the ground rules for confidentiality and information sharing are set differently across professions. There can be uncertain boundaries between who does what even between professions working under the same roof of a children's centre. Anomalies can complicate secure practice on crucial issues such as the shared safeguarding obligation.

Pause for reflection

Cummings (2008) reports using the critical incident technique within two children's centres. Her aim was to support those separate teams to explore issues around their work where collaboration was needed with other agencies.

- One general finding was that a team would sometimes attribute problems over trust, shared aims or mis-communication, to the approach of other agencies. Use of the technique within an in-house development day enabled practitioners to recognise and accept that some of these problems existed within the mixed staff group.
- The leadership challenge was to address the need for regular communication, to iron out different use of the same words and establish shared aims which incorporated active respect for different sections of a large centre.

The report provides very practical pointers for leadership of integrated children's centres, such as the need to give value-based reasons for contentious decisions. Many of the ideas are applicable to other kinds of settings. Look at Alison Cummings' report (online address on page 146) and consider which issues that she raises echo situations which you face now, or have in the past.

Children's centre teams will sometimes be part of a referral of children and families to an outside agency. However, equally an outside agency will refer parents to the centre for one or more of their services. Reflection on past misunderstanding and frustration can lead to better practical decisions for the future. A valuable rule of thumb, shared by more than one head of centre, is to make sure that the view of the family is clear. What do parents or other family carers believe – informed or possibly misinformed by another agency – that your centre is likely to offer to their children?

For example, why does this family think you are making a home visit? Do they, for instance, believe that a pattern of home visits will continue as long as they would welcome them? However, the centre approach is that only a limited number of home visits are currently made available for parents, who would not otherwise feel confident, or sufficiently organised, to go to the centre. Should the centre's policy change here? Or, on reflection, are there good reasons not to offer a full-scale home visiting service? With clear explanation, with repetition if necessary, will most parents accept what is a less good option from their standpoint?

Whose vision, values and priorities?

Klavins (2008) reviewed some key issues arising from the requirement that children's centres should involve parents in the process of evaluating current services and future directions. She draws out serious tensions and occasional conflicts that have to be resolved by leaders of these integrated services.

Klavins points out that the dominant approach over the 1990s (including Sure Start) was to consult with parents in order to identify what would be the top priorities on a local basis. By the middle of the following decade, children's centre leaders found themselves in the position of inviting parents to evaluate services that would not have been in their top priority list had they been asked. Centre leadership could be under pressure, directly linked with government funding streams, to meet national health targets over reduction of smoking or obesity. Yet professional judgment, arising from an effective partnership with local families, could be that parents would more welcome support on other issues or specific activities like craft classes. Some centres found that the childcare element of the service offer did not meet local family preference to spend time with their children and have a community focus. The pressure on children's centres to offer childcare was part of the government agenda to get more women as mothers into, or back into, the workforce.

The centre leader had to address the implications of developments that were clearly wanted by local families. One example was parents' request for more services to be available at weekends and evenings. The provision of such services would have implications for working conditions for the team and, much like other partnership issues in any early years provision (Lindon, 2009a), contrasts a clear preference from parents with the preference of staff not to work outside usual hours.

Considered choices and overall responsibility

Klavins' overall point, that centre heads have to make some tough choices, was echoed in conversations with heads that have contributed to our ideas for this book. One head was clear that centre staff must be able to articulate shared answers to deceptively simple questions: 'why are we doing this?', 'who is it for?' and 'so what?' You can be clear about the answer to a question and yet uncertain how, in detail, to implement it to make it work. Another centre articulated a core value of 'children first, everybody else afterwards': a stance that led them to evaluate everything against what was the impact on the children, what made a positive difference for the individuals who only had one go at their early childhood.

Effective leadership depends upon gathering reliable information from service users, never forgetting that the children themselves will have views.

- A centre could focus on developing services that would be actively welcomed by the local community and find some way to deal with national pressures. They could try for some middle ground or aim to tailor what they offered to fit government priorities.
- The commitment to consultation with parents highlights that, of course, there will be different views within the group, even when the centre serves what looks like a relatively homogeneous local community.
- Some services will aim to meet specific needs of children or families. Centre heads pointed out that a warm, personal welcome, enabling parents or other family carers to feel comfortable, at home in the centre, is at the heart of avoiding the negative message of services that stigmatises families.
- Wheeler and Connor (2009) make a valid criticism of over-use of the phrase 'hard to reach', pointing out that some families take the view that services or practitioners, not them, are the ones hard to reach. Centre heads often agree with this and stress the importance of avoiding any sense that the problem with under-used services or events must lie with the sub-group of families at which they were targeted.

- If a centre team, led by their head, is serious about gaining feedback from families then they have to make it easy for these fellow adults to express doubts as well as enthusiasm (more about this aspect of partnership in Lindon, 2009a).

Some children's centres are in urban areas, but not all of them. So a city or large town model cannot apply to all centres. Heads need to understand what parents and families in more rural areas need and want. The head of the centre in a small town pointed out to us that it was fairly obvious for them when they saw a family who they realised used none of the facilities. Centres in much larger communities don't know everyone and so will not succeed with this visual check. The family support officer in one centre we visited had introduced postcode tracking to identify the take-up on services by smaller sections of the catchment area.

Constructive discontent and wicked problems

Leadership in and for children's centres can undoubtedly be complicated by the shifting expectations set by the government, and the sometimes poor fit with what is assessed to be the wiser next step based on extensive local knowledge. One of the heads of centre in Klavins' (2008) study had a wall poster with the message 'keep swimming against the tide' which was rather depressing, in our view.

Grenier (2003) talks of 'constructive discontent' (see also page 137) to sum up the challenge of identifying how an existing nursery school could transform itself into a children's centre which was, and was seen as, directly relevant to the immediate local community. The concept of constructive discontent – called 'intelligent dissatisfaction' in the organisational behaviour literature – is often used as part of creative problem solving. The aim is to express dissatisfaction with the current situation, but to go beyond griping to reach a clearer idea of what is the matter and how might the situation be improved. Constructive discontent is necessary to deal with problems that do not have an easy, tried-and-tested solution.

Grint (2005, 2009, 2010) discusses the difference between critical, tame and wicked problems. These link to the three types of change, as described from page 71.

- *Critical* problems may be urgent, even a crisis, but there are systems and procedures in place and staff know what to do. Often these result in 'everyday' change.
- *Tame* problems are relatively familiar, although not necessarily easy to resolve. Similar situations have arisen before and there is understanding about what will most likely work best. Both of these are clearly management problems and often are solved through 'enhancement' change.
- In contrast, *wicked* problems are complex issues which have a high level of uncertainty and isolating cause-and-effect is not at all clear. Even very experienced staff will not have all the answers. Furthermore, they may have an accurate view of what needs to be done, but they and their team are not able to make everything happen. These are more clearly leadership issues.

Children's centres, and to a lesser extent other early years settings, are being tasked with wicked problems requiring 'radical' solutions. A key example is the expectation that what happens in children's centres will make a significant difference to the life chances of children from vulnerable households and will therefore help to close the poverty gap. Such social problems are highly complex because the possible solutions are not located exclusively in the organisation itself. Hence they are out of your control. Closing the poverty gap, addressing rising obesity levels or reducing smoking cannot be resolved in a children's centre. Yet these are all issues that have been placed within the responsibility of children's centres at some point.

Children's centres have been pushed in opposite directions by trying to reconcile serving the local community, giving an active welcome to all families and yet targeting services to those who could most benefit. This dilemma has been fuelled by unhelpful official statements that allegedly sharp-elbowed middle-class parents fill the baby massage classes or whatever at the local centre. There seems to be more assertion than evidence in some of these statements. Some children's centre leaders and teams take a more pragmatic view, not least that children, and sometimes their parents, can benefit from a mixed group of needy and non-needy families. A considered choice is necessary if an event or series of events is offered to a specific group. Part of this care is to avoid the impression that the service is just for 'incompetent' families, who will then feel stigmatised, as equally the 'competent' will become deterred from using the service.

Finding your contribution to wicked problems

Wicked problems have much in common with no-right-answer dilemmas.

- Trying in vain to reach the one right answer is less important than leadership that ensures collaborative discussion and commitment to the chosen way forward. Everyone needs to understand the advantages and disadvantages of the chosen course and grasp why this choice has been made.
- The constructive approach to wicked problems is to recognise that they highlight inconsistencies in practice, or shine a bright light on the contradictory requirements placed on this service from different sources.
- The best course will be the most realistic option that is compatible with non-negotiable values in the setting. If there is uncertainty around core values, then this has to be addressed, otherwise possible solutions that try to help can go against the principles of the service.
- Finally, no service can risk accepting the full responsibility for resolving wicked problems; who else shares this responsibility?

As told to us, the confident leader of early years services in one local authority was willing to speak out in joint meetings. She stated that it was unacceptable for other services to talk about early years provision as if this service was the main, or only, one which should be closing the poverty gap. The task was complex and involved everybody, so what were the health or housing services or the schools doing – and in detail? Three cheers for that challenge – which was apparently met with some surprise around the table in question.

Leaders and their teams have no choice but to cope with a situation that cannot be problem-solved out of existence. In fact, misery results from trying to change things that cannot be changed. Coping better through continued discussion is critical, as uncertainty and a level of ambiguity will remain. Keith Grint advises that such a situation often requires a 'clumsy' solution rather than an 'elegant' one. There will be loose ends, all issues will not be solved but this resolution is the best way forward, given all the information. It may not be perfect, but it enables everyone to cope better.

The C4EO (2010) report about approaches to effective early intervention uses the fine phrase 'grasping the nettle' to sum up the complexities of balancing active respect for families with the professional judgment that parents could be doing much better by their children. An unavoidable challenge for any early years leader is to acknowledge that bed of nettles, grasp the relevant bunch and, with the full support of her or his team, deal with the inevitable stings that will come their way with the more intractable problems.

Resources

- **Anning, A., Cottrell, D., Frost, N., Green, J. and Robinson, M.** (2006) *Developing Multiprofessional Teamwork for Integrated Children's Centres.* Maidenhead: Open University Press.
- **Aubrey, C.** (2007) *Leading and Managing in the Early Years.* London: Sage.
- Centre for Excellence and Outcomes in Children and Young People's Services (2010) *Grasping the Nettle: Early intervention for children, families and communities.* www.c4eo.org.uk/themes/earlyintervention/files/early_intervention_grasping_the_nettle_full_report.pdf
- Children's Workforce Development Council (2010) *On the Right Track: Guidance to the standards for the award of Early Years Professional Status.* Leeds: CWDC. www.cwdcouncil.org.uk/assets/0000/9008/Guidance_To_Standards.pdf
- **Cummings, A.** (2008) *Only Connect: Using a critical incident tool to develop multi-agency collaboration in two children's centres.* National College for School Leadership. www.nationalcollege.org.uk/docinfo?id=17322&filename=only-connect-full-report.pdf
- **Day, C., Sammons, P., Hopkins, D., Harris, A., Leithwood, K., Gu, Q., Brown, E., Ahtaridou, E. and Kington, A.** (2009) *The Impact of School Leadership on Pupil Outcomes: Final Report.* Department for Children Schools and Families with National College for School Leadership. Full report as below, for summary search by RB108. www.education.gov.uk/publications/eOrderingDownload/DCSF-RR108.pdf
- **Dickins, M.** (2010) *Leadership for Listening.* London: National Children's Bureau.
- **Doyle, M.E. and Smith, M.K.** (2001) 'Shared leadership'. *The Encyclopaedia of Informal Education.* www.infed.org/leadership/shared_leadership.htm

- **Duffy, B. and Marshall, J.** (2007) 'Leadership in multi-agency work'. In Siraj-Blatchford, I. Clarke, K. and Needham, M. (eds) *The Team Around the Child: Multi-agency working in the early years.* Stoke-on-Trent: Trentham Books.
- **Dunlop, A.W.** (2008) *A Literature Review on Leadership in Early Years.* Search by title on www.ltscotland.org.uk
- **Grenier, J.** (2003) *Small Steps, Slippery Mud: 100 days as a nursery school head.* www.tinyurl.com/slipperymud
- **Grint, K.** (2005) 'Problems, problems, problems: the social construction of "leadership"'. *Human Relations,* 58, 11, 1467–94.
- **Grint, K.** (2009) *Wicked Problems and the Role of Leadership.* www.informalnetworks.co.uk/Wicked_problems_and_the_role_of_leadership.pdf
- **Grint, K.** (2010) *Leadership: A very short introduction.* Oxford: Oxford University Press.
- **Hadfield, M., Jopling, M., Royle, K. and Waller, T.** (2010) *First National Survey of Practitioners with Early Years Professional Status.* Wolverhampton: Centre for Developmental and Applied Research in Education. www.cwdcouncil.org.uk/assets/0001/1377/First_National_Survey_of_Practitoners_with_EYPS.pdf
- **Harris, A.** (2002) *Distributed Leadership in Schools: Leading or misleading?* www.icponline.org/index.php?option=com_content&task=view&id=130&Itemid=50
- **Harris, A. and Spillane, J.** (2008) *Distributed School Leadership: Developing tomorrow's leaders.* Abingdon: Routledge.
- **Henderson-Kelly, L. and Pamphilon, B.** (2000) 'Women's models of leadership in the child care sector'. *Australian Journal of Early Childhood*, 25, 1, 8–12, March.
- **Klavins, L.** (2008) *Parents Matter: How can leaders involve parents in the self-evaluation process and further development of children's centre and extended school services?* National College for School Leadership. www.nationalcollege.org.uk/docinfo?id=17325&filename=parents-matter-full-report.pdf
- **Lawrence, Y., Robins, D. and Twells, B.** (2008) *Teachers into Leaders: Networking and leadership development.* www.nationalcollege.org.uk/docinfo?id=17422&filename=teachers-into-leaders-summary.pdf
- Learning and Teaching Scotland (2005) *Let's Talk About Pedagogy: Towards a shared understanding for early years education in Scotland.* Glasgow: Learning and Teaching Scotland. www.ltscotland.org.uk/Images/talkpedagogy_tcm4-193218.pdf
- **Lee, M.** (2009) 'Being an inspiration'. *Early Years Educator*, 11, 5, 4. www.bestpracticenet.co.uk/eye-v11-n5-sep09.html#p10
- **Leithwood, K., Day, C., Sammons, P., Harris, A. and Hopkins, D.** (2008) *Successful School Leadership: What It Is and How It Influences Pupil Learning.* Department for Children Schools and Families with National College for School Leadership. http://education.gov.uk/publications/eOrderingDownload/RR800.pdf
- **Lindon, J.** (2009a) *Parents as Partners: Positive relationships in the early years.* London: Practical Pre-School Books.
- **Lindon, J.** (2009b) *Guiding the Behaviour of Children and Young People: Linking theory and practice 0–18 years.* London: Hodder Education.

- **Lindon, J.** (2010b) *Reflective Practice and Early Years Professionalism.* London: Hodder Education.
- **Lingard, B., Hayes, D., Mills, M. and Christie, P.** (2003) *Leading Learning: Making hope practical in schools.* Maidenhead: Open University Press.
- **Muijs, D., Aubrey, C., Harris, A. and Briggs, M.** (2004) 'How do they manage? A review of the research on leadership in early childhood'. *Journal of Early Childhood Research,* 2, 2, 157–89.
- **Munton, A. and Mooney, A.** (2001) *Integrating Self-assessment into Statutory Inspection Procedures: The impact of the quality of day care provision.* http://education.gov.uk/publications/standard/publicationDetail/Page1/RR285
- National College for Leadership of Schools and Children's Services and C4EO (2011) *Resourceful Leadership: How directors of children's services improve outcomes for children.* www.nationalcollege.org.uk/docinfo?id=144732&filename =resourceful-leadership-dcs.pdf
- **Pound, L.** (2008) 'Leadership in the early years', in Miller, L. and Cable, C. (eds) *Professionalism in the Early Years.* London: Hodder Education.
- **Raelin, J.** (2003) *Creating Leaderful Organisations: How to bring out leadership in everyone.* San Francisco, CA: Berrett-Kohler.
- **Raelin, J.** (2010) *The Leaderful Fieldbook: Strategies and activities for developing leadership.* Boston, MA: Nicholas Brealey Publishing.
- **Rodd, J.** (2006) *Leadership in Early Childhood.* Maidenhead: Open University Press.
- **SEDL** (2011) *Leadership Characteristics That Facilitate School Change.* www.sedl.org/change/leadership/character.html
- **Siraj-Blatchford, I. and Manni, L.** (2007) *Effective Leadership in the Early Years Sector.* London: Institute of Education.
- **Spillane, J.** (2005) 'Distributed leadership'. *The Educational Forum,* Winter. http://course1.winona.edu/lgray/el756/Articles/Spillane.htm
- **Spillane, J., Halverson, R. and Diamond, J.** (2001) *Investigating School Leadership Practice: A distributed perspective.* www.sesp.northwestern.edu/docs/invldrshpperspective.pdf
- **Thornton, K.** (2006) 'Notions of leadership in the New Zealand ECE Centres of Innovation Programme'. *New Zealand Annual Review of Education,* 15, 153–67. http://www.victoria.ac.nz/nzaroe/subject-area/.%5C../1996/.%5C../2005/pdf/text-thornton.pdf
- **Waniganayake, M.** (2002) 'Growth of leadership: With training can anyone become a leader?' In Nivala, V. and Hujala, E. (eds) *Leadership in Early Childhood Education: Cross-cultural perspectives.* Oulu: Oulu University Press. http://herkules.oulu.fi/isbn9514268539/
- **Waniganayake, M., Morda, R. and Kapsalakis, A.** (2000) 'Leadership in child care centres: is it just another job?' *Australian Journal of Early Childhood,* 25, 1, 13–20.
- **Wheeler, H. and Connor, J.** (2009) *Parents, Early Years and Learning: Parents as partners in the Early Years Foundation Stage – principles into practice.* London: National Children's Bureau. www.peal.org.uk/resources/practice-examples

Developing your transactional management expertise

In this chapter we will explore the interpersonal aspects of the leadership role: the leadership and management of individuals and groups. We focus on the two key areas of skills: task and maintenance skills. These emerged initially from the study of group dynamics and were extended by research around the contingency theories of leadership discussed in Chapter 2.

We will return to our stance (on page 74) that transactional leadership is not actually leadership at all, but a key interactive side of management. Therefore, from here on we use the phrase *transactional management* in order to distinguish the concept from true leadership based on transformation and personal qualities (the focus of Chapter 7).

In this chapter we start by looking at the more technical side of management. We then move on to explore the complexity of interpersonal relationships at work and their significance for transactional management.

The main sections of this chapter are:
- the management arena
- leading an effective work group
- transactional behaviours for the manager.

The management arena

In discussing what leadership means, we have been concerned to stress the importance of management and what managers need to do. Any organisation will struggle if the person allegedly in the role of manager is unable, or disinclined, to use the skills discussed in this section. In this sense early years provision is no different from any other organisation. Your core work should focus on the children and their families, who are poorly served in settings with weak or inconsistent management. Without a firm foundation, there will be little point in getting excited about ideas around visionary leadership; there will be no basis from which to lead. We expressed reservations about the concept of distributed leadership in Chapter 5. A considerable amount of what is meant in the more practical discussions of that model is covered within this chapter.

The core task of managers

If you look back to page 78, Figure 3.2 gave a full organisational model. In this chapter, we are going to focus on the separate elements of that model. So, first of all, Figure 6.1 shows only the managerial aspects.

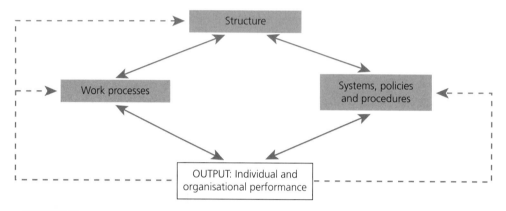

Figure 6.1 The managerial organisational set

The managerial role revolves around sorting out the best structure for the organisation. It is focused on the details of the work itself, and the task behaviours necessary to accomplish the results that matter:

- Who should report to whom? As a manager, you want to avoid a situation in which the holiday scheme team bring every little detail to your office. On the other hand, you do not want them making significant decisions, such as taking the children on a full day train journey, without talking with you or your deputy.
- How is the physical environment organised? Have you made best use of the available space and do individual practitioners fulfil their shared responsibility for ensuring a welcoming and safe environment for children and families?
- What are the systems, policies and procedures needed to ensure that your regular work runs smoothly, avoidable mistakes are not repeated and you are as prepared as possible for the unexpected or emergencies?

Necessary skills of the manager

All managers need three broad kinds of skill: technical, people and conceptual skills. You might like to look back at page 37 when we discussed qualities that are needed in a leader, including confidence, sociability and the skills of thinking. These qualities also apply to being an effective manager.

Technical skills encompass the knowledge about methods, processes, procedures and techniques for the work of this organisation and the skills to use relevant tools and equipment. Managers need to understand the details of child development in order to have realistic expectations for young children's progress and behaviour.

They need to determine how children's development is tracked, so that they can offer effective support to practitioners who are unclear. They implement accepted procedures for recruitment of new staff and thoroughly understand the process of referral, if there are safeguarding concerns about a child.

Managers inevitably have to complete a fair amount of paperwork, or the computerised equivalent. Even if they have someone else who is responsible for doing tasks like book-keeping, managers need to know enough to check that all is well. There are telephone calls, scheduled and unscheduled meetings (some more formal than others) and it is crucial to keep an eye on what is happening in the organisation: what is sometimes called 'managing by wandering around'. A very great deal of a manager's work is communicating. According to McCall *et al.* (1978), low to middle levels of management spend well over half their time talking to other people, a figure rising to 90 per cent at the top level. The average proportion of time spent communicating for managers was between 65 per cent and 75 per cent.

So, managers need *people skills*. Managers require the ability to communicate clearly and effectively and to establish effective co-operative relationships. Dealing with others requires knowledge about human behaviour and interpersonal relationships. Managers need to understand the possible links between feelings, motives and attitudes to the behaviour they see. These issues are discussed from page 153, later in this chapter.

Managers also need *conceptual skills*. They need analytical ability and logical thinking. They also need concept formation skills – the ability to see the wood for the trees – creativity in idea generation, problem solving, anticipation of change and the recognition of both problems and opportunities. The concept of reflective practice familiar within the early years sector (Lindon, 2010b) is part of this set of skills.

Power and influence

Influence is about gaining and using power (discussed earlier on page 5). This may be done sensitively and pleasantly, or inappropriately in an abrupt or confrontational way. The objective for the manager is to make it easier for practitioners to accept your suggestions, by using your power in an authoritative way when required – rather than making it harder for them by using power inappropriately, or not drawing on it at all.

Legitimate power should be used appropriately, and by 'appropriate' we mean that:
- It is reasonable for a superior to ask practitioners to cover responsibilities that are within their job description, such as completing the records of their key children or having regular conversations with parents.
- It is not appropriate for a manager to ask practitioners to 'do it for me', or to imply that their reluctance makes life difficult for the manager.

The second approach muddies what should be a clear work relationship (using legitimate power) with the emotional dimension of a personal relationship. This confusion erodes legitimate power being used credibly by the manager. It devalues that source of appropriate influence when it is critical, for example when a practitioner's work falls well short of the standards for the job.

Figure 6.2 summarises the likely effects of using different forms of power as a transactional manager to influence your team. While each of these types of power can be identified as separate sources, they are usually intermixed.

Legitimate or position power is the source most closely tied to formal organisation and hence to management. Legitimate power carries with it reward power (giving interesting work, praising) and coercive power (including reprimands and formal warnings over poor practice). Managers may have higher levels of expertise which have helped the person to reach this position of greater authority. A current view is that managers should have expertise (expert power), otherwise why are they in this senior position? Expert power carries with it information power, reward power (so long as colleagues value this person's expertise) and possibly some coercive power (maybe colleagues want to feel knowledgeable and in tune with this person).

People who reward others informally within an organisation are likely to be given referent power, and hence may become leaders of a sort, as can those with 'charisma'. However, such sources of power alone are insufficient for these people to become managers. You have to be appointed into the position of manager. However, individuals with considerable referent power can exercise a form of leadership within a setting that any manager is unwise to ignore.

Coercive power is, in general, to be avoided unless all other options have failed and the manager is at her or his wits' end. If necessary, coercive power must be based on legitimate power. As the manager you have the right to expect compliance to your requests, especially when these reflect the job description for this practitioner. It may feel like your most disliked option, but there are times when it is fully appropriate to use coercive power in a forceful way. Perhaps you need to make crystal clear to one practitioner that, 'Keeping the records of your key children up to date is not optional'. Maybe another practitioner has yet again broken confidence about families, despite very clear guidance from you in the past. Now could be the time for, 'I'm writing a formal warning about your

behaviour. Recognise that this is the first step in the disciplinary procedure.'
Managers sometimes need to use coercive power in an assertive way, stating quite
clearly the rules of employment and the way the hierarchy works.

Source of leader	Type of outcome for staff member		
Influence	Commitment	Compliance	Resistance
REFERENT POWER	LIKELY	*POSSIBLE*	*POSSIBLE*
	If request is believed to be important to leader	If request is believed to be unimportant to leader	If request is for somthing that will bring harm to leader
EXPERT POWER	LIKELY	*POSSIBLE*	*POSSIBLE*
	If request is persuasive and subordinates share leader's task goals	If request is persuasive but subordinates are apathetic about task goals	If leader is arrogant and insulting, or subordinates oppose task goals
LEGITIMATE POWER	*POSSIBLE*	LIKELY	*POSSIBLE*
	If request is polite and very appropriate	If request or order is seen as legitimate	If arrogant demands are made or request does not appear proper
REWARD POWER	*POSSIBLE*	LIKELY	*POSSIBLE*
	If subtle, used very personally	If used mechanically, impersonally	If used manipulatively, arrogantly
COERCIVE POWER	VERY UNLIKELY	*POSSIBLE*	LIKELY
	If used helpfully, unthreateningly	If used aggressively or maniplatively	

Figure 6.2 Major sources of leader influence and the likely response from staff

Focus on the process of getting things done

Blanchard and Lorber (1984) developed the *One Minute Manager* approach,
which emphasises the importance of making every moment count. They propose
an 'ABC' of management. Readers will be familiar with the ABC approach to
observing in order to make sense of children's behaviour. In that case the three
elements are antecedent, behaviour, consequence – the management version is
very similar. Blanchard and Lorber describe it as follows:

- A stands for *activator* – what the manager has to do before anyone can be
  expected to accomplish a goal.

- B is for *behaviour* – what the other person says or does related to this aspect of their work.
- C is for the *consequences* – what the manager does when someone accomplishes or fails to accomplish the goal.

For example, in an early years setting, the *activator* could be the necessary explanations required for Nancy, a new member of staff, to operate properly as a key person to named children. The *behaviour* is what Nancy is observed to do in terms of behaving as a key person. The *consequences* would be praise for what Nancy has understood and implemented, such as establishing the key person time with her children as agreed. Nancy is clearly uncertain about how informal observations are shared between staff in the room, because she is reluctant to accept the post-it notes from Sean about her key children. Her manager needs to tell her those aspects of behaving as a key person that Nancy has not yet implemented.

In order to help all the staff, the manager needs to implement what Blanchard and Lorber call 'the nuts and bolts' of the one minute manager which have the acronym PRICE:

- *Pinpoint* – you define what you want staff to do in observable and measurable terms. For example, Nancy needs to be ready with a personal welcome and goodbye to the parents of her key children each day. If she is not in the nursery, then Sean will do this in her place, because he is her partner in key working with these families.
- *Record* – ensure you are accurately recording what happens. Does Nancy have a key person time each day? Does she have a suitably flexible plan for what will happen in that time slot over the next week?
- *Involve* – share what you have noticed with Nancy and be specific. Let her know that her focus on short-term planning and children's current interests is right for the special key person time. However, she has misunderstood about taking responsibility for the records of her key children. She does not have to make all the observations. Within the room, her colleagues will contribute what they have noticed, as Sean offered. Nancy is responsible for integrating the observations into the personal records. Nancy's manager will explain and describe, not criticise, and will let Nancy respond with her own questions or comments.
- *Coach* – if necessary, the manager will help Nancy to work with her colleagues over observations and how these are shared. As appropriate, the manager will also make sure that Nancy understands the partner key working system with Sean.
- *Evaluate* – after a reasonable period, evaluate how Nancy is progressing. Have any problems emerged? Is she still confused about some issues? If so, then more work may be needed, as you pinpoint exactly what now needs to be done, and begin the process again.

It is critical for managers to remember that the most important part of the job within the centre is to achieve high standards in the provision for children and families, and any related services that are offered. Managers have to focus on the satisfactory performance of every practitioner in completing the necessary and agreed tasks. Ideally, you wish that everything will be done with a strong sense of commitment from every member of staff – with minimal effort or pressure from you as a manager. Some settings may come close to this ideal, but it will not happen all the time.

It is unrealistic to struggle for high levels of commitment from less motivated staff, or those who are still on the journey towards fully understanding, for example, why they should help young children tidy up materials into the right basket. You continue to explain why staff must not heave play resources into any old basket. For the time being their compliance with your clear instruction will be sufficient to get toys into the right basket and children will be able to make choices and resource their own play. It is not necessary that doubtful staff are happy about it. Simply telling the practitioners 'this is how it will be' may not make you feel comfortable or happy, but sometimes firmness is needed to get things done in a timely fashion. Obviously, you look for every opportunity to show the staff why you have given them this direction, through what is happening with the children.

Figure 6.3 presents another part of the full organisational model (from page 78) in which we focus on just the transactional aspects. The focus on people, their individual motivation and the morale of the group is crucial. It is also necessary to get the job done by ensuring that individual capabilities meet – or exceed – the requirements of this job. Managers typically like staff who directly report to them to be effective in working with others, and also to perform their work well. Managers have a much tougher role if they have to deal with staff who are either abrasive or passive, and who do not fulfil the responsibilities of their job. It is often difficult to deal with the staff member who is interpersonally skilled and well liked – even charming – who really does not perform well in the job.

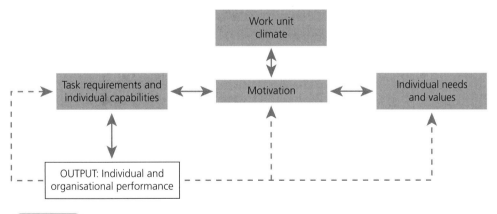

Figure 6.3 The transactional organisational set

Primarily, managers need to monitor what individual staff do on a continuous basis and keep their eye on the goals that are meaningful for the setting. This means keeping track of what is going on in an objective way. Furthermore, managers need to make clear people's roles and responsibilities, both on an individual basis and within the group. Only within this context can managers provide regular, accurate and useful information to staff about how they are working, on a more or less constant basis – certainly not just in official (maybe annual) appraisal sessions.

Skills in group working as a manager

In this section we look at how the basics of working with groups underlie effectiveness as a manager. A group of individuals working in the same place does not automatically operate as a team. The words 'group' and 'team' have a recent history with parallels to 'management' and 'leadership'. The word 'team' has become fashionable and is often applied to any group of people working together, even briefly.

Teams are not necessarily better than groups; the people involved are just working in a different way. A group of people may sometimes work as a team and a team may sometimes divide in separate groups. These days, 'team' has become the preferred word across work organisations and 'teamworking' is used instead of the previous term 'group working'. The same basic skills underpin an effective group or team; these are the task and maintenance skills designed to get people to work well together. These terms will be familiar to you, because we discussed them in Chapter 2.

Individuals and groups are better at different tasks

The early years literature places a strong value on collaborative communication and consensus in the staff team. However, it is important to remember that open discussion in groups is not always the best way to make decisions. Managers can operate with a high commitment to communication, without trying to ensure that everything gets discussed at length in team meetings.

Typically, individuals will handle small and routine problems more efficiently and faster than groups. Only individuals can solve very subtle reasoning problems – particularly those where it would be impossible to show that the solution was correct enough to satisfy all people present in a meeting. Finally, unless individuals are allowed to make some decisions alone, they will not develop the skills necessary to take responsibility. Practitioners who always have to check with colleagues or the whole team, will not develop the personal confidence to take on positions of greater responsibility.

Make the connection with ... **your practice**

Reflect on your approach as a manager.

- What range of decisions do you make alone, or with the input only of your deputy?
- Consider examples of decisions that you have brought to a team meeting. What kind of decisions were these and what did a group discussion add to the quality of the final decision? Did you use something like leadership decision styles (page 50)?

- Thinking of the practitioners in your team – what kind of decisions do you want them to be confident of making on their own, or with a room colleague? What kind of decisions should not be brought to you, or to a whole team meeting?

In contrast, groups will generate more ideas, and decisions made are more likely to be broadly correct. The effects of averaging means that fewer major mistakes are made by groups, because the social arena makes all members look more broadly into problems than they might have done otherwise – so long as discussion is not dominated by some individuals or cliques (see the discussion from page 161 about group dynamics). Group discussion can also curb the power of managers by making information public and therefore open to debate. Only meetings can effectively co-ordinate the work of different specialists, where team members with particular knowledge bring that to the discussion. Most importantly, involvement in the group brings enthusiasm to implement decisions that everyone feels they helped to make.

Group working, effectiveness and trust

Early years provision operates in a rapidly changing environment. There is built-in uncertainty to days with children and families; you cannot predict what children or parents will do or say today. Additionally, settings, like other organisations, exist in a climate of change. In particular this requires that all levels and all parts of the provision work well together so that they can flex more easily to new demands. The power of groups working together is far greater than that of an equal number of individuals operating on their own.

Research in a wide variety of organisations consistently identifies one issue as critical for maintaining group effectiveness. That single factor is an atmosphere characterised by trust; people behaving in ways that lead others to trust them.

In working relationships, trust of individuals is usually based on four elements:
- *Dependability* – they are there when they are needed; you do not wonder, 'Will he write the report?' or, 'Do I have to remind her to pass on the letter to Kayleigh's mother?'
- *Consistency* – they regularly help or contribute as part of their usual behaviour
- *Predictability* – they do not give you nasty surprises; good work is not dependent on their mood
- *Reliability* – what they offer is almost always useful.

When people talk about trusting someone, they most often talk about one of three components: information, judgement and execution (what is done). We have added a few examples below. Please reflect on this discussion of trust in the individuals at work and add examples from your own experience.

You can trust these people's *information* because:
- It is usually timely. In other words this person enables you to do something about the information. You have been told this morning that Rory's mother is cross because his clothes are muddy from the gardening project. You can plan

to be available to talk with her this afternoon and have another conversation about your commitment to outdoor play. If you talk to her quickly, you are confident you can defuse the situation.

- It is accurate and unbiased. You can trust that Razia's concern about the way her colleague regularly interrupts the children (expressed in a recent supervision session) is genuine.
- It is given in your own best interest to help you do your work better, not loaded with a hidden agenda. For example, the deputy asks you to change your practice over story time to benefit the children, rather than to make her look good on 'leadership' in front of the manager.

You can trust these people's *judgement* because:

- You understand how they have reached a decision; what they say seems thoughtful and not off-the-cuff. Naomi is able to explain and describe why she believes that the rolling snack time is no longer working well for the current group or children in her room.
- You do not get conflicting signals from these colleagues, for example, joking about something they claim to value.
- They do not talk about others behind their back in a negative fashion. If they have concerns, these are expressed constructively (page 112).

You can trust these people in the *execution* of their responsibilities because:

- They follow through; they do what they say they will do.
- You can count on them to tell you if they cannot keep a commitment. Occasional problems happen over the weekly Speech and Language session, but the therapist always lets you know early enough if she cannot run it.
- They behave with proper regard for confidentiality. They do not gossip about children or families. They understand when information must be shared and ask for advice if they are uncertain.

The ideas above are focused on working relationships with individuals. Trust in the group is equally important but focuses on slightly different areas. The key issues for trust in effective group working are:

- being open and accessible
- being both consistent and reliable – there is no doubt about who is doing what.

Lack of trust within a group does not necessarily mean that people are deceitful or dishonest; it may mean more that communication is unclear, decisions are interpreted differently or that words like 'confidentiality' are used with a different meaning by group members from different professional backgrounds. The manager may need to address the dynamics of meetings when decisions fail to be implemented, as well as having a conversation with individuals. Why has Seema not contacted the story teller at the library, when she promised in our last staff meeting to do so? How come Sam is still late in joining the after school club each day – were we not crystal clear in the team meeting about when he leaves the 3–5s group?

These examples around the importance of trust bring us back to power (page 153), and the likely effects of people accepting or refusing requests from the manager.

Leading an effective work group

Unlike social groups, work groups typically meet primarily to solve problems or to exchange information. You may have a cup of coffee, maybe some cake and the atmosphere of the meeting is friendly. However, your unchanging goal is to improve the standards of your joint work. Chapter 4 covered the skills of personal effectiveness, focusing on individuals. Now we focus on the skills of working with people in groups.

Assertiveness and group meetings

From page 104 we discussed the need for assertiveness (or dominance) as part of the skills of personal effectiveness. An assertive approach was distinguished from the alternatives of aggression or submissiveness (a passive approach). Like individuals, groups too can show varying degrees of dominance, from passivity or submissiveness through to aggression. Figure 6.4 shows these tendencies within the group.

Group tends to passivity	
• Unchecked assumptions • Wasted abilities	• Lack of valid information • Low level of commitment • Sub-optimal performance
Appropriate assertiveness	
• Issues surfaced, high levels of valid information flow • Good quality of decision making	• Clarity of purpose and role • Commitment and ownership • High performance and trust
Group tends to aggression	
• Winners and losers • Cliques, scapegoating • See things as stark choices: this or that, either-or	• Fear and incapacitation of some people • Motivation, morale and commitment low

Figure 6.4 Groups and assertiveness

Each group has its own character which must be borne in mind by anyone, but by the transactional manager in particular, who seeks to improve the way the team communicates and functions. Of course, you will adjust the ideas in this section in line with your detailed knowledge of your own staff. However, a consistent skill base is needed for the effective working of any group. The focus of group working here focuses on more formal meetings in the practice, most of which are designed to solve some problem or other, and a few to act as briefings or information exchanges.

The context of meetings

As a manager or chair, the first step is always to be clear why you have a meeting and not to have a meeting unless it is necessary. For example, is your objective to come up with new ideas for making the most of our communal space or to solve a problem in organising cover for summer holidays? Having decided that, the next question is who should attend – everyone or just a representative from each room? Furthermore, bear in mind that the more people you invite, the more difficulty in reaching an agreement. Invite those staff who can and will contribute. Is this a topic on which it would be appropriate to invite any parents at a later meeting, if not the first one?

A different structure, with different ground rules of interaction (see *standard-setting* on page 163), will be suitable given different aims. Discussion about the communal space may benefit from a brainstorming approach, when ideas are invited and all noted before any criticism is allowed of the ideas. If there is disagreement within the group about the different views on weaning and naps, it is important to ensure views are heard without interruption. All the issues need to be surfaced, so that they can then be resolved. As such the manager or deputy will need to ensure that everyone is listening, and not jumping in prematurely with comments or questions.

On the other hand, the meeting might be specifically designed to develop the sense of a team in the nursery. Again, this kind of meeting needs a different structure and you will not succeed in airing how staff feel and think about current group working within the same meeting as one in which you work through an agenda of day-to-day operational issues. For meetings that build a sense of being a team, we have found it crucial to get everyone's perceptions (about current group working, and possibly about everyone individually within the group) anonymously in advance. Comments are then collated, randomly, on flip charts. This approach allows for all information to be surfaced, without requiring the more hesitant members to own up to their own contributions. Ideally, you involve an outside consultant in this kind of meeting.

Whatever the precise objective of the meeting, it is critical to have all the information available in order to reach the best outcome. Look back at the discussion about Leader Decision Styles on page 49. Similarly, all of the skills we cover below are required.

Effective group working skills

The fundamental communication skills can be grouped into task and maintenance behaviours. This approach to group dynamics is widely used and was summarised well by Kolb *et al.* (1979). The skills are the abilities to behave in certain ways that support the ability of groups to do things well. The behaviours are what can be seen: the visible manifestation of someone's skills in action.

- *Task behaviours* are designed to develop people's knowledge and skills to be able to do their work effectively. We will look at these first.
- *Maintenance behaviours* are designed to develop motivation and commitment to the outcome in this group and to ensure that all relevant points are raised before a decision is taken. These are discussed from page 163. In situational leadership, maintenance behaviours are called supportive behaviours. They are basically the same.

Task behaviours in the group

Task behaviours for effective group working draw on the ability and talent of people, their 'technical competence', which can be extended through continued professional development. The transactional manager needs the skills to behave in the ways outlined in Figure 6.5 in order to promote the kind of interaction within groups that means everyone is enabled to do the best job possible for children and their families. The transactional manager sets a good example: a role model who shows these ways of behaving in action. There is every reason to suppose that other staff will begin to behave in this way and the manager may not need to step in all the time.

Behaviour	*Specific objective ... to*
• Initiating–structuring	• guide and sequence discussion
• Information giving and seeking	• clarify and increase quality of data processed
• Challenging	• increase quality of analysis
• Building–elaborating	• develop ideas in the group
• Summarising	• check understanding and monitor progress
• Consensus testing	• explore potential disagreements and actively check levels of support

Figure 6.5 Effective group working skills – 1: the *task* behaviours

Initiating–structuring

These behaviours could come from anyone in the group. These include making suggestions for how to improve the way the group is operating in a meeting. For example, the proposal that someone summarises comments on a flip chart, or to use a new problem-solving process recently learned on a course. The suggestion might be to break the full meeting into room groups at a particular point, to agree their views on the weaning and naps issue before presenting back to the full group. Other behaviours that come under Initiating–structuring include proposing solutions, on the basis of reliable information, or different ways of organising material.

Information giving and seeking, challenging, building–elaborating

These behaviours require both assertiveness (to give) and listening skills (to receive) that information – look back at the discussion in Chapter 4. This group of behaviours includes asking for clarification, asking for more information and equally offering information about the topic in hand. A prevailing pattern of assertiveness in the group – rather than a submissive or aggressive style – means that *challenging* can be done and experienced in a constructive way. There is much more about, 'I can't see how that idea links with …', rather than 'that'll never work!'. Well-informed and courteous challenge leads naturally to *building– elaborating*, in which opinions and beliefs are given and asked for, with efforts made to build on each other's approaches towards a possible solution. It can include giving examples to help others understand what you mean, and showing how a number of ideas may relate to each other.

Summarising

This skill enables you to pull everything together and is designed to ensure that everything relevant is noted and made clear to everyone. You will also use this skill in more formal conversations with individual practitioners, for instance within a supervision session. In a group, the focus of summarising may be about the content of the discussion – 'what we've talked about so far is … ' and checking with the group, 'Is this right? Has anyone got anything to add?' You might summarise the process of the meeting, for example: 'We started slowly on this knotty problem of partnership with parents and whether tired children should have an afternoon nap. Then good ideas came out from everyone. I think we've made real progress.'

Consensus testing

Finally, this behaviour is designed to see how close the group is to a decision by exploring any disagreements for the purpose of resolving them and reaching an agreement to move forward. This testing can be gentle. An example would be, 'Do we all agree – this is the way [*details would be here*] we'll handle conversations with parents when they ask for routines that we feel aren't in their child's best interests?' Alternatively consensus testing may need to be far more assertive, especially if there has been sustained disagreement. An example would be, 'Ten of us are happy that the new schedule will work for how we'll use the communal space. Jane and Katja – you both still say it won't work. We need to hear and understand your objections. You first, Jane, then it'll be Katja. Explain what you see as the problem.'

You hear, understand and ideally overcome the objections so that full agreement is reached. However, time here is a critical variable; this discussion cannot go on forever and neither can the current situation with the communal space. If Jane or Katja hold to their objections, you may opt for voting – the majority decision – in order to save time. The quality of the decision reached, and your prediction of commitment in the team, is likely to be less good than if true consensus was reached. It is a perpetual challenge for a leader to balance demands for the best decision, with the most commitment, against the demands of limited time. You may need to work individually afterwards with Katja and Jane to help them save face or to welcome their acceptance of the decision, even though they find it hard.

Managing the group, both together and individually, helps to make outcomes better.

Maintenance behaviours in the group

Task behaviours are not sufficient for effective group working; you also need those focused on the maintenance skills. These are designed to help people **want to** do what is necessary and to manage the pattern of interaction and communication as the group works. Whereas task behaviours focus on ability, maintenance skills focus on motivation. These are summarised in Figure 6.6.

Behaviour	Specific objective ... to
• Gate-keeping	• increase and equalise participation
• Compromising	• admit error, ease discussion
• Harmonising	• confront hostility/disagreements
• Humour	• reduce tension
• Encouraging	• praise to prevent withdrawal
• Standard setting	• regulate behaviour and discussion
• Process analysing	• discover and resolve issues in working practice as a group

Figure 6.6 Effective group working skills – 2: the *maintenance* behaviours

Standard-setting

This maintenance behaviour is closest to a task behaviour. Standard-setting determines the rules by which the meeting will operate and everyone needs to agree. Standard-setting should be done at the beginning of the meeting (or in advance), as well as when needed later on. Practical decisions include if anyone needs to take notes in the meeting and managing how the group deals with the absence of a member whose input is relevant.

Sometimes standard-setting is called having ground rules. These might relate to having a timed agenda which is followed. Perhaps you spend only five minutes discussing the date for the Teddy Bears Picnic – it is urgent to set a date, but the decision is not complex and should not take up lots of time. Basic standard-setting that applies to all meetings could include, 'One person speaks at a time, without interruption.' The manager (or whoever is chairing the meeting) needs to be ready to challenge with, 'Sylvia, we agreed on no interruptions. That's the second time you've interrupted Britney.' Lively groups in which practitioners compete for the floor might need full team commitment to a further ground rule such as nobody can criticise another person's contribution unless they first say 'three good things' about it. This additional loop helps stop people from not really listening, and instead to consider other views – however different from their own – before they have earned the right to make their own points.

Complex issues that need to be aired within the team might need a ground rule about sensible sequencing. An example would be: first get the information, second, share opinions about it, and only then decide what to do about it. To do this well, the leader needs to be able to summarise and conclude openly that all information is in to the satisfaction of the group, before moving on – and so on. Members who try to bring in opinions too early need to be asked to wait until all the information is gathered. Standard-setting is critical, as it provides the agreed basis of authority by which you can act.

More complex standard-setting and time management are needed in a large meeting that, say, brings together different agencies working within the same children's centre. A clear agenda and ground rules need to ensure that everyone has the floor at some point and that the meeting is not dominated by one agency or kind of professional. Maybe there needs to be a clear message, in advance, that in the planned information exchange everyone has a ten-minute slot to present their case. If they want to make a PowerPoint presentation, then copies need to be available at the meeting. Again the chair of the meeting has to be ready to enforce the agreed timing; 'Simon, you've had your two-minute warning, your time is now up. Yes, I know you've got ten more slides. You'll have to email that data to us.'

Make the connection with ... **your own practice**

An example from our own experience of the importance of standard-setting was of a large meeting with people from different locations. The members were very lax about time-keeping and several were nearly always late. Having agreed to be timely, at the very next meeting, the first presenter, whom we will call Andrea, arrived 15 minutes late. The chair refused to hear her presentation, on the grounds that Andrea had missed her allocated slot by being late, and the meeting had to move on. It was a powerful lesson to Andrea and the rest of the group.

- Do you have similar examples from your own experience, when a firm line was needed?
- On the other hand, reflect on experiences when you can see that failure to act decisively, with further chances being given, disrupted the work of a meeting.

Other maintenance behaviours for group working
The remaining behaviours all contribute to creating the best environment for everyone to make their contribution.
- *Gate-keeping* is about asking quieter members to contribute so that everyone gets a fair chance to speak on an issue, or making sure that each person, in turn, speaks on an issue. It 'opens the gate' to let people in and you judge how you make that invitation from your knowledge of individual staff. It particularly applies to the more passive members of the group. For example, 'We haven't heard much from you, Zoe. What do you think about…?'
- *Encouraging* supports the contributions of members by praising them, or agreeing with them, rather than just carrying on with the point you wished to make. This behaviour draws on using reward power (page 7) and helps the contributors to want to contribute more.

- *Harmonising* is about helping to resolve differences of opinion between other group members. This behaviour could also be called mediating. You help colleagues to reach common ground – often by summarising their areas of agreement as well as where they differ. For example, 'Nicki and Issak, you both agree that we should not keep exhausted children awake. You seem to disagree only over the length of naps needed. Is that right?' This helps to move the discussion forward by showing a reduction in the areas that are still contentious, and therefore makes these easier to solve.
- *Compromising* is when you, yourself, admit error: 'Sorry. I didn't realise that Sarah finalised Dads' Day in the last meeting, when I was away.' You also offer a compromise when you amend your position in response to what the group is saying: 'I hadn't thought of it that way.' By doing this, you prevent others having to press their case against what they may see as your opposition, as well as coming across as reasonable and flexible.
- The main point of *humour* is to reduce tension within the group. Light-heartedness can be useful on occasion to place things in context; 'Come on folks. It's really no harder than making a cup of tea.' An injection of humour may also relieve pressure, so that the group becomes more energised. Of course, any humour must be used sparingly and not demean anyone in the group, nor belittle anyone's contribution. Such a discourtesy is likely to inhibit their further contributions, and may make the rest of the group feel sympathy for that colleague and sceptical of the person who has mis-used humour.

Finally, *process analysis* looks directly at the way the group operates in order to be clear about the dynamics: are some issues actually problems that need to be resolved in order for the group to work more effectively? Some typical questions are:

- Who speaks most and who least? Does this matter? If so, how? Are we doing anything to bring in the largely silent team members?
- Do we use certain words a lot, such as 'try' or 'ought' or 'should'? Are these stopping us making best choices, or committing fully to a new course of action?
- Who is sceptical and who is committed? What tends to energise this group and what seems to bore them? Does one person or clique always have a 'yes, but…' response to any proposal that would mean spending more time outdoors?
- Are we spending our time wisely? Are we spending most time on important things, or those where decisions are needed urgently? Does our discussion focus on the work or do we digress into general conversation or moaning about other agencies? Can we manage our social need to chat in some way?
- Are we talking about issues in full staff groups that would be better covered in a room meeting? Or further, who needs to be at this meeting? Who has something valuable to contribute, who is not really involved in this issue?
- Is the leader too dominant in discussion? Has the leader checked this recently? She or he has a responsibility to tolerate silence. Equally, the rest of the team has a responsibility to speak up in meetings, rather than talk about important issues covertly and only when they get back to their room.

- How do we stop meetings overrunning, how can we address time keeping? What can we do about Sarah who is nearly always late? Should we start without her? Is there a better time to have our meetings?
- Do we need as many meetings? Does everyone need to be at all of them?

Pause for reflection

The list of points in the above section includes elements of task behaviour; many of these ideas are interrelated in practice. Please look back at consensus testing, on page 162, and reflect on ways in which a willingness to analyse what is happening in the group will shine a light on whether consensus testing is operating as you believe it should.

- Consensus testing does not mean using voting as a frequent or first choice. Has it become the established pattern here that whoever chairs this meeting uses 'let's take a vote' as a way of avoiding thorough discussion or resolving differences in the group?
- Is the group impatient to get the meeting finished, and will agree to anything to get home?
- Is the phrase 'We're all agreed then?', followed by silence, the way this manager deals with reticence to speak up in this group, rather than finding ways to invite quiet practitioners to express a view?

Please think about your own experience in meetings and consider whether the questions apply.

Worthwhile consensus testing means an awareness of the process in this group: actively exploring specifically that each person agrees and dealing with any concerns that they may have. This exploration in turn uses many of the behaviours discussed in this section.

In what ways can you apply those ideas to group situations in which you are involved?

Self-orientated behaviours in the group

In opposition to all of the task and maintenance behaviours are those which are designed to protect individuals from threat: behaviour that is orientated to personal needs only and will operate to block effective group working. For example: Cathy does not really want to be in this staff meeting and she has a poor opinion of the colleagues whose 'stupid ideas won't work'. Britney is very nervous about speaking up and, unless someone deals with Sylvia's entrenched habit of interruption and talking over people, Britney will withdraw into herself. Sean is not giving the discussion his full attention because he now has a major concern about how soon he can leave to pick up his daughter, given that the meeting is already well beyond its finish time.

We call these reactions self-orientated behaviours, all of which place personal needs above those of others – including the entire group. These behaviours, shown in Figure 6.7, are designed to defend yourself from worry, pain and upset: to overcome frustration of one sort or another.

Behaviour	Specific objective ... to
• Fighting, controlling and shutting out	• dominate position and to win irrespective of best solution
• Pleading and emotional appeals	• draw attention to personal weakness to get group's attention
• Pairing	• support another to offer mutual protection/comfort
• Withdrawal and tuning out	• physically or psychologically leave the group to avoid further strain
• Dependency and couter-dependency	• avoid initial conflict, but prevent doing work not really agreed to

Figure 6.7 Self-orientation in groups: the *blocking* behaviours

In the following discussion we have made links between these behaviours and Relationships Awareness Training™ (RAT) – the Red–Blue–Green preferred styles (discussed from page 87).

Fighting, controlling and shutting out

This reaction is one of the major 'fight' defences in a group. The person will attempt to dominate discussion, speaking louder (and longer) than anyone else in order to win in the end. For example, Charlene has a track record of blaming colleagues for mistakes. She accuses them of stupidity, timidity or being overly intellectual – anything to deflate what she sees as the opposition as she tries to ensure that her views win.

Individuals like Charlene are very disruptive to group working. They actively challenge people who oppose them, often by dismissing their contributions and belittling them as individuals. They interrupt others frequently and the style is one of aggression rather than assertion (page 104). In terms of task behaviours, the manager needs to shut them up and make space for the others. Certainly you could argue that these are Red-emphasising people who try to resolve issues on the basis of 'I'm stronger than you.'

Pleading appeals

Maintaining this link with RAT, Blue people, who would far rather resolve problems along the nice–nasty dimension, are more likely to make pleading appeals. A typical introduction of such an appeal is, 'This may not be important, but …', which actually means, 'Please listen to me and give me space.' Sometimes the emotional appeal is based on someone's own hobbyhorse. There may be value in Beth talking about the nursery website or problems with parents who fail to shut the front gate, but this is only appropriate if her comments are relevant to what the group is currently discussing. Beth's continued focus on these two points is not relevant to all discussions. She chooses to place her pet issues above those of the group. Again it is a plea to 'listen to me' and to have her contribution recognised. A good leader will acknowledge Beth's points in the group, move back to the topic being addressed, and could arrange to talk to her privately about her concerns afterwards.

Pairing

This pattern occurs when two members usually work in tandem in a group. The staff will feel they have something in common; it might be a similar age in a group that is mainly younger or older, they trained together or work in the same room. If Annie makes a comment, then Betty will immediately support her, regardless of the topic of discussion. If Betty's comment is questioned by anyone, then Annie leaps to her defence. They cling together for support. Each has a friend, and that makes them feel more secure. They are not comfortable in the group, and the leader should find out why – so that necessary changes can be made. Typically those who pair have the same first preference in RAT, most likely Blue, then Green and (more rarely) both Red.

Withdrawal and tuning out

This behaviour is visible when people doodle, daydream, gaze at their nails or mobile phone. They are not interested in the current topic of discussion. Everyone loses concentration from time to time but, as with pairing, this must be addressed when the behaviour becomes habitual. Standard-setting in a group can address what kind of behaviour is discourteous to others, and possibly also unprofessional. An example would be staff who whisper to each other in meetings, but then decline to voice the comment out loud. We cannot see any links to RAT here – everyone gets bored from time to time – but the issue is how you deal with that feeling. At its most extreme, withdrawal can mean a person walks out of the meeting.

Typically, however, withdrawal is behaviour that is passive, unassertive and submissive. These people may be learning something from the group, but they are not developing – or contributing – interpersonally. It is hard to get these individuals to speak; it is as if they believe the quickest way to get out of the meeting is to stay silent. These people do not want to be there and you need to raise the question of 'why?'.

Maybe Ujala believes that no one will listen anyway if she does speak up, because of all the talking over and shutting out that is common for this group. Maybe Theresa prefers greater formality and more rules for the staff meeting and believes this is likely to save time. Be careful of assumptions about Daisy, just because she is quiet. However, Daisy will implement the group decision – even more willingly without what she views as 'all this waffle' – so let her get on with it! However, in this case, consider whether Daisy needs to be at all of these meetings or merely a few. Perhaps she is showing the behaviour that follows now.

Dependency and counter-dependency

This phrase is a mouthful, we know, but the concept is very useful. This situation is horrible for the rest of the group and it goes like this: Lucy goes along with the decision that the group makes about reorganising lunch time, without any apparent problem. If asked, she says, 'It's fine', 'whatever you want' or something similar. Lucy is showing dependency. She has chosen not to explore her concerns, nor to develop a real understanding of what has been proposed and her implied commitment to the outcome. However, when the reorganisation of lunch time (to which Lucy said she agreed) brings several problems which were not anticipated, then Lucy announces, 'Well I never believed in changing the old system anyway. I could've told you the reorganisation wouldn't work.'

This is classic counter-dependency, and often comes over as cynical – not to mention being infuriating to colleagues. Lucy is dependent on the group to make decisions (for her) and when these do not work, then she will blame others (counter-dependency). The only way to overcome this behaviour is through considerable patience from the manager, and diligent work with Lucy to understand her feelings and thoughts. However, part of these discussions will involve bringing home to Lucy the impact of her behaviour on her colleagues. The manager needs to believe that his or her effort is going to be – on balance – worthwhile for the team, as this is likely to take a lot of valuable managerial time.

None of these self-orientated behaviours are easy to overcome. They are all, in one way or another, a cry for help. Ujala does not feel able to contribute; she needs to be encouraged and the combative nature of this group modified. Lucy may feel she does not get the recognition or status she is owed. They all need their positive contributions to be recognised, and their less helpful ones ignored or challenged. There is a parallel here with guiding the behaviour of children. A wise approach with people of any age is to consider whether it is better not to respond to some irritating behaviours: you ignore the behaviour; you do not ignore the person. Task and maintenance skills, both in the group and one-to-one interaction, are the best way to reduce – if not completely overcome – these self-orientated behaviours.

Getting the best out of the group

We discussed SYMLOG in Chapter 2 and you can refresh your memory from page 61. This analysis provides a useful baseline to assess how your own workgroup functions. Figure 6.8 shows all the SYMLOG statements as used in their values-based questionnaire, developed from research by Robert Freed Bales and the SYMLOG Consulting Group. The statements are grouped to show how well each value, shown through visible behaviour, contributes to effective teamwork.

Notice the checks and balances in the classification. For instance, effective teamwork is supported by willingness to sacrifice one's own interests to reach organisational goals when that is necessary. However, it is rarely effective for teamwork if individuals give up their personal needs and wishes in a passive way, when this self-denial is not necessary.

Values in behaviour that help and hinder good teamworking

Thirteen values that **almost always** contribute to effective teamwork:

- Popularity and social success, being liked and admired
- Active teamwork towards common goals, organisational unity
- Efficiency, strong, impartial management
- Having a good time, releasing tension, relaxing control
- Protecting less able members, providing help when needed
- Equality, democratic participation in decision making
- Responsible idealism, collaborative work
- Change to new procedures, different values, creativity
- Friendship, mutual pleasure, relaxation
- Trust in the goodness of others
- Dedication, faithfulness, loyalty to the organisation
- Obedience to the chain of command, complying with authority
- Self-sacrifice if necessary to reach organisational goals.

Five values that are **necessary sometimes, but can be dangerous:**

- Individual financial success, personal prominence and power
- Active reinforcement of authority, rules and regulations
- Tough-minded, self-orientated assertiveness
- Conservative, established, 'correct' ways of doing things
- Restraining the individual's desires for organisational goals.

Eight values that almost always **interfere** with effective teamwork:

- Rugged self-centred individualism, resistance to authority
- Self-protection, self-interest first, self-sufficiency
- Rejection of established procedures, rejection of conformity
- Passive rejection of authority, going it alone
- Admission of failure, withdrawal of effort
- Passive non-cooperation with authority
- Quiet contentment, taking it easy
- Giving up personal needs and desires, passivity.

Figure 6.8 Values in behaviour that help and hinder good teamworking (Bales and Cohen)

Pause for reflection

We find the SYMLOG classification offers a useful guide towards how an effective group, or an organisation, may be characterised. Please look carefully at Figure 6.8 and take each statement in turn.

Consider the way that they are classified.

- Does this classification square with your own experience in work?
- Are there any surprises here for you?
- Discuss the ideas with colleagues at work or on your leadership programme.

Support for the group

Not forgetting trust (beginning on page 157), the manager needs to provide support to the group and to individuals in the group. In summary, this is accomplished in three general ways:

1 Encouraging others to air their views and concerns. The key word here is encouraging – be proactive in this area, and if necessary, actively seek out views and concerns. The manager also needs to act so as to prevent a few members dominating the team.

2 Establishing clear ground rules – assuring that all members are aware of and support the manner in which you work as a team. Everyone's duties and obligations should be clear to all.

3 Empowerment.

So far we have not talked much about the third area for effective teams: empowerment. We have a bit of a problem with the term 'empowerment' and how it is often used. The intent of empowerment in the work context is positive: to give everyone the chance to say what they mean, to contribute more – even to take a leading role. However, too often the working definition of empowerment in many organisations is 'doing the boss's job for the subordinate's pay'. We have seen this as a reality for empowerment in action too often and it is unacceptable.

More accurately within a team, empowerment should centre on sharing power among all team members. This involves two general areas of activity:

1 Encouraging team members to look for and articulate alternative approaches to problems, actions and ideas: behaviours like asking and gate-keeping.

2 Working towards a team consensus, neither a vote nor an autocratic decision, but true consensus, so that all members give their genuine real support of actions taken or decisions made. Consensus is the active process of exploring and resolving all of the members' concerns about the issue in hand before reaching the final decision and specifically gaining each member's commitment to the agreed course of action. To gain this commitment may mean that the manager has to go to each group member in the meeting in turn. Each person is asked to personally commit, in public, to actively support the decision taken.

If managers continuously work on these factors, an effective team can be built and maintained. To maintain a well-operating group requires that process analysis (page 165) is conducted almost continuously to ensure that the group is still working well. Periodically asking and answering the following questions can help:

- What do we do well?
- Should we spend more or less time on some parts of the work? Overall are we doing more than we need, perhaps in terms of repetitive paperwork over children's records or risk assessment? What can we cut out or reduce without losing the necessary focus on good documentation and safety? Can we do elements of the work in a different order – or in parallel?

- How can we test any constraints in the flow of what we do? What or who causes delays and can these be avoided?
- Do we build enough space into our timing to prevent unexpected events affecting the achievement of our goals?
- Are we agreeing on issues too easily? Are we wary of airing disagreements when these issues need to be brought into the open?
- Are staff all clear on their roles, goals and responsibilities?
- Is everyone sufficiently involved in forward planning? As a manager, am I relying on some staff more than others? Is this sensible?
- What turns this team on and off? What enthuses them and what drains their energy?

Finally, experience and research has shown that there are a number of areas for focus with groups at work which are often overlooked. Time spent on the following can bring great benefit. As a group leader, which of these could you use?

- Choose one job-related skill that you would like to develop. Make space for this focus in your individual plan for continued professional development.
- Find ways to make your team's work more interesting or enjoyable. This may mean removing elements of the work that people dislike and which serve little purpose. For instance, be ready to check whether you do have to complete this kind of paperwork or to this extent.
- Find out what you personally do – with the best of intentions, of course – that your staff find unhelpful and which wastes their time – and stop doing it! According to Drucker (2007), this is a hallmark of the effective manager.
- Identify one material resource that can help your team to do better in their work and obtain that resource. It could be buying a set of safe steps so that toddlers can climb up to the changing table. Explain how this resource will help: independence for toddlers (who are safe because the key person is right beside them) and protection for the adult's back. Let staff know why this new resource is, in your considered opinion, important for the work.
- Clarify your team's purpose both internally and externally to keep everyone on track and feeling valued by the organisation. Set realistic goals with your staff, and establish quality standards for what you all do.
- In terms of your line management, seek clarity about what your superior values from you and hence how you could help him or her to do better. Focus your efforts here.
- A key part of management is keeping your own line manager from the kind of direct involvement that interferes with your team and erodes your credibility as a manager with your staff. For instance, as leader of the 3–5s room, you welcome your manager's good ideas, but would much rather she discussed suggested changes in your regular meeting and did not come into the room and make those changes herself.
- Define what information would help you and your team to make better informed decisions and seek to acquire it. Be open-minded about the source of new information: local authority and national sources, published material and the internet or the expertise of parents.

- Get to know your colleagues better – understand how their life outside work will influence their life inside work. There is obviously a balance to be kept here and some staff may choose to keep the two separate.
- At least once a year, make space with your team to plan and agree both processes – how you do the work – and direction – where you are going. Ideally have this meeting away from work, and if you can get a trusted outsider to facilitate it, so much the better.
- Allow your people the opportunity to stretch and grow, as appropriate to their capabilities. You wish them to take a manageable risk – not one that is terrifying. Offer a more challenging assignment, with the possibility that it might not work, but in an atmosphere where mistakes are an opportunity to learn and to develop. (A message that everyone should be communicating to the children; it is all about learning.) 'No mistakes' in a team probably means that people are not trying hard enough, living with habits of caution and an unwillingness to take risks.

Task and maintenance skills are not only critical to the operation of effective groups, they are also critical to the transactional world of the manager-leader.

Transactional behaviours for the manager

We now move on to your working relationships with individual staff. However, many of the skills are in common with effective group working. In transactional management terms these are:
- Directive (Concern for Task) behaviours that provide necessary direction and structure: these communicate what people are to do (where, when and how) and follow up to ensure satisfactory completion.
- Relationship (Concern for People) behaviours that give appreciation and recognition: these encourage and reinforce good work, check that the people are all right or want help, and improve the motivation of staff.

Adjusting managerial behaviour to the situation

In this section we return to Hersey and Blanchard's model of situational leadership, which we first discussed in Chapter 2 (page 50) – see Figure 6.9. They use the terms 'leader' and 'leadership'. However, to remain consistent with our clarification that this pattern of behaviour is not really about leadership, we will use the word 'manager'. By this term we are referring to either the manager or the deputy of an early years setting who has the responsibility, and authority, for individual staff.

To recall, the basic proposal of situational leadership is that managers' behaviour should change to reflect the characteristics of individual staff who report directly to them. The characteristics fall into three areas:
- staff ability and skill level
- their level of motivation
- their capacity to assume responsibility.

These three components go to make the concept of Development Level. So that, for example, someone with low motivation and skill would be at Development Level 1 (D1), whereas someone highly skilled, highly motivated and able to take responsibility would be Development Level 4 (D4). This model matches the style of leader (S1 to S4) with the Development Level of the staff member (D1 to D4). Matching the style to the level is seen by Hersey and Blanchard as the best way to enable your staff to perform and develop further. For ease of reading, we have reproduced the model from Chapter 2.

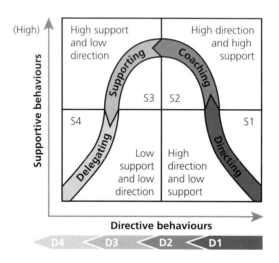

Figure 6.9 The situational leadership model

Leadership Styles and Development Levels

Suppose your staff are new to your organisation, they have little experience of doing the task or they are unwilling to do a task – they are at Development Level 1. Also staff who feel insecure and lack self-confidence are D1 as they need more structure and direction to perform. They will be best served by being told what to do, with clear explanations of how to do it. They need the guidance of being closely monitored until their performance picks up – the Structuring (S1) Style characterised by *high direction* and *low support*.

Only limited attention is paid to the motivation of staff – note that this is little attention, not none at all. In this lower right-hand box *low support* means that the member of staff needs direction, rather than the support to be able to perform without help. S1 is not about being unsupportive in the sense of being cold and unfriendly. The manager should therefore be demonstrating the task behaviours outlined earlier (page 161) – initiating and structuring, information giving and receiving, and so on. The manager will be very clear on what is expected and the performance standards sought. She or he helps the person to deliver on what is expected in the job, and spends a lot of time showing this member of staff how to do things, checking that tasks have been done reasonably well, and offering constructive comments (page 112).

As the person improves their performance, then the manager should move into S2. Here the manager is certainly not reducing their attention on getting the job done; *direction* and task focus are still high. However, in S2, the level of motivational *support* increases use of maintenance skills (such as encouraging and gate-keeping) to do so – perhaps by asking the staff member what the manager can do to help. The staff member is praised (specific positive feedback) for work well done, and recognising what has been learned. Encouragement is given, perhaps to do some parts of the job alone without supervision, or to seek help from colleagues rather than the manager. Encouragement is important in S2, as most people find it de-motivating if their manager shows high levels of task orientation (*direction*) and little else for a long period of time.

In terms of the theory of situational leadership, the operation of S2 should lead to the staff member's performance improving, so that it at least reaches the basic standard required, and ideally higher than this minimum. If the person is now performing at or above standard, the manager should now move to S3. The focus of this stage is to see whether or not the person can take responsibility alone for maintaining this standard. If the person cannot take that responsibility, there is no choice for the transactional manager other than to retreat back to S2, with all the extra supervisory work that this involves. Otherwise, important aspects of the work will not get done.

The model seeks to enable all staff to reach the Developmental Level D4. In D4, individuals will need far less managerial time (as the S4 shows less of both *directive* and *supportive* behaviours). So, if the person can take responsibility, and continues to perform well, the manager moves to S4, giving little help or encouragement (both *direction* and *support* are *low*). Note it is low or 'little' help – not none at all.

Here, the manager could ask the practitioner, 'How are things going?', or 'Do you need any help from me?' The manager trusts the reply of, 'No thanks, I'm fine' and does not press to offer more help. In S4, managers are testing to see whether this practitioner can now deliver best practice with hardly any supervision – in other words they are at D4 rather than D3. If this is the case, and they perform well independently, practitioners are ready for further responsibility or, in some circumstances, to apply for a more senior position. At this point, of course, the whole process starts again. Everyone has to learn in a new job and needs some structure and direction.

Situational leadership states that if staff members are unwilling to do a part of their job, then for that task, the Structuring Style (S1) is mandatory.

- Think about the non-negotiable aspects of working with children and families in early years provision. Have you struggled with staff who are reluctant to chat with babies at nappy changing time or claim that they 'don't have time' to talk with parents? These parts of the job are not up for a 'maybe' discussion; they are at the core of practice.

- The S1 style of high direction with very clear instructions is needed. Focusing on support and empathy will not do the trick. It can be counter-productive to give too much attention to the excuses that uncooperative practitioners give for not talking with the parents of their key children. This communication is not optional.

Situational leadership focuses usefully on the different needs of staff members. One or two practitioners may be at D3, another person is at D4 and three newly arrived practitioners are at D1. It would be irresponsible as a leader to try to treat everyone the same. Ken Blanchard and his colleagues express this view well with, 'There is nothing so unequal as the equal treatment of unequals' (Blanchard *et al.*, 1986, page 33). You need to adjust your style to their development needs.

- Reflect on the current situation in your team. Can you see where different individuals could be placed on D1–4?

- Are you aware of your style and matching it to the professional needs of the team? Be honest with yourself, do you find some styles more of a personal struggle? Most managers, even in some of the most cut-throat areas of business, find it hardest to do S1 and S4, as S1 is too hard and cold, and S4 is not doing enough.

The progress from S1 to S4 is not inevitable, because some staff cannot progress through all the development levels. They may not have the ability, the motivation or the self-confidence to assume responsibility for their own level of performance. If a staff member does not move beyond Development Level 2, then it is unsafe for the manager to move from the S2 Coaching Style, as performance would suffer. High direction is necessary to get the work done to the standard required. Furthermore, some people will always need high support. They want the manager to be actively concerned about them.

None of these shifts is as stark as the model implies; they are gradual. Similarly, if the shift from one style to another is made too soon – before the subordinate is ready – be ready to circle back.

- If you move from S2 to S3, and the subordinate keeps asking you how to do new assignments – you would circle back to S2 and so on.

- If a group of highly competent subordinates (D4) cannot solve a problem, you may need to help them (S3).

- A move to the low support of Delegating (S4) may be interpreted as the manager no longer caring. The staff member can feel hurt and abandoned – even though his or her performance is excellent. Hence the sensible manager would circle back to re-establishing the Encouraging Style (S3), realising that this person needs high support to maintain their motivation.

- This flexibility from the manager keeps the subordinate involved. If done well, staff at whatever level get whatever they need from their manager to optimise their performance and development.

Ability and motivation – keys to performance

At the root of this model is the ability and motivation of the practitioner. If both of these are high, then the practitioner should be able to do the job very well. The focus then moves to see whether the person can take personal responsibility for performing well, or whether the manager still needs to be checking up.

A quick equation may help: *Ability x Motivation = Performance*. The relationship is multiplicative. If either ability or motivation is zero, then performance too will be zero. The relationship between ability and motivation cannot be additive. Think about it – if this were the case, then someone with ability = 1, for example, but with motivation = 0 would show job performance = 1. This situation is impossible. If you have no motivation, it does not matter how able you are – you will not bother to turn in good work in your job. The manager's job is to get the best standards of practice for children and families. So if the staff member is turned off – for whatever reason – their motivation has suffered and so will their performance. Similarly, it does not matter how motivated someone is to do something (say = 5) – if they have no ability (= 0), there will be no performance (5 x 0 = 0). For instance, a practitioner who is deaf will not be able to respond to a conventional telephone. He or she does not have the ability in this situation.

Figure 6.10 shows the options given in an identified motivation or ability problem. Look at the possible courses of action and reflect on how they work in theory, and could operate in practice in your work as a manager.

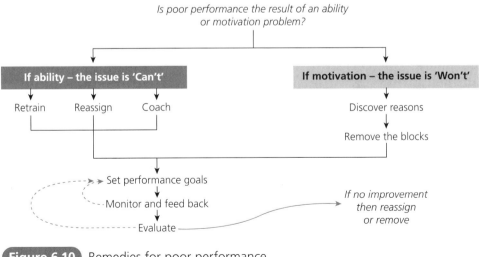

Figure 6.10 Remedies for poor performance

The 'reassign or remove' option following 'no improvement' has to be applied, of course, with due attention to your procedures. For example, perhaps the manager's decision is that Simone's temporary role as room leader cannot be extended. Currently, Simone cannot cope with giving colleagues directions but, if she is motivated to extend her skills, then she could improve. In contrast, serious and sustained failure to meet the basic requirements of the job will raise the question of whether disciplinary action is triggered.

Development Levels

Figure 6.11 summarises the characteristics of each Development Level and the matching management style – emphasising the motivation and ability of the practitioner. If you compare this directly with the Figure 6.9 on page 174 you will see that we have moved Development Level into the main graph and placed the leadership style along the base.

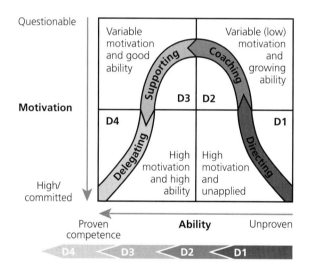

Figure 6.11 Direct report development levels D1–D4, adapted from Blanchard.

Look at the options and consider how these are reflected in your experience as a manager. You cannot, for instance, safely move into D4 (Delegating) if you are uncertain about this person's capacity to take responsibility for doing the job well. When there is a problem over performance – doing a good job in this part of practice – the manager needs to assess and decide whether the problem is due to lack of ability on the part of the staff member, or whether it is more a problem of motivation.

When staff motivation is likely to be questionable, they will need *high support* from the manager. Similarly when their performance is low (or the person is unwilling) *high direction* is needed to get them to do the work required. With highly committed, motivated staff of proven competence (D4) *low support* and *low direction* are the order of the day. It is only in the case of those staff with growing ability whose motivation may have been knocked a bit by the *high direction* S1 style, that high levels of both *support* and *direction* are required – the S2 Coaching style.

Consistency and an individual approach

A question often asked of transactional management is what happens when staff talk to each other about the manager? Suppose a D1 practitioner talks with a colleague whom the manager assesses to be at D3 and is therefore treating appropriately for this level? If these two practitioners compare their experiences, will the manager be seen as inconsistent (at best) or manipulative (at worst)?

Broadly, there should not be a problem, for these reasons:
- The manager has the consistency of being the same person, and performing an appropriate role of managing her or his staff.
- The practitioners at levels D1 and D3 are both getting what they need in terms of direct help from their manager.
- Practitioners expect to be treated differently by their line manager if they are skilled and experienced, rather than new and inexperienced. In fact, many people will get cross when their level of experience fails to be recognised. If practitioners consistently over- or underestimate their own ability, then the manager has to address this issue directly.
- The final important point is that the transactional manager should be open and candid in communicating what she or he is doing and why. Part of the process has to be talking with practitioners about their level of ability or motivation and for the manager to explain the situational leadership approach.

Match and mismatch of management styles and development levels

Problems only really occur when there is a mismatch: for example, the manager treats a D2 subordinate as if she were D3. This error occurs because the manager has not analysed the situation correctly, and/or has not involved and briefed the staff member properly. Figure 6.12 shows the responses of people to such mismatches. In particular, this highlights the potential problem of the all-singing all-dancing operation of the Coaching (S2) style.

Basic style	a) Effective/consistent use (Development Level)	b) Ineffective use (Development Levels)
S1 Structuring High Task – Low Relationship	Leaders seen as having well-defined and sensible structures and procedures for doing work and achieving targets that are useful to subordinates, helping them to perform well. (D1)	Leader seen as being too controlling and prescriptive, and trying to force a regime of rules and regulations on others. Appears only interested in 'the numbers' and doesn't value the people. 'A petty dictator.' (D2, D3, D4)

[Figure 6.12 continues overleaf]

Basic style	a) Effective/consistent use (Development Level)	b) Ineffective use (Development Levels)
S2 Encouraging Low Task – High Relationship	Leader seen as involving the team in goal setting and the definition of work processes and standards, while providing high levels of encouragement and support for them as individuals. (D2)	Leader seen as offering more procedures than are necessary, and too many meetings. Although concerned about subordinates, the genuineness of this is highly suspect. 'I'm not sure he or she is trustworthy.' (D1, D3, D4)
S3 Encouraging Low Task – High Relationship	Leader seen as having implicit faith in people to be able to do their work, so is primarily concerned with ensuring that their goals are met and their motivation is maintained. (D3)	Leader seen as placing harmony above all else, and unwilling to compromise relationships in order to accomplish tasks to a better performance standard. 'A nice person, but gutless.' (D1, D2, D4)
S4 Delegating Low Task – Low Relationship	Leader appropriately delegates to subordinates how work should be done and gives little support and encouragement where little is required. (D4)	Leader seen as providing little in the way of support for them or for doing their work. 'Leaves us to sink or swim.' (D1, D2, D3)

Figure 6.12 Consequences of good or poor application of styles, adapted from Blanchard

We stress the limitations of S2 Coaching, as this is where most people profess to be. It is very safe in that the manager keeps control and hence not much can go wrong technically with the performance of the team. They will perform to standard, maybe not best practice, but satisfactorily. The drawbacks of S2 are that it takes a lot of time, which arguably could be better spent by the manager doing non-supervisory work or dealing with their own superiors and other external pressures. Staying with S2 also fails to allow staff members to develop fully, which, in turn, builds frustration in the most competent staff. This is a situation to be avoided; you need your best performers and potential leaders. It undermines best practice in the team and may be a warning sign that the manager wants to keep control of everything – for personal reasons or from the belief that the S2 style is what managers should do.

Finally, there is the issue of what style should be used when you have meetings with your team. In short, meetings are interactive and they need to be managed (*high direction*). As such the manager would be unlikely ever to move out of the S1 or S2 style, otherwise the necessary structure would be lacking. This direction can include standard-setting, consensus testing and the like. Most meetings are best run in the S2 Coaching style to get the most commitment from the group to decisions taken. The exception is when there is no choice and something has to be done or decided now, and people are unwilling to do it. The meeting should then be run in the *high direction – low support* style of S1 Directing. The manager cannot waste time on trying to convince hard-line doubters. Such effort is unrealistic and reduces the perceived seriousness of the situation. The goal is to do it now.

Make the connection with … **your own practice**

- Can you think of a time when you experienced a mismatch between what you judged you needed and the response from your manager – in terms of the styles in Figure 6.12?
- How you made that kind of mis-judgement as a manager yourself?

Final tips for the transactional manager

Transactional management works if done openly and well. It involves people appropriately, gives high levels of feedback and rewards staff members both for performing well and taking more responsibility. Considered use of the different styles can also reduce the manager's supervisory workload; you are not checking up on people to whom you can now safely delegate.

- Equally with the transformational leader – the focus of the next chapter – treat your people in terms of what they are and how they actually behave, not how you wish they would behave or act. For example, you might really like a staff member as a person. This may mean that you see her as more competent than she actually is and treat her as a D3, with the S3 Encouraging style, when she actually needs the greater direction of S2 Coaching.
- Focus on solving problems between people, not on seeking rights and wrongs or apportioning blame. Again, the rule is to use the same approach which should be applied in interaction with the children: you accept this person; you take issue with their behaviour.
- Tell your people on what you would welcome feedback and respond positively when it is given (page 114). Resist the temptation to justify your behaviour as this only tends to stop people giving you feedback in future. Most often this justification begins with 'because …'. It can be a daunting prospect for practitioners to give feedback to their manager – it needs to be made easy and non-threatening. Seek specific examples when you are not clear – usually when you find the feedback (either positive or negative) to be surprising. You may even ask for feedback anonymously (on paper) if it helps to start the process.
- Overall, focus more energy on rewarding behaviour you want than on highlighting and criticising unwanted behaviour from your staff. Once again, managers need to set a good example for the kind of interactions they would like to happen between colleagues and this attention to balance is also completely consistent with how everyone should be guiding children's behaviour. Praise is to the spirit as oxygen is to the body.

Resources

- **Bales, R. and Cohen, S.** (1979) *SYMLOG: A system for the multiple level observation of groups.* New York: Free Press.
- **Blanchard, K. and Lorber, R.** (1984) *Putting the One Minute Manager to Work.* London: Fontana/Collins.
- **Blanchard, K., Zigarmi, P. and Zigarmi, D.** (1986) *Leadership and the One Minute Manager.* London: Fontana/Collins.
- **Drucker, P.** (2007) *The Effective Executive: The definitive guide to getting the right things done.* Oxford: Elsevier.
- **Kolb, D.A., Rubin, I.M. and McIntyre, J.M.** (1979) *Organizational Psychology: An experiential approach.* Englewood Cliffs, NJ: Prentice Hall.
- **Lindon, J.** (2010b) *Reflective Practice and Early Years Professionalism.* London: Hodder Education.
- **McCall, M., Morrison, A. and Hannan, R.** (1978) *Studies of Managerial Work: Results and methods.* Technical Report No. 9: Greensboro, NC: Center for Creative Leadership.
- The SYMLOG Consulting Group, (1993) *SYMLOG Practitioner Training Materials.* San Diego: The SYMLOG Consulting Group.

The transformational leader – bringing about change

We now address transformational leadership, which we previously described (from page 54) as genuine leadership, rather than management. This chapter covers specific practical issues for the early years sector in bringing about change. We then focus on the way in which a transformational leader creates a shared vision and works to create change. Finally, we explore how transformational leaders show active consideration for other people as well as the importance of also paying attention to their own well being.

The main sections of this chapter are:

- the context of change in early years
- harnessing vision and values
- continual learning and responsiveness
- valuing people.

The context of change in early years

Grenier (2003) recounts his experiences as the head of a nursery school tasked with bringing about significant change in practice, which included becoming a children's centre. He points out that the impact of a large-scale change in practice can be emotionally draining. It is crucial that neither children nor families are left just ticking over because the team is focused on the upheaval of change.

Make the connection with ... **your practice**

Grenier describes the process of bringing about significant change as, 'much like taking little steps in slippery mud. Take too big a step and you will fall, or slip backwards. The skill is in searching for a bit of firm ground, or being absolutely sure of your balance before you make a move' (2003, page 24).

Please read Grenier's account of his first 100 days as a nursery school head at **www.tinyurl.com/slipperymud**

- Note down what you feel are the main points that could support you in understanding your role as someone tasked with bringing about positive changes in the team.

- By all means, also note situations that Grenier faced, but which you judge are not current issues for your setting.
- Ideally, discuss your ideas with colleagues or fellow students who have also read the report.

Grenier's account aims to capture the feelings of uncertainty and muddle that is usual in trying to change practice. He expresses concern, which we share, about the negative impact on the self-esteem of Early Years Professionals when they are faced with this reality – particularly after having been given a sanitised version of the change agent role seasoned with an enthusiastic portrayal of inspirational leadership. All change looks like a disaster in the middle – think about being half way through redecorating a room at home! The problem for any work sector is that a less than realistic portrayal of the change process leaves practitioners thinking it is their personal failure that the planned change does not work as well as they anticipated.

In contrast, EYPs can be relieved to hear from experienced practitioners and leaders that change takes longer than you thought, especially if a staff group has not established a tradition of talking and listening, or of working like a team. Part of responsible EYP programmes – or any modules on leadership – has to be an honest acknowledgement that the process of change can be some steps forward and some back, even with the keenest of practitioners.

Pause for reflection

In talking with EYPs and heads of centres, it was quite usual to hear that a significant change had taken between one and two years to establish fully within the team.

- These were examples of important shifts in early years practice, like moving towards flexible planning that follows children's interests, rather than detailed forward activity planning by the adults alone.
- It had taken an equivalent amount of time in more than one setting to bring round less than enthusiastic practitioners to the value, and need, for generous time outdoors with children, as to make the change itself.

It is also worth noting the finding from organisational behaviour that significant change within any service or organisation is unlikely to be secure in less than two years. The problem often is that by then another reorganisation is under way, which makes it hard to know whether the initial change actually worked.

Consider your professional experience of being part of significant change in practice, and compare notes with other people: managerial colleagues or fellow students on the EYP pathway or degree courses. How long did it take before a major change was fully established as part of everyday practice? What were the major problems faced?

Key issues in bringing about change

This section draws on accounts of the change process in early years and from informal conversations with the experienced leaders thanked in the acknowledgements. You might also find it helpful to look again at approaches to organisational change, from page 85.

Vision is necessary but not sufficient on its own to support reflective and purposeful changes in practice. Enthusiasm for a changed future in the setting is crucial. Yet, accounts of what actually happens in settings which have successfully implemented change shows how much sheer staying power and emotional energy is needed before it is established. Key points raised included:

- If you are new to the setting, or coming in from the outside to advise on change, then time has to be spent becoming familiar with the working environment. Assumptions can derail successful implementation of change later. Do the practitioners with whom you will be working think there is scope or need for improvement? If they are not supportive, your work will be harder.
- What is the existing situation in the group? If you are already part of it, then reflect on what you know of your colleagues and ensure that you are fully alert to the diversity of views in the team. Specifically, what do your colleagues feel about the focus for change? Do some oppose it?
- What have they experienced in recent times and has this left them confident that they have good practice, which is respected, so they can consider further improvements? Or have recent events left the team doubting their skills, convinced any suggestions are criticisms and disinclined to listen to yet another 'fad'?

Choices and priorities

Even in a more stable staff group with experience of operating as a team, the change agent still needs to make choices about priorities, because sensible changes cannot be made in many different ways at the same time.

- The initial diagnostic phase is critical to fully understand what is going on and the strengths and weaknesses of the provision. You should then be able to focus on critical elements.
- If you are not focused in your lead towards improved practice, then your colleagues will be confused about where to put their energy and what you want them to do.
- You will lose focus if you spread your energy too widely. It makes good sense to consider and discuss which aspect of practice needs most improvement. Seek to find a small change that will bring most improvement first before tackling more challenging ones. Which would bring most benefit to the children, or the families, if the chosen focus is related to partnership?
- Can you start by using the existing strengths of individual practitioners? For instance, this room team has the ability to be encouraging about children's behaviour. What you have observed is that their ability seems to be applied mostly to the girls. The boys in the room are on the receiving end of much low-

level nagging from the adults. Can the encouragement being given to girls be applied to the boys?

Change depends on good quality information

Whether you are the manager or an EYP tasked with bringing about improvements, you need the firm base of knowing what is happening at the moment. For instance, the Early Years Foundation Stage (for England) highlighted the importance of child-initiated play and conversation, but a recent history of adult-led planning left many practitioners uncertain about how to bring children's interests back to the forefront (Lindon, 2010d).

Does the team really understand how you envisage the improvements? For instance, you may be concerned about the tendency in the team to over-direct children's play. However, do they understand what you mean by the difference between organising for possibilities in play and organising the details of what children will do as they play? One centre head who spoke to us had made the decision to gather observational evidence on the adult-led activities in the centre and monitored how practitioners responded to individual children's ideas and interests. This information highlighted practitioners' uncertainty over how to be an effective play partner. They did not know how to respond spontaneously to how children reacted. This led to team development, acknowledging practitioners' experience in overall planning and organisation of play activities, while addressing the benefits of being more responsive.

You need to track changes through monitoring to see if what practitioners have agreed to do is actually happening. Having a goal for change without monitoring is rather like having nicely drafted and healthy menus, without checking that the cook prepares what is on the written menu and that the children eat it. Monitoring systems are about good management and are linked with sufficiently detailed records of plans from team or room meetings. The skills of monitoring are a reminder that leadership needs to co-exist respectfully with management.

Harnessing vision and values

Much of the focus on transformational leadership is on what previously had been either ignored in the literature on organisations, or felt to be invisible: the emotional arena.

The transformational leader in action

Transformation leadership is about vision, values, norms and the organisational culture. It is orientated towards the social, psychological and process aspects of working, and includes areas such as:

- Emergent power and influence patterns: who is influencing whom, who is following, who is leading?
- Individuals' views of their organisation, and their views on their own and others' competence.

- Patterns of informal groups and their relationships – networks within this organisation.
- What are the real links between people – at the same and different levels? How much trust and openness is visible?
- How willing are people to take risks within their work: to strive to continually learn and improve?
- How people see their own role, and their underlying values.
- What are people's feelings, their needs, wants and fears?

Transformational leadership focuses on the organisational culture as well as developing strategy. Transformational leadership is big; it has a very wide scope.

Figure 7.1 is an edited version of our organisation model from Chapter 3, featuring only the transformational aspects. You will see the dotted feedback loop from the 'output' box, as the results in terms of individual and organisational performance influence both the mission and the organisational culture. For example, if a nursery has been significantly criticised by the inspectorate, morale is likely to drop, which affects the organisational culture and reduces willingness to put in the extra effort required. Changes will need to be made to strategy to overcome the problems.

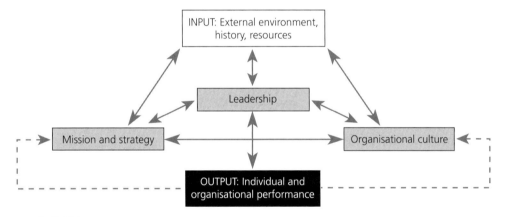

Figure 7.1 The transformational set organisation

For the leader of any large organisation, for example heads of children's centres, the overall context is much more complex than for a small setting. The history will be more diverse, the environment (including the local community) more multi-faceted, demands for resources (both physical and human) broader. Self-management is critical for transformational leaders (remember Chapter 5), as is their quest for learning and continued professional development – both for themselves and everyone responsible to them.

Figure 7.1 highlights the key roles of the transformational leader to:
- model and demonstrate effective leadership skills
- work on and develop a mission (or vision) and a strategy to achieve this
- understand and develop a positive organisational culture of improvement and energy where issues are surfaced and dealt with.

Once more, the ultimate outputs are improved performance and job satisfaction.

A wide range of terms is used in the literature, and also in practice, to describe elements of the organisational mix. It is not at all unusual to find different meanings applied to the same terms within a profession, let alone in different professional areas. For example, one of us (LL) worked as a consultant with two organisations concurrently which both used the terms 'policy' and 'strategy'. However, for one organisation, 'policy' was defined in practice as the overall direction of the business and 'strategy' was the route to achieve the policy. For the other organisation, the use of terms was exactly reversed.

So it is important to know what we mean by key terms, and these are outlined below:

- Vision – the long-term overall aim of this organisation.
- Mission – a major step in the achievement of the vision. The written statements for a vision, the mission or of goals never have words like 'try' in them. They define results, what you are committed to make happen, measurable outcomes and not a commitment to do your best, with the built-in proviso that you may not succeed.
- Goal – an objective, which is a specific part of the mission. If all goals are successfully achieved, the mission will be accomplished. If the missions are achieved, then the vision will also be achieved.
- Strategy – the agreed ways in which to achieve your objectives, and hence the mission(s) and vision.
- Policy – the ways in which you wish to treat the customers of your service or your staff.
- Values – what everyone, as part of this organisation, holds to be true. Values are important in their own right. Values are typically short, simple and all-encompassing.
- Beliefs – the operating principles that derive directly from the values.

For example, a value could be 'Children are paramount'. Beliefs deriving from this single value could be: 'We always put children's needs first,' 'Children are the most important members of society as our future depends on them,' or 'We consider parents' requests in terms of what it means for their children.'

Make the connection with … **your practice**

Have you drafted a vision statement for your own provision? Consider the details in the light of the ideas in this section.

Vision statements are best if brief. However, what is important about vision statements is that these should satisfy the setting – and needs for detail differ. Do what is needed to get ownership and clarity internally.

We advise that it is better to address the vision and values as separate, though related, issues. This helps later when defining goals and developing a strategy to reach your destination.

Having a vision and making it real

A key component of transformational leadership is having a vision of where the organisation needs to be. The same – or similar – concept to a vision is sometimes called a mission. Visions and missions are confusing, in that the terms are sometimes interchangeable, and sometimes not. Typically, if both crop up together, 'visions' tend to be farther away (say 10 or 20 years hence), whereas missions are nearer (three to five years is usual). In this section we use the word 'vision' – as that is common usage within the literature about early years leadership – although we note that the 'mission' time scale is more used in early years.

Warren Bennis commented, 'All leaders have the capacity to create a compelling vision, one that takes people to a new place, and the ability to translate that vision into reality' (1990, page 46). The image of travel to a new place is a useful one, as it includes not only the definition of your destination – where are you going? – but also details of the necessary arrangements – how will you get there? To extend the travel analogy a bit more – sensible choices need to be made about which sort of transport to use: how long can you spend travelling, how much money have you got and what are the preferences of your fellow travellers?

Consistent research shows that it is the presence of this personal vision of a leader, shared with members of the organisation, which differentiates leaders from managers. The importance of the vision has been emphasised in the literature about school leadership, just as much as in the world of business (SEDL, 2011). One reviewer expressed the idea as, 'Future vision is a comprehensive picture of how an organisation will look at some point in the future, including how it will be positioned in its environment and how it will function internally' (Manasse, 1986, page 157).

Making the vision real is a key task of the transformational leader, and we argue that making this meaningful to everyone is absolutely fundamental. Even the most energetic transformational leader cannot work alone. She or he needs to create, and maintain, a sense of shared responsibility for change in the provision. Staff must believe and actively commit to the way forward. It is not enough to just share a vision – what it means to everyone involved must be actively managed. This typically involves deciding the facts that staff need to know, and what you want them to believe as a conclusion. Together these should result in people forming an emotional attachment to the vision. A transformational leader will get nowhere with a personal vision which nobody else shares. It will be worse than useless, as the leader's credibility in this case will tend to zero.

The vision is the over-riding aim of your service; it sums up your reason for existence, the critical function of your provision, what you strive to achieve and what motivates you. The whole organisation should want to achieve it.

- The vision is demanding but not impossible to achieve. Visions are not a pipe-dream. In early years practice, you should be able to achieve your vision within a few years. It is not about the short term – neither is it necessarily about envisaging your provision decades into the future.

- Visions focus on *one* critical element – for example, the children or the parents – not both. A vision is very clear in its intent.
- The statement of your vision is ideally (and usually) quite brief; it is the hub around which all your other efforts gather. A short vision is also far more memorable – for if hardly anyone can remember the vision, it is highly unlikely ever to be fulfilled. It is often useful to discuss the values (those things we hold dear and fundamental) to lock into people's motivation to achieve the vision.
- The details are credible: people can see that they can do it – albeit with some stretch. Therefore, in organisational terms, the vision needs to be realistic, given the capabilities and motivation of the staff, and their scope for continued development.
- The vision is expressed in a way that you can assess whether it has been achieved, or to what extent. Going back to the travel analogy, it will be possible to know that you have reached your destination. You are not trying or hoping to get to Edinburgh; you will reach Edinburgh and not Glasgow. By the way, reaching Newcastle (because it is on the way and we are nearly there) is neither all right nor acceptable.

Make the connection with ... **early years practice**

Here are some vision statements from fictional early years settings.

- Crocus Playgroup will be at the heart of the local community
- Meerkats Day Nursery will be an outdoor nursery
- Princes Children's Centre will be the most innovative setting in the county
- Greyhorse Road Nursery and Primary School will improve the life chances of all the children.

We discuss some of the examples in this section, but first of all:

- How would you know if you had realised any of these visions?
- What goals would you set to measure achievement?
- How do you feel a parent would respond to hearing these statements?

Linking the vision to the values and 'the heart'

The vision makes most sense in the context of your core values: statements you find worthwhile, respect and esteem in their own right. The core values of an early years team will inform anyone else of what you care about deeply. Values are strongly held and are emotional in nature – you feel deeply about them and they are *very* resistant to change. Your route to achieving the vision has to be consistent with your values. Often values can be identified by asking the question 'how' of the vision statement, or 'we will do this by...'.

Scenario

Wesley, the head of Greyhorse Road Nursery and Primary School, says that they will achieve their vision to improve the life opportunities for all the children in accord with their value of being in partnership with parents.

This stance may make achieving the vision more difficult than going it alone. However, Wesley can make a strong case that the non-negotiable value of working in partnership with parents is also strengthened by research about parental engagement in their children's learning. Finding effective ways to bring parents on board (the details of their strategy) is more likely to improve the children's prospects and so to realise the vision.

Wesley will need to agree how to measure 'improved life opportunities' and set criteria for what this means. Furthermore, the Greyhorse Road team will have to decide the boundaries of their responsibility. For example, 'getting children into their parents' preferred secondary schools' is not under their control. Their strategy, however, will definitely not be to meet targets about children's progress by sidelining any parents who object.

Please use this fictional example to highlight the decisions that you have made in your setting as you worked on the vision, values and strategy.

The transformational leader is active in clarifying and developing the vision and values that determine what is done in this setting and how to do it. For instance, if push comes to shove, whose best interests have to prevail: those of the children or their parents? Of course, you seek a form of partnership in action which respects family choices. However, the leader is responsible for guiding the team when agreement with a parent's request would, in your professional judgement, undermine children's well being or actually put them at risk. The transformational leader acknowledges the confusion that can be experienced in the team when it seems as if any decision taken will be wrong in some way. She or he guides them through problem solving appropriately by recalling the core values for this provision. The leader supports and encourages staff for acting in accord with these values.

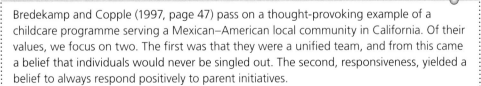

Take another **perspective**

Bredekamp and Copple (1997, page 47) pass on a thought-provoking example of a childcare programme serving a Mexican–American local community in California. Of their values, we focus on two. The first was that they were a unified team, and from this came a belief that individuals would never be singled out. The second, responsiveness, yielded a belief to always respond positively to parent initiatives.

As a result, the centre team were very uneasy when parents wished to give gifts to individual teachers. The parents wanted to express their appreciation and gift-giving was a habit rooted in the local culture. The team wanted to show respect but felt that individuals should not be singled out.

This dilemma is a values example of changing an either-or problem into a both-and situation. The director of the foundation running the programme worked with the team to resolve the impasse over the team accepting or rejecting the gifts as both actions went against a core value. They reached an agreement to accept the gifts, but not as individuals. This was fine with the parents and hence resolved the dilemma. Any gifts were taken on behalf of the whole centre and used for the benefit of everyone.

Think of an example when you have had to problem solve because two equally important values pulled the team in opposing directions.

Bringing out 'the unmentionables'

The process of working through vision and values can raise a whole bunch of issues which may force everyone to challenge their own views. This is a fundamentally transformational process, not merely the instruction and support a practitioner should get from the transactional manager. Sometimes these views are called the 'unmentionables'. Even though these are usually hidden they affect individual practitioners or, more significantly, exert an impact on the whole group.

An individual example would be that Claire truly struggles with one of her key children, Joshua, who has a severe disability on the autistic spectrum. She finds Joshua's repetitive behaviour hard to accept and continues to try to stop his all-consuming interest in wheeled vehicles. Claire finds it very hard to talk about positive strategies with Joshua as she feels that she just 'ought' to be more relaxed with him. The reality is that Claire cannot stop herself being impatient with Joshua, with the result that she is miserable and he is distressed by her actions. The only way to help Joshua, and Claire, is to bring the issues out into the open, and find changes that will help both of them.

The transformational leader supports a commitment to learning in the team by being clear about the ways in which choices are made and the nature of problem solving. Too often decisions can be made on the basis of either-or. In the example above this would be expressed as *either* Claire learns to be more relaxed with Joshua *or* she will have to give up being his key person. The approach can be one of both-and. Claire feels very strongly that she does not want to cease being Joshua's key person. She is motivated *both* to work on stopping herself from proposing activities in which Joshua has no interest *and* to accept direct help from Joshua's father, who has practical ideas for how to widen his son's interests a bit.

Unmentionables often involve the entire group – either because the view is shared by many staff or because the strong view of a few practitioners affects the working atmosphere. Examples of views that need to be brought into the open and resolved could be: 'Hetty can't really be committed to the children; she keeps putting herself up for promotion,' 'Not another kid from the Harris family!' or 'Children should just eat what we put on their plate. Why are we giving them any choice?' It is necessary to confront such views in order to remove the blocks to acting differently and more effectively.

Addressing issues like these is not easy; there is almost certainly more than one room or full team discussion involved – and outside help may be needed. However, if the views are not challenged and thoroughly talked through, then it is likely that the unmentionable will derail the process of change. This discussion can be a key part of the transformational process from which better understanding emerges, and with it greater commitment to the vision and the setting.

Making the vision tangible through goals

The vision will only come alive if the leader works with the team to determine specific and realistic goals to which staff commit. These goals are derived directly from the vision. So the vision is broken up into goals (some people use the word 'objectives' instead), and the achievement of all of these specific, measurable goals will result in the achievement of the vision. The strategy will include how the goals link together, and what has to be done to reach them in accord with the setting's values and beliefs. We have highlighted these ideas through some fictional examples.

Scenarios

Please consider these two examples and use them to reflect on your own practice.

Meerkats Day Nursery

Becky and Jo, joint owner/managers of Meerkats, need to be clear with the team about what they mean by being an outdoor nursery. It is that a free-flow system will enable children and staff to spend most of the day outside.

Given the current situation, goals are needed to enable the under-twos to enjoy safe free flow. Another goal relates to reorganising the garden to make the most of spaces. The team shares the belief that involving the children in decisions that directly affect their life at nursery is beneficial. So any changes will be informed by finding out what the children currently enjoy doing outdoors and any special places that they would not want to be changed.

Notice here that goals can be sequential. For example, until the goal of safety for the youngest children is achieved, it is pointless to reorganise the outside space, as doing this first might compromise the safety goal.

Princes Children's Centre

A vision will not come alive if the meaning and implications are not made clear to all. The leader must identify which members of staff are fundamental to delivering the vision, and focus attention on these.

Brigid, the head of Princes Children's Centre, is especially proud of the centre's innovatory approach to establishing healthy habits for children over diet and physical activity. It is critical that Brigid works closely to address the initial reluctance of Lottie, the centre's new cook, to lead in the achievement of the goal for children to be helping prepare food. Lottie is crucial to elements of achieving the vision. Her involvement will also be central if the centre is to meet the expressed wishes of a large group of parents for practical sessions on how to cook.

Brigid needs to find ways to address the sources of Lottie's resistance. The cook needs to be brought into line with the vision, and – if necessary – reminded that her job description includes the expectation that the centre's cook will work alongside the rest of the team for the well being of children and families.

....

We suggest you read some vision statements from other (actual) settings. Examples come up if you Google 'vision statement+nurseries'. Some are brief, while others include considerable detail about underpinning values and goals that will contribute rather than a vision as we have described it. Sometimes people in a setting are so proud of what they achieve from working on missions, goals, strategy, values and beliefs that they make it all public. This decision needs to be a careful choice. The purpose of the vision and values is to get everyone in the organisation pulling willingly in the same direction. It is a marketing decision about whether it is published in full or not, on the setting's website or fixed to a notice board. The issues involved are described in the following scenario.

Scenario

The team of Crocus Playgroup may all fully understand their '22 principles', but other people may find them confusing. The manager, Natalie – acting as a transformational leader – has to confront the reality of emotional work. She has to disappoint the staff, as she recognises that it is better for the playgroup's future if much of the material is kept in-house.

Natalie is aware that some of the statements are very demanding, and some may not be realised quickly. She does not want a father reading, 'Children will leave our nursery smiling' and then challenging the key person over why his daughter was upset when he picked her up on Thursday. Natalie will have to deal with her staff's initial disappointment and continue forward.

● Have you experienced a situation like this? What did you learn?
● What decisions have you made about how much you make public of your setting's vision and values?

....

To achieve the vision requires people to work well: transformational leaders show a passion for performance and what is achieved – the results. Vision without appropriate action is just a fantasy. Actions, without the context of a unifying vision, can be disconnected or have hard-working staff groups heading in different directions. A familiar phrase is, 'We're all in the same boat' and this is a good way of looking at a setting. You want everyone pulling in the same direction. You cannot have one member drilling a hole in the boat, saying, 'I have complete responsibility for this bit of the boat, and can drill if I choose.'

Transformational leaders emphasise outcomes: the actual achievements rather than being a nice person and working hard but not actually achieving anything. Of course, practitioners need, and deserve, support and guidance to turn best efforts into actual results. But in the end satisfaction and excitement in the work comes from achieving goals leading to the shared vision.

Continual learning and responsiveness

Transformational leaders will provide the positive environment that is crucial to support the development of the skills needed by groups and individuals. To do this they ensure that the necessary resources, both human and material, are in place to make the shared vision a reality.

Leaders set a good example

The emphasis on constantly developing skills should be exemplified by the leader. She or he is constantly, and visibly to the staff, learning through all possible strands of continued professional development, including seeking informative feedback from others. This information can come from both inside the setting and outside. Transformational leaders seek to compare their operation to different enterprises to see what insights can be applied to make improvements to practice.

Focus on learning is crucial to developing an organisational culture based on being responsive to the needs of parents and children and one that can continually adapt to change. For example, Brigid, the head of Princes Children's Centre, listens to the receptionist's valuable feedback that parents were complaining to each other when they came out of the first session of the new parenting programme. Brigid is ready to discuss with the person running the course what is happening and how to respond before the situation gets out of hand.

Learning from other settings

Some early years settings, their leader and the team, can be rather isolated and this situation generates suspicion about the motives of outsiders, especially those whose setting is in competition.

Henry (2010) describes the key issues for encouraging partner settings to benefit from visits and the value of a fresh pair of eyes and constructive comments from a fellow professional. She raises these key points from the leadership programme which she runs:

- The early sessions enabled participants to get to know and trust each other. Settings were paired and so the process of visiting and constructive feedback involved both giving and receiving.
- Part of the accreditation process for the programme was that everyone had to write up their visit within the same pro forma.
- There was a clear purpose for visiting. Information was generated on an area of practice which the visiting manager judged was a good standard, an aspect of practice which could be improved and something from this practice that visitors would like to apply within their own setting.

This even-handedness, alongside the continued professional relationship within the programme, meant that understandable unease could be overcome. When an atmosphere of trust has been established, then managers can be pleased to realise that other local managers face similar challenges – and may have some answers. Sharing practice experiences enables everyone to focus on the best strategies, for example, how to best link observation into worthwhile planning. The nursery across town had not solved all the problems about guiding children's behaviour, but together better ideas emerged.

Purposeful visiting between the paired settings also supported more consideration by managers about their own current practice and the extent to which they were reflective. Sometimes, this further thought about what and why confirmed that the current way of organising did work best in this setting. However, through discussions, the manager and staff had a better grasp of the reasons for continuing this approach. This sense of a more active, reasoned choice made it easier to support it if queried by parents or the inspectorate.

A key feature of the EYP programme, and sometimes of modules on Early Childhood Studies degrees, has been that practitioners visit the settings of fellow students who are part of the same programme. From our informal conversations with EYPs, the consistent message has been that EYPs appreciate the expectation that they should spend time in another setting. They had emerged with fresh ideas and some EYPs had forged a relationship with another setting that continued after the completion of their pathway. Building on this, local authorities, sometimes in combination with neighbouring authorities, have developed EYP networks that meet on a regular basis for continued professional development.

Welcoming fellow practitioners into your setting necessitates trust that you have a shared understanding about confidentiality: they will be observing daily events in your setting. Trust also encompasses a secure level of confidence in visiting professionals' skills of observation and constructive feedback, when the agreement is that they offer a review of your practice.

Focusing on both how and what

Transformational leaders spend as much time managing *how* things are done as well as *what* is done.

For example, although the recent parents' evening in FineStart nursery went very well, the success was down to Theo's very hard work, rather than to that of the entire group. It is acceptable that one person takes responsibility to coordinate an event, but it was never the plan for Theo to do everything himself. Katy, the manager, works to ensure better participation and a more equal workload in the future. After praising Theo, Katy takes an informed and realistic view of new tasks and roles for which other practitioners, like Sadie and Kim, are actually capable, even though they may doubt it themselves.

Even when an event or other new development does not go as well as planned, the message of the transformational leader is clear: *how* can we do better, not *why* we failed, why it would never work, or whose fault it was. Failures and mistakes are seen as an opportunity to learn and to improve. Typically, trying new ideas, and sometimes not succeeding, is much better than always playing it safe and not taking any risks at all. Without taking some risks, there will be no new learning and hence there is very limited scope to develop new skills and boost self-confidence. Sometimes the leader has to offer staff the chance to 'fail', by giving then a very challenging task – in order to see what they can actually achieve. Once more, it is not failure if they do not make it – they have just not succeeded – yet.

Valuing people

Leaders go beyond the development of a common vision; they provide an environment that promotes individual contributions to the enterprise.

Time for communication

Transformational leaders ensure that staff are confident their opinions and concerns are fully worthy of the leader's time and serious consideration. Only then will practitioners feel valued and able to devote their full attention to children and parents. If, say, the concerns of parents seem always to out-rank those of the staff, then there is a real danger that practitioners will not feel valued. As such, they are likely to put in less effort to improve practice. The needs of the children should be to the fore, but 'the children come first' is not a mantra to be repeated in order to dismiss the opinions of staff.

Transformational leaders have the ability to harness and channel the collective ambitions and aspirations of the workforce to a common goal. In other words, staff support the leader and the vision, because they see that by so doing *they are doing something in their own best interest.* That term sounds familiar, because it was part of the discussion about 'acceptance and rejection of authority' on page 41. Continued communication further supports the sense of being 'in this together'. The leader manages staff's expectations on a daily basis to keep everyone on track about what is happening – particularly for events that are not usual. So no practitioner is surprised when a consultant appears, because everyone knew that this person was arriving today and with what purpose.

Collaboration, courtesy and respect

Transformational leaders develop and maintain collaborative relationships. They identify and nurture key supporters as well as form and support teams towards the common vision. Leaders behave in this way because they genuinely value individuals – not just as a bunch of people who happen to work here and do a good job – but as whole individuals with hopes, aspirations, feelings and a life outside work.

Relationships are approached in terms of the present, not of the past. What is done is done, and if there were problems, corrective action should have been taken at the time; raking over past errors is unhelpful and disheartening. Critically, the transformational leader accepts people as they are, not how they would like or want them to be.

For instance, Michaela is a thoughtful and responsible practitioner in this pre-school team. Helen, her manager, is sure that Michaela is ready for the deputy's position and outlines a plan for Michaela to extend her qualifications. Yet Michaela turns down this offer, explaining that currently she needs a job without pressures in order to focus on her young family. It would be inappropriate for Helen to express frustration, because Michaela did not embrace the plan or was ungrateful for the confidence shown in her. Helen has to absorb her frustration that Michaela is not really like her. Helen has always thought, if she had been given just such a chance, she could have become a manager ten years earlier.

Transformational leaders treat every member of staff with the courtesy and respect that is often reserved for unknown visitors arriving at the setting. Perhaps parents who are interested in the nursery or professional visitors receive a more polite and assiduous response than familiar colleagues – particularly if, like inspectors, they are seen as powerful. You are careful to get their names right, perhaps offer a coffee. If you know in advance, you prepare for the arrival of such visitors. Too often at work, it is tempting not to bother to prepare. Perhaps familiarity breeds, if not contempt, but a reduced level of respect. Knowledge of colleagues may be used to wind them up or humorously reject their comments, perhaps quoting past history. The transformational leader, in particular, cannot afford to be dismissive of others in any way.

Emotionally literate leaders

We discussed emotional intelligence from page 58. It is useful to return to the ideas here, since they contribute to the picture of a transformational leader who values people. Emotional literacy is part of this complex.

Goleman *et al.* (2002) remind us that people may forget exactly what you said or did, but are very likely to recall clearly the feelings that you evoked in them by what you did in a given situation. Goleman *et al.* warn against what they call a 'toxic' form of leadership, where leaders use their position and understanding of emotions to undermine people within the group. They focus primarily on dictatorial approaches and carping criticism. However, in early years provision there can also be the toxic effect of a manager who is nearly paralysed by anxiety. This dominant emotion may be linked with external figures, like the inspectorate, but it could also be an internal dynamic: the manager feels unable to challenge more powerful staff members or to dismantle disruptive cliques.

Two styles identified by Goleman *et al.* are relevant here.

1 The emotionally intelligent leader is able to *command*, in order to remind the team about issues that are non-negotiable when children are involved. Effective, and safe, early years leaders learn how to be forceful, straight-talking at the appropriate time, with the correct people, in the right place and in the best way. This might be in a group context, when the team needs to be reminded of the task at hand. For an individual, it could mean a private conversation that in some cases will only be fully effective when there is thorough back-up in the management systems for supervision, and if necessary, for disciplinary procedures.

2 The *affiliative* style focuses on creating harmony in the team, with the aim of supporting individuals to connect in working relationships. The positive impact in early years provision will be a commitment to nurture for adults as much as for children. The potential downside arises if harmony in the team becomes a higher priority than resolving issues or shaky practice that should be sorted out. Goleman *et al.* describe this as an anxious affiliative approach. Harmony cannot be held as more important than a shared vision for the team and the leaders' ability to ensure the necessary skills are in place to achieve that vision. An excessive focus on the affiliative style raises problems over conflict. Too much conflict can undoubtedly be disruptive and can lead to hurt feelings and scapegoating. Too little conflict leads to poor information exchange, difficulty in raising any disagreements, and staff padding around issues rather than dealing with them directly.

Human nature has been a constant over the centuries. Aristotle, an ancient Greek philosopher, said, 'Anyone can be angry, that is easy. But to be angry with the right person, to the right degree, at the right time, for the right purpose, and in the right way – that is not easy' (from *The Nicomachean Ethics*). As a manager, it may be appropriate to be angry about a clear breach of practice, but this should not just come out uncontrollably. The leader should have planned, in this case, that expressing the anger she genuinely feels will be the most effective way to get the errant practitioner to mend her ways.

Often the leader will be very sympathetic to the real difficulties faced by staff members in their personal life. However, leaders have to temper their empathy for staff's domestic difficulties, when there is an observable negative impact on practice. In some cases, the manager has to communicate that unless a practitioner's performance improves (in specific ways), his or her future in the setting is at risk. Leadership is not easy.

It is a major challenge for the transformational leader to use emotion, yet regulate feelings with a conscious awareness of not only what is felt, but also a choice whether or not to express that emotion openly. Remember Helen's frustration with Michaela on page 198.

Celebrating accomplishments

Transformational leaders publicise successes widely – both about the organisation and about individuals. Praise is widely (not narrowly) given – they match rewards to desired behaviours. The preferred approach is small rewards for many, rather than large rewards for a few. Praise is typically done in public (so that other staff may learn what achievements are rewarded and hence to see the practices that are valued), with reprimands or help to overcome a setback done in private. Recall the ABC of management from page 153.

There is plenty of informal recognition day by day and regular praise builds pride, enthusiasm and commitment in the workforce. Special events to celebrate achievements regularly occur. For example, if Lottie involves the children in food preparation, a meal may be provided for parents where she is enthusiastically thanked by all for her contribution. A proud leader may put the setting or individual team members forward for awards such as those run by specialist early years magazines.

Trust – the glue that holds an enterprise together

Trust is critical to running effective organisations; they simply will not work without it. You may ask or tell people what to do, but ultimately you trust them to do it. You cannot supervise everyone doing everything all of the time. Can you imagine a major event functioning without trust? The royal wedding of William and Catherine in April 2011 is a good example. The media, horse riders, police, clergy and guests were trusted to do what was expected. If they had not – or in fact if any had not – the ceremony and the spectacle would have been disrupted.

Trust is also a key issue for professional networking (page 195) and a sound reason why local networks, as a way to build competence, need to be established and supported with care. This trust needs to be established initially between the managers of each setting. They will be crucial in explaining to the whole team what will happen and why during any of these visits. The same professional courtesy applies whenever someone is visiting a setting in an advisory or consultancy context.

Believing that others are trustworthy is the default setting. It is also the best way to find out whether someone can be trusted. Only if there is compelling evidence to the contrary should this trust be suspended – and even so, be wary of generalising. Remember the discussion of trust from page 157. For example, if Tyrone has twice given you inaccurate information about the timing of the next school half-term, it is tempting to say that he cannot be trusted to get the dates right for the holiday play scheme. However, Tyrone has never failed over his timings related to the scheme; he is trustworthy in terms of execution. It may be that Tyrone needs to double-check his information before telling you. He may need to be checked for a while before you trust him fully.

It is vital for the transformational leader to develop and build trust. To recap, this means: doing what you say you will do, giving accurate information at all times, and updating people in timely fashion if things change.

Managing yourself

The transformational leader has to be self-disciplined and conscious of what he or she is doing all the time – a point that is raised through many of the examples in this chapter. McClelland and Boyatzis (1982) point out that leaders need to exercise regular self-control, by placing the needs of the organisation above their personal wishes. This self-management necessarily requires energy and increases the level of stress experienced by the leader. Leaders have to balance the demands of logic and emotion, control and freedom by focusing on what is important, and carefully choosing when and where to confront what is not working. The process is truly 'hearts and minds' because, as we know, people are not exclusively rational.

Leaders need to be self-aware (an important element in reflective practice, Lindon, 2010b) and part of this is understanding your own feelings about using power and authority. The major sources of power at the leader's disposal – legitimate, expert, reward and coercive power, discussed from page 151 – may be required to help the setting to realise the vision. If you have difficulty using any of these, then your overall capacity to influence others may be significantly reduced.

Caruso and Salovey (2004) talk about a leader's ability to change or switch emotional gears. Done in an authentic way, it can be positive for a leader to bring another emotion to the forefront, even if it is not the first feeling you experience. For instance, there could be times when the team will benefit from the leader's honesty that, 'My first reaction to this news was to start getting anxious. I decided

I'm not going that way.' Of course, the leader then has to effectively deal with whatever could provoke anxiety in this news. Leaders need to be emotionally honest, yet fulfil their obligation to support the team. Sometimes it is important to use positive emotion to overcome a negative mood.

Like other leaders, those in early years provision have to resist the pressure to do everything themselves as the best way to ensure best practice. Realistically, you cannot do everything; you need to trust that practitioners will do their jobs well and to give guidance is needed – as discussed in Chapter 6. Otherwise, everyone is under pressure. The leader is doing too much and the rest of the staff feel watched all the time. As a result practice is less good and the organisational culture suffers. The consequence is that the dominant approach in the setting becomes 'We're doing the best we can,' or 'We're no worse than anyone else.' This is when mistakes and failures are accepted as normal and falling short of good practice becomes part of the organisational culture.

Make the connection with … **your own practice**

Please look through this section and consider what applies to you. For instance:

- Can you identify areas in which you find it hard to keep your opinions to yourself?
- Are there some areas of work that you enjoy so much that you are reluctant to let go of them?

Valuing and taking care of yourself

Generally speaking, as Kotter (1979) identified, the higher up a person is within the organisation the more power and responsibility is involved in their role and consequently the more stressful their situation can be. The leader of an organisation is dependent on others to do their work, and on other levels of the hierarchy who are responsible for ensuring that junior colleagues work to a high standard. Top leaders feel, and in our view *should* feel, responsible for the collective results of the organisation. Transformational leaders are able to function without the approval or permission of others to maintain direction and focus and to protect their organisation. There is no doubt that being a transformational leader can be lonely. Effective leaders have the courage, self-confidence and capability to make difficult choices, and stand by them.

Inevitably leaders have to learn to tolerate periods of pressure and feeling under stress; it comes with the position. A level of stress which feels manageable to you is not necessarily negative. Effective leaders often feel a real buzz of operating under pressure: focusing utterly on the task in hand to succeed – 'Yes, I've (or we've) done it!' As a concept 'stress' is neutral. We would not do anything without some kind of stress – we eat when we feel hungry, we sleep when we feel tired. It is distress that is negative. However, unrelenting pressure will overload – and distress – even the most resilient of leaders.

- Sustained and unrelieved stress has a negative effect, often called 'burn-out' in the organisational literature and that of counselling (Lindon and Lindon, 2008).
- Burn-out has well-defined physiological effects: ill health, sleep disturbance and greater propensity to pick up infections (Sapolsky, 1999).
- The physical impact takes a toll on psychological well being so that an emotionally exhausted leader becomes short-tempered or looks to staff for the support that leaders themselves should offer.
- If this downward slide continues, the leader (or anyone for that matter) risks becoming spiritually drained, summed up by a feeling that everything is meaningless – 'What is the point of anything?'

Helping others can help you, too

Interestingly, Boyatzis *et al.* (2006) argue that the stress levels of the leader can be significantly reduced by having caring and compassionate relationships with staff as a coach or mentor to them. This important working (and essentially transactional) relationship will help to sustain their leadership effectiveness over time. Without great personal resilience, the greater the duration of stress, the more likely it is that a leader will become ineffective. Leaders need the level of self-awareness that enables them to recognise what is happening and the humility to accept support, particularly from others going through similar experiences. Informal and formal networks can help leaders to share their stresses and strains, successes and setbacks, with others who can empathise. Sometimes outside consultants or coaches can provide a safe place for the leader to discuss issues in confidence. We keep saying that leadership can be lonely – these are a couple of ways to make it less so!

Resources

- **Bennis, W.** (1990) 'Managing the dream: Leadership in the 21st century'. *Training: The Magazine of Human Resource Development*, 27, 5, 44–6.
- **Boyatzis, R., Smith, M. and Blaize, N.** (2006) 'Developing sustainable leaders through coaching and compassion'. *Academy of Management Journal on Learning and Education*, 5, 1, 8–24.
- **Bredekamp, S. and Copple, C.** (eds) (1997) *Developmentally Appropriate Practice in Early Childhood Programs.* Washington, DC: National Association for the Education of Young Children.
- **Caruso, D. and Salovey, P.** (2004) *The Emotionally Intelligent Manager: How to develop and use the four key emotional skills of leadership.* San Francisco, CA: Jossey-Bass.
- **Goleman, D., Boyatzis, R. and McKee, A.** (2002) *The New Leaders: Transforming the art of leadership into the science of results.* London: Time Warner.
- **Grenier, J.** (2003) *Small Steps, Slippery Mud: 100 days as a nursery school head.* www.tinyurl.com/slipperymud
- **Henry, L.** (2010) 'Open the door to new ideas'. *Nursery World*, 28 January, 26–7.

- **Kotter, J.P.** (1979) *Power in Management.* New York: Amacom Books.
- **Lawrence, Y., Robins, D. and Twells, B.** (2008) *Teachers into Leaders: Networking and leadership development.* www.nationalcollege.org.uk/docinfo?id=17422&filename=teachers-into-leaders-summary.pdf
- **Leithwood, K., Day, C., Sammons, P., Harris, A. and Hopkins, D.** (2008) *Successful School Leadership: What It Is and How It Influences Pupil Learning.* Department for Children Schools and Families with National College for School Leadership. http://education.gov.uk/publications/eOrderingDownload/RR800.pdf
- **Lindon, J.** (2010b) *Reflective Practice and Early Years Professionalism.* London: Hodder Education.
- **Lindon, J.** (2010d) *Child-initiated Learning: Positive relationships in the early years.* London: Practical Pre-School Books.
- **Lindon, J. and Lindon, L.** (2008) *Mastering Counselling Skills.* Basingstoke: Palgrave Macmillan.
- **Manasse, A.** (1986) 'Vision and leadership: Paying attention to intention'. *Peabody Journal of Education,* 63, 1, 150–73.
- **McClelland, D. A. and Boyatzis, R.** (1982) 'Leadership motive pattern and long term success in management'. *Journal of Applied Psychology,* 67, 9, 737–43.
- **Sapolsky, R.M.** (1999) 'The physiology and pathophysiology of unhappiness'. In Kahneman, D., Diener, E. and Schwarz, N. (eds) *Well-being: The foundations of hedonic psychology.* New York: Russell Sage Foundation.
- **Schein, E.H.** (1997) *Organizational Culture and Leadership.* San Francisco, CA: Jossey-Bass.
- SEDL (2011) *Leadership Characteristics That Facilitate School Change.* www.sedl.org/change/leadership/character.html

References

Alvesson, M. and Billing, Y. (2009) *Understanding Gender and Organizations.* London: Sage.

Anning, A., Cottrell, D., Frost, N., Green, J. and Robinson, M. (2006) *Developing Multiprofessional Teamwork for Integrated Children's Centres.* Maidenhead: Open University Press.

Antonakis, J., Voilio, B. and Sivasubramaniam, N. (2003) 'Content and leadership: An examination of the nine-factor full-range leadership theory using the Multifactor Leadership Questionnaire'. *Leadership Quarterly,* 14, 3, 261–95.

Aubrey, C. (2007) *Leading and Managing in the Early Years.* London: Sage.

Avolio, B. and Gardner, W. (2005) 'Authentic leadership development: Getting to the root of positive forms of leadership'. *Leadership Quarterly,* 16, 315–38.

Back, K. and Back, K. with Bates, T. (1991) *Assertiveness at Work,* 2nd edition. Maidenhead: McGraw-Hill.

Bales, R. (1950) *Interaction Process Analysis: A method for the study of small groups.* Cambridge: Addison-Wesley. Reprinted 1976, University of Chicago Press.

Bales, R. (1999) *Social Interaction Systems: Theory and Measurement.* New Brunswick: Transaction Publishers.

Bales, R. and Cohen, S. (1979) *SYMLOG: A system for the multiple level observation of groups.* New York: Free Press.

Barnes, L.B. and Kriger, M.P. (1986) 'The hidden side of organizational leadership'. *Sloan Management Review,* 28, 1, 15–25.

Bass, B. and Bass, R. (2008) *The Bass Handbook of Leadership: Theory, research, and managerial applications,* 4th edition. New York: Free Press.

Baumrind, D. (1967) 'Child-care practices anteceding three patterns of preschool behaviour'. *Genetic Psychology Monographs,* 75, 43–88.

Bennis, W. (1990) 'Managing the dream: Leadership in the 21st century'. *Training: The Magazine of Human Resource Development,* 27, 5, 44–6.

Bennis, W. and Nanus, B. (1985) *Leaders: The strategies for taking charge.* New York: Harper and Row.

Blake, R. and McCanse, A. (1991) *Leadership Dilemmas: Grid Solutions.* Houston, TX: Gulf Publishing Co.

Blake, R. and Mouton, J. (1964) *The Managerial Grid: The key to leadership excellence.* Houston, TX: Gulf Publishing Co.

Blanchard, K. and Lorber, R. (1984) *Putting the One Minute Manager to Work.* London: Fontana/Collins.

Blanchard, K., Zigarmi, P. and Zigarmi, D. (1986) *Leadership and the One Minute Manager.* London: Fontana/Collins.

Boyatzis, R., Smith, M. and Blaize, N. (2006) 'Developing sustainable leaders through coaching and compassion'. *Academy of Management Journal on Learning and Education,* 5, 1, 8–24.

Boyle, M.E. and Smith, M.K. (2001) 'Classical leadership'. *The Encyclopaedia of Informal Education.* **www.infed.org/leadership/traditional_leadership.htm**

Bredekamp, S. and Copple, C. (eds) (1997) *Developmentally Appropriate Practice in Early Childhood Programs.* Washington, DC: National Association for the Education of Young Children.

Burgess, D. and Borgida, E. (1999) 'Who women are, who women should be: Descriptive and prescriptive gender stereotyping in sex discrimination'. *Psychology, Public Policy and Law,* 5, 665–92.

Burke, W. and Litwin, G. (1992) 'A causal model of organizational performance and change'. *Journal of Management,* 18, 3, 523–45. http://documents.reflectlearn.org/Offline%20OA%20Models%20and%20Frameworks/BurkeLitwin_ACausalModelofOrganizationalPerformance.pdf

Burns, J. (1978) *Leadership.* New York: Harper & Row.

Caruso, D. and Salovey, P. (2004) *The Emotionally Intelligent Manager: How to develop and use the four key emotional skills of leadership.* San Francisco, CA: Jossey-Bass.

Catalyst (2006) *2005 Catalyst Census of Women Board Directors of the Fortune 500.* New York: Catalyst.

Centre for Excellence and Outcomes in Children and Young People's Services (2010) *Grasping the Nettle: Early intervention for children, families and communities.* www.c4eo.org.uk/themes/earlyintervention/files/early_intervention_grasping_the_nettle_full_report.pdf

Children's Workforce Development Council (2010) *On the Right Track: Guidance to the standards for the award of Early Years Professional Status.* Leeds: CWDC. www.cwdcouncil.org.uk/assets/0000/9008/Guidance_To_Standards.pdf

Chinn, R. and Benne, K.O. (1976) 'General strategies for effecting change in human systems'. In Bennis, W.E.; Benne, K.O.; Chinn, R.; and Carey, K.E. (eds) *The planning of change,* New York: Holt, Rinehart and Winston.

Coleman, P. and LaRoque, L. (1990) *Struggling to be 'Good Enough': Administrative practices and school district ethos.* New York: The Falmer Press.

Cummings, A. (2008) *Only Connect: Using a critical incident tool to develop multi-agency collaboration in two children's centres.* National College for School Leadership. www.nationalcollege.org.uk/docinfo?id=17322&filename=only-connect-full-report.pdf

Dana, D. (1990) *Talk It Out: Four steps to managing people problems in your organisation.* London: Kogan Page.

Day, C., Sammons, P., Hopkins, D., Harris, A., Leithwood, K., Gu, Q., Brown, E., Ahtaridou, E. and Kington, A. (2009) *The Impact of School Leadership on Pupil Outcomes: Final Report.* Department for Children Schools and Families with National College for School Leadership. Full report as below, for summary search by RB108. www.education.gov.uk/publications/eOrderingDownload/DCSF-RR108.pdf

Dickins, M. (2010) *Leadership for Listening.* London: National Children's Bureau.

Doyle, M.E. and Smith, M.K. (2001) 'Shared leadership'. *The Encyclopaedia of Informal Education.* www.infed.org/leadership/shared_leadership.htm

Drucker, P. (2007) *The Effective Executive: The definitive guide to getting the right things done.* Oxford: Elsevier.

Duffy, B. and Marshall, J. (2007) 'Leadership in multi-agency work'. In Siraj-Blatchford, I. Clarke, K. and Needham, M. (eds) *The Team Around the Child: Multi-agency working in the early years.* Stoke-on-Trent: Trentham Books.

Dunlop, A.W. (2008) *A Literature Review on Leadership in Early Years.* Search by title on www.ltscotland.org.uk

Eagly, A.H. and Johnson, B. (1990) 'Gender and leadership style: A meta-analysis'. *Psychological Bulletin*, 108, 2, 233–56.

Ebbeck, M. and Waniganayake, M. (2003) *Early Childhood Professionals: Leading today and tomorrow.* Sydney: MacLennan and Petty.

Eliot, L. (2009) *Pink Brain, Blue Brain: How small differences grow into troublesome gaps and what we can do about it.* New York: Houghton Mifflin Harcourt.

Ellis, L., Hershberger, S., Field, E., Wersinger, S., Pellis, S., Geary, D., Palmer, C., Hoyenga, K., Hetsroni, A. and Karadi, K. (2008) *Sex Differences: Summarizing more than a century of scientific research.* Hove: Psychology Press.

Fiedler, F. (1967) *A theory of leadership effectiveness.* New York: McGraw-Hill Book Company.

Garfield, C. (1987) *Peak performers: The new heroes of American business.* New York: Harper Paperbacks.

Garvey, D. and Lancaster, A. (2010) *Leadership for Quality in Early Years and Playwork: Supporting your team to achieve better outcomes for children and families.* London: National Children's Bureau.

George, B. (2003) *Authentic Leadership: Rediscovering the secrets to creating lasting value.* San Francisco, CA: Jossey-Bass.

Glick, P. and Fiske, S. (1999) 'Sexism and other "isms": independence, status, and the ambivalent content of stereotypes'. In Swann, W. Jr. and Langlois, J. (eds) *Sexism and Stereotypes in Modern Society: The gender science of Janet Taylor Spence.* Washington, DC: American Psychological Association.

Goleman, D. (1996) *Emotional Intelligence: Why it can matter more than IQ.* London: Bloomsbury.

Goleman, D., Boyatzis, R. and McKee, A. (2002) *Primal Leadership.* Harvard Business School Press.

Goleman, D., Boyatzis, R. and McKee, A. (2002) *The New Leaders: Transforming the art of leadership into the science of results.* London: Time Warner.

Graen, G.B. (1976) 'Role making processes within complex organizations'. In Dunnette, M.D. (ed.) *Handbook of Industrial and Organizational Psychology.* Chicago, IL: Rand McNally.

Graen, G.B. and Uhl-Bien, M. (1995) 'Relationship-based approach to leadership: Development of leader-member exchange (LMX) theory of leadership over 25 years: Applying a multi-domain perspective'. *Leadership Quarterly,* 20, 371–82.

Grenier, J. (2003) *Small Steps, Slippery Mud: 100 days as a nursery school head.* www.tinyurl.com/slipperymud

Grint, K. (2005) 'Problems, problems, problems: the social construction of "leadership"'. *Human Relations,* 58, 11, 1467–94.

Grint, K. (2009) *Wicked Problems and the Role of Leadership.* www.informalnetworks.co.uk/Wicked_problems_and_the_role_of_leadership.pdf

Grint, K. (2010) *Leadership: A very short introduction.* Oxford: Oxford University Press.

Hadfield, M., Jopling, M., Royle, K. and Waller, T. (2010) *First National Survey of Practitioners with Early Years Professional Status.* Wolverhampton: Centre for Developmental and Applied Research in Education. www.cwdcouncil.org.uk/assets/0001/1377/First_National_Survey_of_Practitoners_with_EYPS.pdf

Hard, L. (2005) *How Is Leadership Understood and Enacted within the Field of Early Childhood Education and Care?* Unpublished doctoral thesis, Center for Learning Innovation, Queensland University of Technology. http://eprints.qut.edu.au/16213/1/Louise_Hard_Thesis.pdf

Harris, A. (2002) *Distributed Leadership in Schools: Leading or misleading?* www.icponline. org/index.php?option=com_content&task=view&id=130&Itemid=50

Harris, A. and Spillane, J. (2008) *Distributed School Leadership: Developing tomorrow's leaders.* Abingdon: Routledge.

Haslam, S.A., Reicher, S.D. and Platow, M.J. (2010) *The New Psychology of Leadership.* London: Psychology Press.

Henderson-Kelly, L. and Pamphilon, B. (2000) 'Women's models of leadership in the child care sector'. *Australian Journal of Early Childhood*, 25, 1, 8–12, March.

Henry, L. (2010) 'Open the door to new ideas'. *Nursery World*, 28 January, 26–7.

Hersey, P. and Blanchard, K.H. (1969) *Management of Organizational Behavior – Utilizing Human Resources.* Upper Saddle River, NJ: Prentice Hall.

Hersey, P. and Blanchard, K.H. (1974) 'So you want to know your leadership style?'. *Training and Development Journal,* American Society for Training and Development, Feburary.

Herzberg, F. (1959) *Work and the Nature of Man.* Cleveland: World Publishing.

House, R. (1971) 'A path-goal theory of leadership effectiveness'. *Administration Science Quarterly,* 16, 3, 321–39.

Hujala, E. (2002) 'Leadership in a child care context in Finland', in Nivala, V. and Hujala, E. (eds) *Leadership in Early Childhood Education: Cross-cultural perspectives.* Oulu: Oulu University Press. http://herkules.oulu.fi/isbn9514268539/

Judge, T., Bono, J., Ilies, R. and Gerhard, W. (2002) 'Personality and leadership: A qualitiative and quantitative review'. *Journal of Applied Psychology,* 87, 765–80.

Kagan, S. and Bowman, B. (eds) (1997) *Leadership in Early Care and Education.* Washington, DC: National Association for the Education of Young Children.

Kanter, R.M. (1983) *The Change Masters: Corporate entrepreneurs at work.* London: Unwin Paperbacks.

Kate Greenaway Nursery School and Children's Centre (2009) *Core Experiences for the Early Years Foundation Stage.* Distributed by Early Education. Also information on www.coreexperiences.wikia.com

Kelley, R.E. (1992) *The Power of Followship.* New York: Doubleday.

Kirby, P., Paradise, L. and King, M. (1992) 'Extraordinary leaders in education: Understanding transformational leadership'. *Journal of Educational Research*, 85, 5, 303–11.

Kirkpatrick, S. and Locke, E. (1991) 'Leadership: Do traits matter?' *Academy of Management Executive*, 5, 2, 48–60. http://sbuweb.tcu.edu/jmathis/Org_Mgmt_Materials/ Leadership%20-%20Do%20Traits%20Matgter.pdf

Klavins, L. (2008) *Parents Matter: How can leaders involve parents in the self-evaluation process and further development of children's centre and extended school services?* National College for School Leadership. www.nationalcollege.org.uk/docinfo?id=17325&fil ename=parents-matter-full-report.pdf

Klenke, K. (2007) 'Authentic leadership: a self, leader, and spiritual identity perspective'. *International Journal of Leadership Studies*, 3, 68–97. www.regent.edu/acad/global/ publications/ijls/new/vol3iss1/klenke/Klenke_IJLS_V3Is1.pdf

Kolb, D.A., Rubin, I.M. and McIntyre, J.M. (1979) *Organizational Psychology: An experiential approach.* Englewood Cliffs, NJ: Prentice Hall.

Korsvik, T. (2011) 'Childcare policy since the 1970s in the "most gender equal country in the world": a field of controversy and grassroots activism'. *European Journal of Women's Studies,* 18, 2, 135–53.

LEADERSHIP AND EARLY YEARS PROFESSIONALISM

Kotter, J.P. (1979) *Power in Management*. New York: Amacom Books.

Kouzes, J. and Posner, B. (1993) *Credibility*. San Francisco: Jossey-Bass.

Lawrence, Y., Robins, D. and Twells, B. (2008) *Teachers into Leaders: Networking and leadership development*. www.nationalcollege.org.uk/docinfo?id=17422&filename=teachers-into-leaders-summary.pdf

Learning and Teaching Scotland (2005) *Let's Talk About Pedagogy: Towards a shared understanding for early years education in Scotland*. Glasgow: Learning and Teaching Scotland. www.ltscotland.org.uk/Images/talkpedagogy_tcm4-193218.pdf

Lee, M. (2009) 'Being an inspiration'. *Early Years Educator*, 11, 5, 4. www.bestpracticenet.co.uk/eye-v11-n5-sep09.html#p10

Leimon, A., Moscovici, F. and Goodier, H. (2010) *Coaching Women to Lead*. Hove: Routledge.

Leithwood, K. (1992) 'The move toward transformational leadership'. *Educational Leadership*, 49, 5, 8–12.

Leithwood, K. and Steinbach, R. (1991) 'Indicators of transformational leadership in the everyday problem solving of school administrators'. *Journal of Personnel Evaluation in Education*, 4, 3, 221–44.

Leithwood, K., Day, C., Sammons, P., Harris, A. and Hopkins, D. (2008) *Successful School Leadership: What It Is and How It Influences Pupil Learning*. Department for Children Schools and Families with National College for School Leadership. http://education.gov.uk/publications/eOrderingDownload/RR800.pdf

Lewin, K., Lippitt, R. and White, R. (1939) 'Patterns of aggressive behavior in experimentally created "social climates"'. *Journal of Social Psychology*, 10, 271–301.

Lindon, J. (2008) *Safeguarding Children and Young People: Child protection 0–18 years*. London: Hodder Education.

Lindon, J. (2009a) *Parents as Partners: Positive relationships in the early years*. London: Practical Pre-School Books.

Lindon, J. (2009b) *Guiding the Behaviour of Children and Young People: Linking theory and practice 0–18 years*. London: Hodder Education.

Lindon, J. (2010a) *Understanding Child Development: Linking theory and practice*. London: Hodder Education.

Lindon, J. (2010b) *Reflective Practice and Early Years Professionalism*. London: Hodder Education.

Lindon, J. (2010c) *The Key Person Approach: Positive relationships in the early years*. London: Practical Pre-School Books.

Lindon, J. (2010d) *Child-initiated Learning: Positive relationships in the early years*. London: Practical Pre-School Books.

Lindon, J. and Lindon, L. (2008) *Mastering Counselling Skills*. Basingstoke: Palgrave Macmillan.

Lindon, L. (1980) *A Re-conceptualisation of Job Satisfaction: Self-referent or job-referent?* Unpublished PhD thesis, University of London.

Lingard, B., Hayes, D., Mills, M. and Christie, P. (2003) *Leading Learning: Making hope practical in schools*. Maidenhead: Open University Press.

Luthans, F. and Avolio, B. (2003) 'Authentic leadership development'. In Cameron, K., Dutton, S. and Quinn, R. (eds) *Positive Organizational Scholarship*. San Francisco, CA: Berrett-Koehler.

Manasse, A. (1986) 'Vision and leadership: Paying attention to intention'. *Peabody Journal of Education*, 63, 1, 150–73.

Manning-Morton, J. and Thorp, M. (2001) *Key Times: A framework for developing high quality provision for children under three years old.* London: Camden Local Education Authority. (The resource was republished in 2006 by Open University Press.)

Maslow, A. (1943) 'A theory of human motivation'. *Psychological Review,* 50, 370–96. http://psychclassics.yorku.ca/Maslow/motivation.htm

Mayo, E. (1933) *The Human Problem of an Industrial Civilization.* Boston, MA: Harvard Business School.

McCall, M., Morrison, A. and Hannan, R. (1978) *Studies of Managerial Work: Results and methods.* Technical Report No. 9: Greensboro, NC: Center for Creative Leadership.

McClelland, D. A. and Boyatzis, R. (1982) 'Leadership motive pattern and long term success in management'. *Journal of Applied Psychology,* 67, 9, 737–43.

McGregor, D. (1960) *The Human Side of Enterprise.* New York: McGraw-Hill.

McKee, R. and Carlson, B. (1999) *The Power to Change.* Austin, TX: Grid International Inc.

Moyles, J. (2006) *Effective Leadership and Management in the Early Years.* Maidenhead: Open University Press.

Muijs, D., Aubrey, C., Harris, A. and Briggs, M. (2004) 'How do they manage? A review of the research on leadership in early childhood'. *Journal of Early Childhood Research,* 2, 2, 157–89.

Munton, A. and Mooney, A. (2001) *Integrating Self-assessment into Statutory Inspection Procedures: The impact of the quality of day care provision.* http://education.gov.uk/publications/standard/publicationDetail/Page1/RR285

Murphy, J.T. (1988) 'The unheroic side to leadership: notes from the swamp'. *Phi Delta Kappan,* 69, 654–9.

National College for Leadership of Schools and Children's Services (2008) *Everyone a Leader.* www.nationalcollege.org.uk/print/index/docinfo.htm?id=21820&filename=everyone-a-leader.pdf

National College for Leadership of Schools and Children's Services and C4EO (2011) *Resourceful Leadership: How directors of children's services improve outcomes for children.* www.nationalcollege.org.uk/docinfo?id=144732&filename=resourceful-leadership-dcs.pdf

Nivala, V. (2002) 'Leadership in general, leadership in theory'. In Nivala, V. and Hujala, E. (eds) (2002) *Leadership in Early Childhood Education: Cross-cultural perspectives.* Oulu: Oulu University Press. http://herkules.oulu.fi/isbn9514268539/

Nivala, V. and Hujala, E. (eds) (2002) *Leadership in Early Childhood Education: Cross-cultural perspectives.* Oulu: Oulu University Press. http://herkules.oulu.fi/isbn9514268539/

Northouse, P. (2010) *Leadership Theory and Practice.* London: Sage.

Owen, C. (2003) *Men's Work: Changing the gender mix of the childcare and early years workforce.* London: Daycare Trust. www.koordination-maennerinkitas.de/uploads/media/Owen-Charlie-Men_s-Work_02.pdf

Pemberton, C. (1995) *Strike a New Career Deal: Build a great future in the changing world of work.* London: Pitman Publishing.

Peters, T. and Waterman, R. (1980) *In Search of Excellence: Lessons from America's best-run companies.* New York: Harper Business.

Porter, E.H. (1973, 2005) Strength Deployment Inventory. Carlsbad, CA: Personal Strengths Publishing.

Porter, E.H. (1976) 'On the Development of Relationship Awareness Theory: a Personal Note'. *Group Organization Management, 1*(3), 302–309.

Porter, E.H. (1996) *Relationship Awareness Theory.* Carlsbad, CA: Personal Strengths Publishing.

Post, J. and Hohmann, M. (2000) *Tender Care and Early Learning: Supporting infants and toddlers in child care settings.* Ypsilanti, MI: High/Scope Press.

Pound, L. (2008) 'Leadership in the early years', in Miller, L. and Cable, C. (eds) *Professionalism in the Early Years.* London: Hodder Education.

Raelin, J. (2003) *Creating Leaderful Organisations: How to bring out leadership in everyone.* San Francisco, CA: Berrett-Kohler.

Raelin, J. (2010) *The Leaderful Fieldbook: Strategies and activities for developing leadership.* Boston, MA: Nicholas Brealey Publishing.

Rakos, R.F. (1991) *Assertive Behaviour: Theory, research and training.* New York: Routledge.

Robins, A. and Callan, S. (eds) (2009) *Managing Early Years Settings: Supporting and leading teams.* London: Sage.

Rodd, J. (1997) 'Learning to be leaders: perceptions of early childhood professionals about leadership, roles and responsibilities'. *Early Years,* 18, 1.

Rodd, J. (2006) *Leadership in Early Childhood.* Maidenhead: Open University Press.

Rosemary, C. and Puroila, A-M. (2002) 'Leadership potential in day care settings: using dual analytical methods to explore directors' work in Finland and the USA'. In Nivala, V. and Hujala, E. (eds) *Leadership in Early Childhood Education: Cross-cultural perspectives.* Oulu: Oulu University Press. http://herkules.oulu.fi/isbn9514268539/

Sapolsky, R.M. (1999) 'The physiology and pathophysiology of unhappiness'. In Kahneman, D., Diener, E. and Schwarz, N. (eds) *Well-being: The foundations of hedonic psychology.* New York: Russell Sage Foundation.

Schein, E.H. (1987) *Process Consultation Volume 1: Its role in organizational development.* Boston, MA: Addison-Wesley.

Schein, E.H. (1997) *Organizational Culture and Leadership.* San Francisco, CA: Jossey-Bass.

Scrivens, C. (2002a) 'Constructions of leadership: does gender make a difference? Perspectives from an English speaking country'. In Nivala, V. and Hujala, E. (eds) *Leadership in Early Childhood Education: Cross-cultural perspectives.* Oulu: Oulu University Press. http://herkules.oulu.fi/isbn9514268539/

Scrivens, C. (2002b) 'Tensions and constraints for professional leadership in the kindergarten service in New Zealand'. In Nivala, V. and Hujala, E. (eds) (2002) *Leadership in Early Childhood Education: Cross-cultural perspectives.* Oulu: Oulu University Press. http://herkules.oulu.fi/isbn9514268539/

SEDL (2011) *Leadership Characteristics That Facilitate School Change.* www.sedl.org/change/leadership/character.html

Sergiovanni, T. (1990) 'Adding value to leadership gets extraordinary results'. *Educational Leadership,* 47, 8, 23–7.

Sergiovanni, T. and Moore, J. (eds) (1989) *Schooling for Tomorrow: Directing reforms to issues that count.* Boston, MA: Allyn and Bacon.

Simkins, T. (2005) 'Leadership in education: "What works?" or "What makes sense?"'. *Educational Management Administration and Leadership,* 33, 1, 9–26.

Siraj-Blatchford, I. and Manni, L. (2007) *Effective Leadership in the Early Years Sector.* London: Institute of Education.

Slater, R.O. and Doig, J.W. (1988) 'Leadership in education: issues of entrepreneurship'. *Education in Urban Society,* 20, 3, 294–301.

Smith, M.K. (2001) 'Kurt Lewin: groups, experiential learning and action research'. *The Encyclopaedia of Informal Education.* www.infed.org/thinkers/et-lewin.htm

Spillane, J. (2005) 'Distributed leadership'. *The Educational Forum,* Winter. http://course1.winona.edu/lgray/el756/Articles/Spillane.htm

Spillane, J., Halverson, R. and Diamond, J. (2001) *Investigating School Leadership Practice: A distributed perspective.* www.sesp.northwestern.edu/docs/invldrshpperspective.pdf

Stanford Encyclopaedia of Philosophy (2011) *Feminist Epistemology and Philosophy of Science.* http://plato.stanford.edu/entries/feminism-epistemology/

Stogdill, R. (1948) 'Personal factors associated with leadership: A survey of the literature'. *Journal of Psychology,* 25, 35–71.

Stogdill, R. (1974) *Handbook of Leadership: A survey of theory and research.* New York: The Free Press.

Tannenbaum, A. and Schmidt, W. (1958) 'How to choose a leadership pattern'. *Harvard Business Review,* 36, 95–101.

Taylor, F.W. (1911) *The Principles of Scientific Management.* New York: Harper Row. Online information at www.marxists.org/reference/subject/economics/taylor/principles/index.htm

Terry, R. (1993) *Authentic Leadership: Courage in action.* San Francisco, CA: Jossey-Bass.

The SYMLOG Consulting Group, (1993) *SYMLOG Practitioner Training Materials.* San Diego: The SYMLOG Consulting Group.

Thornton, K. (2006) 'Notions of leadership in the New Zealand ECE Centres of Innovation Programme'. *New Zealand Annual Review of Education,* 15, 153–67. http://www.victoria.ac.nz/nzaroe/subject-area/.%5C../1996/.%5C../2005/pdf/text-thornton.pdf

Thornton, K. (2007) *Courage, Commitment and Collaboration: Notions of leadership in the NZ ECE Centres of Innovation.* Victoria: University of Wellington. http://researcharchive.vuw.ac.nz/bitstream/handle/10063/124/paper.pdf?sequence=2

Tichy, N. (1983) *Managing Strategic Change.* New York: John Wiley.

van Engen, M. and Willemsen, T. (2004) 'Sex and leadership styles: A meta-analysis of research published in the 1990s'. *Psychological Reports,* 94, 3–18.

Vroom, V. and Yetton, P. (1973) *Leadership and Decision-Making.* Pittsburgh, PA: University of Pittsburgh Press.

Walumbwa, F., Avolio, B., Gardner, W., Wernsing, T. and Peterson, S. (2008) 'Authentic leadership: Development and validation of a theory-based measure'. *Journal of Management,* 34, 1, 89–126.

Waniganayake, M. (2002) 'Growth of leadership: With training can anyone become a leader?' In Nivala, V. and Hujala, E. (eds) *Leadership in Early Childhood Education: Cross-cultural perspectives.* Oulu: Oulu University Press. http://herkules.oulu.fi/isbn9514268539/

Waniganayake, M., Morda, R. and Kapsalakis, A. (2000) 'Leadership in child care centres: is it just another job?' *Australian Journal of Early Childhood,* 25, 1, 13–20.

Whalley, M., Allen, S. and Wilson, D. (2008) *Leading Practice in Early Years Settings.* Exeter: Learning Matters Ltd.

Wheeler, H. and Connor, J. (2009) *Parents, Early Years and Learning: Parents as partners in the Early Years Foundation Stage – principles into practice.* London: National Children's Bureau. www.peal.org.uk/resources/practice-examples

Yukl, G. (1994) *Leadership in Organizations.* Englewood Cliffs, NJ: Prentice Hall.

Index

LEADERSHIP AND EARLY YEARS PROFESSIONALISM